THE WINTER'S TALE

William Shakespeare

THE WINTER'S TALE

William Shakespeare

Lawrence F. Rhu, Editor
University of South Carolina

J. J. M. Tobin, General Editor
University of Massachusetts–Boston

WADSWORTH
CENGAGE Learning

Australia • Brazil • Japan • Korea • Mexico • Singapore • Spain • United Kingdom • United States

WADSWORTH
CENGAGE Learning

Evans Shakespeare Editions:
The Winter's Tale
Lawrence F. Rhu, Editor
J. J. M. Tobin, General Editor

Senior Publisher: Lyn Uhl

Publisher: Michael Rosenberg

Development Editor:
Michell Phifer

Assistant Editor: Erin Bosco

Editorial Assistant: Rebecca
Donahue

Media Editor: Janine Tangney

Senior Marketing Manager:
Melissa Holt

Marketing Communications
Manager: Glenn McGibbon

Content Project Manager:
Aimee Chevrette Bear

Art Director: Marissa Falco

Print Buyer: Betsy Donaghey

Rights Acquisition Specialist,
Text: Katie Huha

Rights Acquisition Specialist,
Images: Jennifer Meyer Dare

Production Service: MPS Limited,
a Macmillan Company

Cover Designer: Walter Kopec

Text Designer: Maxine Ressler

Cover Image: Corliss Preston
(left) as Hermione and Raymond
L. Chapman as Leontes in the
Utah Shakespeare Festival's
2004 production of *The
Winter's Tale*. (Copyright Utah
Shakespeare Festival. Photo by
Karl Hugh.)

Compositor: MPS Limited,
a Macmillan Company

For product information and
technology assistance, contact us at **Cengage Learning
Customer & Sales Support, 1-800-354-9706**

For permission to use material from this text
or product, submit all requests online at
www.cengage.com/permissions
Further permissions questions can be emailed to
permissionrequest@cengage.com

Library of Congress Control Number: 2010942816

ISBN-13: 978-0-495-91122-7

ISBN-10: 0-495-91122-4

Wadsworth
20 Channel Center Street
Boston, MA 02210
USA

Cengage Learning is a leading provider of customized
learning solutions with office locations around the globe,
including Singapore, the United Kingdom, Australia,
Mexico, Brazil, and Japan. Locate your local office at:
international.cengage.com/region

Cengage Learning products are represented in Canada by
Nelson Education, Ltd.

For your course and learning solutions, visit
www.cengage.com

Purchase any of our products at your local college store
or at our preferred online store **www.cengagebrain.com**

Printed in the United States of America
1 2 3 4 5 6 7 14 13 12 11

Other titles in the *Evans Shakespeare Editions*
from Cengage Learning

TABLE OF CONTENTS

Modern Essays

ACKNOWLEDGMENTS

The Winter's Tale is a play remarkable for a failure of acknowledgement. So, it would be a serious lapse not to mention a number of persons who have helped me with this edition. At USC, Jonathan Butler and Nina Levine made the work feasible within the allotted time. Without them the occasion could have slipped away. Elsewhere Glenn Bradie of the Everett Collection, Inc. and Rebecca Oviedo of the Folger Shakespeare Library helped me find apposite images, as did David Howells of the Royal Shakespeare Company and Helen Hargest of the Shakespeare Centre Library and Archive. John Tobin's invitation to join his team of editors was the beginning of a rewarding journey in his excellent company. Heather Dubrow and Katherine Rowe sustained us when we faced seemingly insuperable obstacles. Grace Tiffany recommended a pertinent poem. Susannah Tobin, with her legal acumen, reminded me why her fourth-grade Book Monster remains a legend among those dearest to my heart.

List of Illustrations

THE WINTER'S TALE

William Shakespeare

About this Series

J. J. M. Tobin

THE EVANS Shakespeare Editions are individual editions of essential plays by William Shakespeare, edited by leading scholars to provide college and university students, advanced high school students, and interested independent readers with a comprehensive guide to the plays and their historical and modern contexts.

The volume editor of each play has written an introduction to the play and a history of the play in performance on both stage and screen. Central sources and contexts for the play are included, and each editor also has surveyed the critical commentary on the play and selected representative influential essays to illuminate the text further. A guide to additional reading, viewing, and listening concludes the volume and will continue the reader's relationship with the play.

Each volume includes an overview of Shakespeare's life and the world of London theater that he inhabited. Our goal for these editions is that they provide the reader a window into Shakespeare and his work that reminds us all of his enduring global influence.

The text for these plays comes from *The Riverside Shakespeare*, edited with notes and textual commentary by the late Gywnne Blakemore Evans. Evans was known for his unrivaled scholarly precision, and his *Riverside* text is an essential and much-admired modern edition of Shakespeare. The Evans Shakespeare Editions preserve the *Riverside* line numbering, which is the numbering used in the invaluable *Harvard Concordance to Shakespeare* by Marvin Spevack.

Beyond his scholarly work, Evans was a generous mentor to many of the editors in this series and a tremendous influence on all of us. His kind-hearted nature made it impossible for him truly to dislike anyone. However, despite an identification with the most traditional and canonical of cultural texts, he reserved a raised eyebrow and stern words for those whose politics lacked empathy and understanding for the full diversity of human experience. In this attitude too, as in all his writing and teaching, it was evident that he was a scholar who understood Shakespeare. This series is dedicated to his memory.

SHAKESPEARE'S LIFE

J. J. M. Tobin

SHAKESPEARE WAS a genius, but he was no unreachable ivory-tower poet. Instead, Shakespeare was a young man from the provinces who made good in the big city of London. Just when and how he came from the provinces remains a mystery. He was born in 1564, the eldest son of an initially quite successful father whose position as alderman and then bailiff (mayor) of the town of Stratford allowed his son to attend the local Latin Grammar School. There, Shakespeare received an education that, contrary to some critics' belief, provided him with the historical perspective and verbal flexibility that helped define his writing.

The schoolboy grew into a young man who married an older woman, Anne Hathaway, and became the father of a daughter and a set of twins, a boy and a girl, by the age of twenty-one. The boy, Hamnet, would die before his twelfth birthday. When the playwright's father, John Shakespeare, only recently recovered from two decades of legal and financial difficulties, died in 1601, having earlier secured the coat of arms of a gentleman (Duncan-Jones 90–102), Shakespeare was left in Stratford with a family of four women: his wife, his two daughters, and his mother, Mary, *née* Arden. Shakespeare's own familial experiences, from the fluctuations of his father's fortunes, to the strong influence of several female relatives, to the tragic loss of a beloved son, doubtless added heart and depth to the incisive portrayals of characters that he created in his plays and poems.

Accordingly, given the fact that all description is necessarily selective, Shakespeare often had in mind his own experiences when he chose narrative and dramatic sources for the foundation of his comedies, histories, and tragedies. The few facts of his life that survive are open to all sorts of interpretations, some of which reveal more about the interpreter than about the facts themselves, while others carry with them a greater degree of likelihood. A few critics have noted that Shakespeare was the eldest boy in a patriarchal world, the first surviving child born in a time of plague after the infant deaths of two siblings. As a child, he doubtless saw and remembered his father dressed in the furred scarlet gown of a bailiff in 1568, going about his appointed supervisory tasks, a figure both familiar as a person and strangely exalted as an official, and as Stephen Greenblatt has noted, all by means of a costume (Greenblatt 30–31). He was likely to have been the indisputable favorite of his mother, acquiring a self-confidence that often leads young men with even a modicum of talent on to success.

Richard Wheeler has pointed out that Shakespeare's choice of source material in which a female is disguised as a boy, best illustrated in *Twelfth Night*, has psychological roots in the playwright's wish to have repaired the loss of his son, Hamnet, whose twin sister, Judith, remained a constant reminder of the absent boy (Wheeler 147–53). Finally, although his marriage and fatherhood indicate some clear grounds for heterosexuality, Shakespeare also wrote beautiful poems about a young man, and his plays often feature male bonding and pathetic male isolation when the bond is broken by marriage, as in the instances of Antonio and Bassanio in *The Merchant of Venice* and a second Antonio and Sebastian in *Twelfth Night*. These scenarios offer putative evidence of at least homosociability.

Of course, over-reliance on causal links between the playwright and the experiences of his creations would logically have Shakespeare a conscience-stricken killer like Claudius or Macbeth, a disoriented octogenarian like Lear, and a suicidal queen like Cleopatra—interpretative leaps that even the most imaginative critic is unwilling to make.

Between the birth of the twins in February 1585 and the writer Robert Greene's allusion to Shakespeare as an actor-turned-playwright in September 1592, there is no hard evidence of his whereabouts, although many theories abound. Perhaps he was a schoolmaster in the country; perhaps he was attached to the household of a Catholic landowner in Lancashire. Certainly one of the most plausible theories is that Shakespeare joined the traveling theatrical troupe called the Queen's Men in 1587 as it passed through Stratford and then came to London as a member of their company. If so, he joined an exciting theatrical world with competition for the entertainment dollar among several companies with plays written by both authors who were university graduates and a minority who were not. It was a world that on its stages carefully reflected the political issues and events of the moment, but did so indirectly because of restrictions created by governmental censorship and by the potential dangers posed by a personal response to criticism by the powerful men of the time.

These dramas were composed for a public audience of mixed class and gender, from work-cutting apprentices to lords of the realm and every possible class gradation in between. They were also performed occasionally for a private audience of higher status in smaller indoor venues.

The London of these plays was a fast-growing city, even in a time of plague, full of energy, color, commerce, varieties of goods, animals, and people of all social degrees. The population numbered perhaps 200,000 by the end of the sixteenth century. It was governed by a Lord Mayor and a municipal council quite concerned about issues of crowd control, the spread of disease, crime, and the fallout of all three in neighborhoods either just at the edge of their partial jurisdiction, Shoreditch in the north and Southwark, Bankside, in the south, or fully within it, like the Blackfriars. Playhouses, three-tiered amphitheaters, and the earlier open-plan inn-yards with galleries above, brought together all three of these problems and more, and they were threatened constantly with restriction by the authorities, who also had the subtle financial desire of taxing players whose performances were not protected by aristocratic patronage.

By the time he joined the newly formed Lord Chamberlain's Men in 1594, Shakespeare had already written his first four history plays (*1, 2, & 3 Henry VI* and *Richard III*), the farcical comedies *The Taming of the Shrew* and *The Comedy of Errors*, and the grotesquely interesting tragedy *Titus Andronicus*. Many, but certainly not all, of his 154 sonnets were also written in the mid-1590s. When the Lord Chamberlain's Men moved into the newly constructed Globe theater in late 1599, having had five good years at the Theatre and the nearby Curtain in Shoreditch, Shakespeare had scripted four more history plays, *King John*, *Richard II*, and *1 & 2 Henry IV* (and part of a fifth play, *Edward III*), six comedies, including *The Two Gentlemen of Verona*, *Love's Labour's Lost*, three of the five so-called "golden comedies" (*A Midsummer Night's Dream*, *The Merchant of Venice*, and *Much Ado About Nothing*), and *Romeo and Juliet*, the tragic companion to *A Midsummer Night's Dream*.

The opening season at the Globe doubtless included the last of the English history plays written solely by Shakespeare, *Henry V*, the pastoral comedy both debunking and idealistic, *As You Like It*, and the most frequently taught of the plays focused on Roman history, *Julius Caesar*. Before the death of Queen Elizabeth in late March of 1603, Shakespeare had certainly written his most famous play, *Hamlet*, his most intensely claustrophobic tragedy, *Othello*, the bourgeois domestic comedy *The Merry Wives of Windsor*, the last of the "golden comedies," which we find alloyed with both satire and melancholy, *Twelfth Night*, and the uniquely powerful satirical comedy *Troilus and Cressida*, as well as the enigmatic poem about martyrdom, *The Phoenix and Turtle*.

Outbreaks of the plague affected Shakespeare both as a dramatist and as a poet, for the virulence of the disease, when deaths reached more than fifty a week in London, forced the authorities to close the theaters in order to restrict contagion. Shakespeare was thus left with added time free from the incessant pressure to produce dramatic scripts, and he then composed his two Ovidian narrative poems, *Venus and Adonis* (1593) and *The Rape of Lucrece* (1594). The most extended theater closings were from June 1592 to May 1594 and from March 1603 to April 1604, but there were other, briefer closings. The plague was an abiding and overpowering presence in the lives and imaginations of the poet and his audiences.

After the accession in 1603 of James VI of Scotland as James I of England, when the Lord Chamberlain's Men became the King's Men, and before the company activated for themselves the lease in 1608 of the Blackfriars, a smaller, indoor theater that was to draw a higher and more homogeneous class of spectator, Shakespeare created his other great tragedies, *King Lear, Macbeth, Antony and Cleopatra,* and *Coriolanus,* as well as the bitter *Timon of Athens* (although there is no record of its ever having been performed), and the two "bed-trick" plays, *All's Well That Ends Well* and *Measure for Measure,* comedies in which a lecherous man is fooled by the substitution of one woman for another in the darkness of the night. For that indoor spectacle-friendly Blackfriars theater, Shakespeare wrote the romances *Pericles, Cymbeline, The Winter's Tale,* and *The Tempest,* with their wondrous atmospheres and radiant daughters. By 1611, Shakespeare was moving into partial retirement, co-authoring with John Fletcher, his younger colleague and successor as principal playwright of the King's Men, *Henry VIII, The Two Noble Kinsmen,* and, probably, the lost *Cardenio.*

The division of his plays into these categories—comedies, histories, tragedies, and romances—reminds us that the first step taken by the playwright (indeed any playwright) was to determine the basic genre or kind of play that he wished to write, however much he might expand its boundaries. Genre creates expectations in the mind of the audience, expectations that no dramatist of the time was willing to frustrate. Regarding kind, Polonius tells us with unconscious humor of the versatility of the players who come to Elsinore: "The best actors in the world, either for tragedy, comedy, history, pastoral, pastoral-comical, historical-pastoral, tragical-historical, tragical-comical-historical-pastoral" (2.2.396–399). In that boundary-blurring, increasingly capacious definition of genre, he also informs us of Shakespeare's own gift in all kinds of writing and the fact of his often combining many of these genres in a single work. When, at the end of Plato's *Symposium,* Socrates argues that logically, the greatest tragic writer should also be the greatest comic writer, he was prophetic of Shakespeare, even if he doesn't go on to argue that these principles of tragedy and comedy could and should be connected in the same play. And Shakespeare indirectly repays Socrates for his prophecy by alluding to the philosopher's death in Mistress Quickly's description of the dying Falstaff in *Henry V,* 2.3.

Shakespeare is Shakespeare because of a combination of philosophical tolerance, psychological profundity, and metaphoric genius; that is, he is generous-minded, aware of what makes people tick, and is able to express himself more vividly and memorably than anyone else in the language. And it is his language that truly sets him apart, while simultaneously creating some occasional static in the mind of the modern reader.

There are six areas of this problematic language worth special attention: word choice, false friends, allusions, puns, iambic rhythm, and personification. Shakespeare's vocabulary has words that are no longer part of today's language, chiefly because they refer to things and concepts no longer in use, such as "three-farthings," coins of small value, in the Bastard's metaphoric "Look where three-farthings goes" (*King John*, 1.1.143). Such terms are easily understood by looking at the footnotes, or by checking *The Oxford English Dictionary* or a Shakespearean lexicon, like that of Schmidt; C. T. Onions's *A Shakespeare Glossary;* or *Shakespeare's Words,* by David and Ben Crystal. More difficult are false friends, words spelled the same as words we use today but that have different meanings. One example of this issue is "brave," which as an adjective in the sixteenth and early seventeenth centuries meant primarily "splendid" or "glorious," as in Miranda's expression of awe and excitement in *The Tempest*: "O brave new world/That has such people in't" (5.1.183–84), or "virtue," which in Shakespeare's language usually means "strength or power," as in Iago's argument for personal responsibility to Roderigo and the latter's lament that "it is not in my *virtue* to amend it [being in love with Desdemona]": "*Virtue*? A fig! 'tis in ourselves that we are thus or thus" (*Othello*, 1.3.318–20).

Equally problematic, but just as easily understood by reference to footnotes, are instances of classical and biblical allusion, where Shakespeare assumes a recognition by all or some of the audience of glancing references to Greek and Roman deities, frequently to elements in that most abiding narrative in Western literature, the Trojan War, as well as historical and legendary figures, as in Hamlet's "My father's brother, but no more like my father/Than I to *Hercules*" (1.2.152–53) or his subconscious reminder in the graveyard of the fact that his father was the victim of fratricide, "How the knave jowls it to the ground, as if 'twere *Cain's* jaw-bone" (5.1.76–77).

More difficult at times are Shakespeare's puns—plays on words, sometimes comedic and sometimes intentionally non-comedic, but in each case designed to bring more than one meaning in a single word to the attention of the audience and the reader. Shakespeare's puns are almost always thematically significant, revelatory of character, or both, and attention to the possibilities of the presence of punning can only increase our understanding and pleasure in the lines. There are such simple etymological puns as "lieutenant," the military title of Cassio in *Othello*, where the word is defined as one who holds the place of the captain in the latter's absence—exactly the fear Othello has about the relationship that he imagines exists between his wife, Desdemona, and Lieutenant Cassio. There are also puns that fuse the physical and the moral, as in Falstaff's comment that his highway robbery is condoned by the goddess of the moon, "under whose *countenance* we steal" (*1 Henry IV*, 1.2.29), where the word "countenance" means both "face" and "approval." Falstaff's pun is in prose, a good example of how Shakespeare, commonly regarded as the greatest of English poets and dramatists, wrote often in prose, which itself is full of the linguistic devices of poetry.

When Shakespeare was writing in verse, he used iambic pentameter lines, ten syllable lines with five feet, or units, of two syllables each, in the sequence of short-long or unstressed-stressed. Consider, for example, Romeo's "But soft,/what light/through yond/er win/

Everett Collection, Inc.

Fig. 1. Joseph Fiennes as William Shakespeare fighting through writer's block in the film *Shakespeare in Love*: a handsome dramatist without the receding hairline of contemporary portraits and busts.

dow breaks?" (*Romeo and Juliet*, 2.2.1), or Antony's "If you/have tears/ prepare/to shed/them now" (*Julius Caesar*, 3.2.169).

Scanning the rhythm of these lines is made easier by our knowledge that Shakespeare and the English language are both naturally iambic and that proof of the correct rhythm begins with marking the stress on the final syllable of the line and moving right to left. The rhythm with the emphasized syllables will lead the actor delivering the lines to stress certain words more than others, as we imagine Shakespeare to have intended, even as we know that stage delivery of lines with an unexpected stress can create fruitful tension in the ear of the audience. For example, Barnardo's "It was about to speak when the cock crew" (*Hamlet*, 1.1.147) is a pentameter line, but the expected iambic rhythm is broken in the last two feet, especially in the sequentially stressed final two syllables, which by their alliteration and double stress combine in form to underscore the moment of interruption in the play's narrative. Such playing off the expected is part of Shakespeare's arsenal of verse techniques.

In addition to these issues of unknown terms, false friends, allusions chiefly classical and biblical, meaningful puns, and verse rhythm itself, there is the metaphoric language that is the glory of Shakespeare, but each instance of this feature demands careful unpacking. Consider the early example of Romeo's personifying Death as an erotic figure keeping Juliet as his mistress, linking the commonly joined notions of love and death: "Shall I believe/That unsubstantial Death is amorous,/ And that the lean abhorred monster keeps/Thee here in dark to be his paramour?" (5.3.102–05). This link already had been anticipated by the Chorus in the prologue to the play, which speaks of "The fearful passage of their death-marked love" (1.6).

More compactly, later in his career, Shakespeare will have Hamlet, in prose, combine Renaissance and medieval views in similes and metaphors, comparisons with and without "like" or "as," in order to describe the multifaceted nature of man: "...how like an angel in apprehension, how like a god! The beauty of the world; the paragon of animals; and yet to me what is this quintessence of dust?" (*Hamlet*, 2.2.306–08). Macbeth in his play will argue against his wife's view that a little water will cleanse his guilty hands: "No; this my hand will rather/The multitudinous seas incarnadine,/Making the green one red" (2.2.58–60). Here Shakespeare has been careful to combine the mouth-filling hyperbole and its Latinate terms "multitudinous" and "incarnadine" (an illustration of the technique that he had learned from Christopher Marlowe) with a crystal-clear synonymous expression, "Making the green one red," for the benefit of all in the theater, even as everyone hears the hypnotically mellifluous line that comes before it.

Sometimes Shakespeare scorned the opportunity to use high-flown language, even when one might expect it most, as in the Roman play *Antony and Cleopatra*, when the queen uses a noun as a verb in her bitter image of herself live on the Roman stage played by a child actor, "And I shall see/Some squeaking Cleopatra *boy* my greatness/I'th' posture of a whore" (*Antony and Cleopatra*, 5.2.219–221). Shakespeare gives to Cleopatra's handmaiden Charmian the least hyperbolic expression in a context linking the erotic and funereal (analogous to that situation described by Romeo), "Now boast thee, death, in thy possession lies/A *lass* unparallel'd" (5.2.315–16), where the simple pastoral monosyllable charms the audience, which all along had sensed the antithesis of the playful girl within the cunningly imperious and imperial queen.

While nothing can fully explain the development of this language, its raw material comes largely from Shakespeare's reading, as do the basic elements of plot and character. The same man who was to save and increase his money and property in London and Stratford was, as a craftsman, equally economical, preferring to alter and expand upon material given to him in the literary sources that lie behind all his compositions rather than to create from experience alone. He is the chief counter-example to Polonius's admonition "Neither a borrower nor a lender be" (*Hamlet* 1.3.75)—Shakespeare is a world-class borrower, but one who reshapes and transforms the borrowed materials.

Certainly he had a most retentive memory and could and did recall, at times subconsciously, both single expressions and rather lengthy passages from his reading. "It is often as if, at some deep level of his mind, Shakespeare thought and felt in quotation," as Emrys Jones has noted (Jones 21). Dryden's comment that Shakespeare "needed not the spectacles of books to read Nature; he looked inwards and found her there" ignores Shakespeare's conscious manipulations of his reading as a chief source for his achievement. Nevertheless, Dryden gives us the basic image useful for picturing Shakespeare's genius. The playwright's metaphorical spectacles had two lenses, one of which was focused on life as he knew it and one on the writings of his predecessors and contemporaries: historians both classical and English, proto-novelists, poets, pamphleteers, and essayists, and playwrights who had in their own ways dealt with themes that interested him.

It is by looking at what Shakespeare himself perused that we see his manipulative genius at work, omitting, adding, preserving, and qualifying those plots, motifs, and images viewed through one lens of his binoculars. An important question is just how much of the original theme and significance is brought over in the creative borrowing, a question made more difficult to answer by the fact that in the composition of his plays, Shakespeare often modified and sometimes even

inverted the gender and number of the persons in the original material. See, for example, the model in the story of Cupid and Psyche from
Apuleius' *The Golden Asse* (1566), where Psyche almost murders Cupid,
for the description of the deaths of the little princes in *Richard III*, as
well as for the presentation of the murder of Desdemona in *Othello*.
The closer one looks at this source and the affected passage, the more
one sees that the young man from Stratford, despite being accused by
his London-educated colleague and rival Ben Jonson of having "small
Latin and less Greek," was a sufficiently good Latinist to check the
translation of Apuleius that he was using against the original, even as
he would later check Golding's translation of the *Metamorphoses* against
Ovid's Latin for use in *The Tempest*.

We don't know the workplace of Shakespeare, the desk or table
where he kept his books, nor do we know for certain who provided
him with these volumes, some of which were quite expensive, such as
Holinshed's *Chronicles*, North's *Plutarch*, and bibles, both Bishops' and
Geneva. But, if we imagine a bookshelf above his desk and envision the
titles that he might have ordered there chronologically, we would first
see the classics, most importantly Ovid and Virgil; then the Bible, especially Genesis, the Gospel of St. Matthew, and the Book of Revelation;
medieval and Renaissance writers, including Chaucer and Erasmus;
and then his own immediate predecessors and colleagues, especially
Thomas Kyd, Christopher Marlowe, Robert Greene, and Thomas
Nashe. Sometimes the most unlikely source can provide a motif or a
character, but for more important ideas, we may note what he would
have learned from four exemplary volumes on this imagined shelf.

From Seneca, the Roman philosopher, tutor to the emperor Nero
and playwright of closet tragedies (that is, of plays meant to be read
in the study rather than performed on stage), Shakespeare learned
to balance a sensational theme—fratricide and incest—with a plot
structured with care and characters subtly developed with an attitude
quite fatalistic. From Plutarch, the Greek historian who wrote parallel lives of Greek and Roman leaders, he learned the importance of
the nature of the private man when serving in public office and how
that nature is revealed in small gestures with large significance—what
James Joyce, the "spiritual son" of Shakespeare, would later refer to
as "epiphanies." From Machiavelli, the notorious early-sixteenth-
century political theorist, or from the image of Machiavelli, he saw
what he had already known about the role of deception and amorality
in political life. From Michel de Montaigne, the sixteenth-century
father of the essay, he added to his already operative skepticism, a capacity to question received notions about the consistency of the "self"
and the hierarchical place of human beings in creation.

Mr. WILLIAM

SHAKESPEARES

COMEDIES,
HISTORIES, &
TRAGEDIES.

Published according to the True Originall Copies.

Martin Droeshout sculpsit London.

L O N D O N
Printed by Isaac Iaggard, and Ed. Blount. 1623.

Fig. 2. Later, on other writers' bookshelves, would be Shakespeare's own First Folio (1623), containing thirty-six plays, half of them appearing in print for the first time. It does not, however, include any of the longer poems or sonnets.

To enjoy Shakespeare, it is not at all necessary to understand the sources that he mined, but to study Shakespeare, the better to appreciate the depth and complexity of the work, it is extremely useful to examine the foundations upon which he has built his characters and plots. We can trace, for example, the many constituent elements that have gone into the creation of Falstaff, who, together with Hamlet, is the most discussed of Shakespeare's creations. The elements include, among still others, the Vice of the morality plays; the rogue from Nashe's *The Unfortunate Traveller;* the *miles gloriosus* or cowardly braggart warrior from the Roman comic playwright (and school text) Plautus; the cheerful toper from the Bacchus of Nashe's *Summer's Last Will and Testament;* parodically, the Protestant martyr Sir John Oldcastle from Foxe's *Book of Martyrs;* and even the dying Socrates of Plato's *Phaedo.* Not that Falstaff is at all times all these figures, but in the course of his career in four plays, alive in *1 & 2 Henry IV,* dying offstage in *Henry V,* and radically transformed in *The Merry Wives of Windsor,* he is each of them by turn and counterturn, and still so much more than the mere sum of all these literary, dramatic, and historical parts.

In terms of giving voice to multiple perspectives, to characters of different ages, genders, colors, ethnicities, religions, and social ranks, Shakespeare is unrivaled. No other playwright, then or since, makes other selves live while simultaneously concealing his own self or selves, a talent described by Keats as "negative capability." Shakespeare was also an actor; that is, a person interested in imitating imaginary persons. He was thus doubly a quite creative mimic. Some of the selves mimicked are versions of the "Other," those foreigners or aliens from around the world, including Africans (Aaron, Morocco, Othello), Jews (Shylock, Tubal, Jessica), Frenchmen and Frenchwomen (the Dauphin, Joan of Arc, Margaret of Anjou), non-English Britons (Irish: Macmorris; Scots: Jamy; Welsh: Fluellen), as well as such other continental Europeans as Spaniards (Don Armado) and Italians (including several Antonios), to say nothing of the indefinable Caliban.

Some of his topics, his subjects for dramatic treatment, came often from already set pieces at school, as Emrys Jones, among others, has shown. For example, a set question to be answered, pro and con, was, should Brutus have joined the conspiracy to assassinate Caesar, the answer to which helps create the tensions in *Julius Caesar* (Jones 16). Such an on-the-one-hand and on-the-other school exercise became part of Shakespeare's dramatic strategy, where plays provide the tension created by opposites and the consequent rich ground for multiple interpretations by readers and audiences. There were also sources in earlier stage productions, including plays about Romeo and Juliet, King John, King Lear, and Hamlet. Marlowe especially provided structures to imitate and diverge from in his plays of a weak king (*Edward II*) and of several extraordinary ambitious characters, among whom are a villainous Jew (*The Jew of Malta*), and a rhetorical conqueror (*Tamburlaine*), brilliant efforts which become in Shakespeare's hands the still more dramatic *Richard II*, *The Merchant of Venice*, and *Henry V*.

Shakespeare's borrowing was frequent and pervasive, but his creative adaptations of those raw materials have made him ultimately not just a borrower but in fact the world's greatest lender, giving us four hundred years of pleasure and providing countless artists, whether painters, novelists, film directors, or even comic book writers, with allusive material. Of course, we would happily surrender our knowledge of a number of these borrowings if only we could have some sense of the quality of the voice of the leading man Richard Burbage, of the facial expressions of the comic actor Will Kemp, the sounds of the groundlings' responses to both the jokes and the set soliloquies, and the reactions of both Queen Elizabeth, who allegedly after watching *1 & 2 Henry IV* wanted to see Falstaff in love, and King James, who doubtless loved the image of his ancestor Banquo in *Macbeth*.

Shakespeare's last years before his death in April 1616 were spent back in Stratford. Although little is known of that time, we are left with the enigmatic coda to his life: his will, in which he famously left to his wife, Anne Hathaway Shakespeare, "the second-best bed"—it is unclear whether it was a cruel slight or a fondly personal bequest. Care of his estate went to his elder daughter, Susannah, while a lesser inheritance went to his wayward younger daughter, Judith, and any children she might have. He died a landowner, a family man, and a once well-known playwright. His will did not cite what has become his greatest legacy—the plays and poems that we read today—but the clues that these works leave about his life, and certainly the testament to his talent that they represent, are more valuable than even the most detailed autobiography. To be sure, however, the local boy who made good, worked hard, had flaws, and lived a complicated family life has more in common with many of his readers, then and now, than does the iconic Shakespeare, who has been mistakenly portrayed as a distant genius paring his fingernails while creating many of the greatest works in world literature.

ELIZABETHAN THEATER

J. J. M. Tobin

MASS ENTERTAINMENT today has become ever more fractured as technology provides myriad ways to take in a film (and myriad ways for Hollywood to try to make money). Movie theaters now have to compete with home theaters and couches in a way they never had to before in order to put people in the seats. The attractions of high-definition screens and stereo surround-sound are not the draw they once were now that individuals can access such technology in their own homes, and stadium seating and chair-side concessions don't make up the difference. The appeal of first-run films is fading too, now that movies go to DVD in a matter of weeks and are also available for immediate streaming through a Netflix subscription. All of these technologies, however, whether enjoyed in the cinema or at home, contribute to the moviegoer's sensation of being transported to another time and place (a journey, moreover, that lasts not much longer than an hour and a half). Hard to imagine, then, that a little over four hundred years ago, when the battle for the entertainment dollar took place on the stage rather than the screen, most members of the Elizabethan audience gladly stood for more than two hours without benefit of a padded seat, buttered popcorn, or Junior Mints (although they did have dried fruit and nuts), or the pause button in order to watch the plays of Shakespeare and his fellow dramatists performed. The legendary plays we read today on these pages were once the sixteenth- and early-seventeenth-century equivalents of the *Harry Potter* series or *Avatar*—artistic creations to be sure, but first and foremost moneymakers for their producers.

Theatrical performances in Elizabethan England took place all over the country in a wide variety of venues. As we know from the work of A. Gurr and others, if we put aside the sites used by touring companies like the Queen's Men of the 1580s (to which Shakespeare himself may have been attached), the guildhalls and marketplaces in cities and towns like Norwich, Bristol, and Stratford, or the halls of the universities of Oxford and Cambridge, and instead concentrate on London itself, we see that there were five basic performance locales (Gurr, esp. 115 ff.). There were, of course, the inns and inn-yards, in large part roofed against the weather and useful especially during the winter months.

The most celebrated of these inns in the history of London theater were the Bel Savage, the Bull, and the Cross Keys, these latter two on the same London street. These were the locations most frequently of concern to the mayor and other municipal authorities anxious about unruly crowds and increased chances of plague contagion, until 1594, when it was declared by the Lord Chamberlain of the Queen's court that there would be only two adult companies—his own, the Lord Chamberlain's Men (Shakespeare's group), and his father-in-law's, the Lord Admiral's Men, troupes that would upon the succession of King James be called the King's Men and Prince Henry's Men—and they would not perform anymore in city inns.

Second, there were two indoor halls, one in a building abutting St. Paul's Cathedral, not too far from the Bel Savage Inn, and the other in the refectory of the old Blackfriars monastery, each used by the children's companies of boys who put on plays with adult political and moral themes. Shakespeare and his company in 1596 had hoped to use the Blackfriars because Blackfriars was a liberty—that is, a district that, for reasons of its religious history, was independent of the secular control of the sheriff—but were refused by a powerful NIMBY (not in my backyard) movement of influential residents. They then leased the building to a second generation of a children's company and had to wait until 1608 to take possession of what would turn out to be both a "tonier" and quite lucrative theatrical space.

Third were the dining halls of the Inns of Court, the London law schools or, perhaps, more accurately, legal societies, where noteworthy performances of *The Comedy of Errors* (Gray's Inn) and *Twelfth Night* (the Middle Temple) took place. There, special audiences with their appetite for contemporary satire allowed for the lampooning of particular individuals whose traits and foibles would be represented by grimace, gesture, voice imitation, and even clothing, as in the case of Dr. Pinch in *The Comedy of Errors*, Malvolio in *Twelfth Night*, and Ajax in *Troilus and Cressida*. When these plays were moved to the larger public stage, the personalized elements could be withdrawn and the characters could continue as general, non-specifically humorous figures.

Fourth was the Queen's court itself (after the death of Elizabeth in 1603, it became the King's court), where at Christmastide, the major companies would be invited to perform for the pleasure of the monarch. Indeed, throughout the long period of tension between the city authorities and the court, the justification for allowing the players to perform their craft in public was that they needed to practice in order to be ready at year's end to entertain the monarch. This argument assumed a quite disproportionate ratio of practice to performance, but it was a convenient semi-fiction that seemed to satisfy all concerned. These court performances were rewarded financially by the Master of the Revels and were less expensive than other kinds of royal entertainment, including masques with elaborate scenery and complicated production devices, the high costs of which later contributed to the downfall of Charles I, James's son and successor. Legend has it that Queen Elizabeth so enjoyed some of the performances featuring the character of Falstaff that she wished to see him in love, a comment which was allegedly the stimulus for *The Merry Wives of Windsor*, which was said to have been written in two weeks, the better to satisfy the queen's request. A close look at the multiple sources used in the creation of this middle-class comedy suggests that the legend may be well founded.

Last, there are the purpose-built amphitheaters, beginning with James Burbage's the Theatre (1576) in Shoreditch, just to the north of the city limits; and the Curtain (1578) nearby. To the south, across the Thames, were the Rose (1587), the site of the Lord Admiral's company and most notably the performances of Christopher Marlowe's plays; the Swan (1596); the Globe (1599), built with the very timbers of the Theatre transported across the river in the winter of 1598 after the twenty-one-year lease on the old property had expired and several subsequent months of renting; and, back to Shoreditch in the north, the Fortune (1600), explicitly built in imitation of the triple-tiered Globe.

There was competition for the same audience in the form of bull-baiting, bear-baiting and cockfighting, and also simple competition for attention from such activities as royal processions, municipal pageants, outdoor sermons, and public executions with hangings, eviscerations, castrations, and quarterings, not to mention the nearby temptation of the houses ("nunneries") of prostitution. Nonetheless, these theatrical structures proved that, if you build it, they will come.

And come they did, with hundreds of performances each year of thirty or more plays in repertory for each company, plays of chronicle history, romance, tragedy (especially revenge tragedy), satire, and comedy (slapstick, farcical, situational, verbal, and, from 1597, "humorous"; that is, comedy dependent upon characters moved by one dominant personality trait into behavior mechanical and predictable, almost monomaniacally focused). The two major companies could and did perform familiar plays for a week or more before adding a new play to the repertory. A successful new play would be performed at least eight times, according to Knutson, within four months to half a year (Knutson 33–34). New plays were house-fillers, and entrance fees could be doubled for openings. When sequels created a two-part play, performances were only sometimes staged in proper sequence, even as moviegoers will still watch on cable *Godfather II* or *The Empire Strikes Back* without worrying that they have not just seen *The Godfather* or *Star Wars*.

Fig. 3. Part of J. C. Visscher's view of London (c. 1616 or slightly earlier) looking north from the Bankside and showing the Beargarden theater and, to the right, the Globe theater (or possibly the Swan).

The players seemed willing to play throughout the week and throughout the year, but municipal officials repeatedly insisted that there be no performances on Sundays and holy days and holidays, nor during Lent. These demands had some effect, although their repetition by the authorities clearly suggests that there were violations, with performances on occasional Sundays, even at court, on some holidays, and on some days in Lent.

Of course, even though almost half of Shakespeare's plays had already been performed at the Theater and elsewhere, we think of the Globe, open for business probably in the late summer of 1599, as the principal venue for Shakespeare's work, perhaps with *As You Like It* the first production. The current New Globe on the Bankside in Southwark, erected in careful imitation of what we know to have been the methods and materials of the sixteenth century, allows for a twenty-first-century experience analogous to that of the Elizabethan theatergoer. It may be that the diameter of the current theater, of one hundred feet, is a bit too wide, and that seventy-two feet is rather closer to the exact diameter of not only the Globe but several of these late-sixteenth-century London theaters. If so, the judgment that such Elizabethan theaters could hold between 2,000 and 3,000 people suggests that spectators, particularly the groundlings—those who had paid a penny to stand throughout the two-to-three hour performance—were packed in cheek by jowl.

The geometry of the Globe itself is that of a polygon, but it appears circular. From a distance, one would know that a play was to be performed that day by the presence of a flag flying high above the tiring house, the dressing area for the actors. Once inside the building, the theatergoer would note the covered stage projecting from an arc of the circle almost to the center of the uncovered audience space, such that the groundlings would be on three sides of the stage, with those in the front almost able to rest their chins on the platform which was raised about five feet from the floor. This stage was not raked—that is, inclined or tilted towards the audience—as it often is in modern theaters today. Raking both creates better sightlines and potentially affects stage business, as in the case of a fallen Shylock in productions of *The Merchant of Venice*, who at one point struggled in vain to stand on a pile of slippery ducats (gold coins). This move is made even more difficult by the slight incline. However, instead of raking the stage, the Rose, and perhaps the Globe and the Fortune, had the ground on which the audience stood slightly raked (Thomson 78–79), to the great advantage of those in the back of the theater.

Behind the stage, protected by a backdrop on the first level, was the tiring house where the actors dressed and from which they came and went through two openings to the left and right. There were few surprise entrances in the Elizabethan theater, as the audience could always see before them the places of entry. Covering the upper stage and a large part of the outer stage would be the "heavens," supported by two columns or pillars behind which characters could hide in order to eavesdrop and which could serve metaphorically as trees or bushes. The underside of the "heavens" was adorned with signs of the zodiac, the better to remind the audience that all the world is a stage. At the back of the stage in the center, between the two openings of exit and entrance, was a discovery space within which, when a curtain was drawn, an additional mini-set of a study, a bed, or a cave could be revealed.

From below the stage, figures, especially ghosts, could ascend through a trapdoor, and mythological deities could be lowered from above. From the second tier of the galleries, still part of the tiring house, characters could appear as on battlements or a balcony. Music was a very great part of Elizabethan theater, and musicians would be positioned sometimes on that second level of the tiring house. Less musical but still necessary sound effects, say one indicating a storm and thunder, were achieved by such actions as the offstage rolling of a cannonball down a metal trestle or repeated drumming.

Although the groundlings were the closest to the talented actors, for those members of the audience who wished to sit in the galleries (Stern, esp. 212–13) and were willing to pay more money for the privilege, there would have been the comfort of the familiar, as V. F. Petronella has pointed out, inasmuch as these galleries included rooms not unlike those in the domestic buildings near the Globe. However, the familiar was balanced with the rare via the figures on the stage who represented kings, nymphs, fairies, and ghosts, personages not usually found in the Southwark area (Petronella, esp. 111–25). These audiences themselves came from a great range of Elizabethan society, male and female, from aristocrats to lowly apprentices, with all gradations of the social spectrum in between. The late Elizabethan and early Jacobean period is so special in theatrical history in part because of the work of a number of gifted playwrights, Shakespeare preeminent among them, but also in part because of the inclusive nature of the audiences, which were representative of the society as a whole.

When the King's Men in 1609 began to perform in the smaller, indoor Blackfriars theater while still continuing at the Globe in the summer months, they were able to charge at Blackfriars five or six times the entry fee at the Globe for productions that pleased a grander and wealthier group, but at the cost of having a more socially homogeneous audience. Although the Blackfriars was a more lucrative venue,

Shakespeare's company still profited from productions at the Globe, to the degree that when the Globe burned down during a performance of *Henry VIII* on June 29 1613, the company immediately set about rebuilding the structure so that it could reopen the very next year. One wonders whether Shakespeare came down from semi-retirement in Stratford for the new opening or was already in London working yet again in collaboration with John Fletcher, his successor as principal playwright of the King's Men.

In the more heterogeneous atmosphere at the Globe, whether the first or second version, audiences watched action taking place on a platform of about twelve hundred square feet, a stage which could be the Roman forum at one moment, the senate house at another, and a battlefield at still another. Yet the audience was never at a loss in recognizing what was what, for the dramatist provided place references in the dialogue between and among characters (and some plays may also have featured signs indicating place). The action was sometimes interrupted by informative soliloquies, speeches directed to the audience as if the character speaking on the stage were totally alone, whether or not he or she actually was. By convention, what was said in a soliloquy was understood to be the truthful indication of the character's thoughts and feelings. These soliloquies must have been in their day somewhat analogous to operatic arias—plot-useful devices, but also stand-alone bravura exercises in rhetorical display. Othello's "flaming minister" speech (5.2.1–22) is a good example of the show-stopping effect of the soliloquy, and Edmund's defense of bastardy in *King Lear* (1605; 1.2.1–22), in a passage of identical length, seldom fails to elicit applause at the last line even from today's audiences, who otherwise are accustomed not to interrupt the flow of a performance.

The actors and the audience were proximate and visible to each other during these daylight performances, putting them on more intimate terms than is the case in theaters today. Performers were dressed onstage in contemporary Elizabethan clothing, with the kings and dukes wearing specially purchased, costly garments whose fate as they grew worn and tattered was to outfit the clowns with social pretensions. There were also attempts to provide historical atmosphere when needed with helmets, shields, greaves and togas appropriate to the ancient world. Perhaps as few as ten men and four boys, who would play the women's roles in this all-male theatrical world, could perform all sixteenth-century plays. The boys would remain with the company until their voices cracked, and some then became adult members of the company when places became available. They were apprentices in a profession where the turnover was not great—a bonus to the dramatist who could visualize the actor who would be playing the character he was creating but not so advantageous for a young actor looking for a permanent place within a stable group. Because plays were very seldom performed in an uninterrupted run, actors needed powerful memories. It was a time when the aural rather than the visual understanding was much greater than in our own time, but even so, the capacity of actors to hold in their heads a large number of roles from many different plays was extraordinary, and new plays were constantly being added to the repertory.

Even as one man in his time plays many parts, so did Shakespeare's company of actors. The skills and particular strengths of these actors must have given Shakespeare a great deal of confidence about the complexity of the roles that he could ask them to create. Such an element of the familiar increased the pleasure of the audience when it could recognize the same actor behind two different characters whose similarity might now be perceived. Celebrated instances of doubling include, in *A Midsummer Night's Dream*, Theseus/Oberon and Hippolyta/Titania; and, in *Hamlet*, Polonius/First Gravedigger and, most strikingly, the Ghost/Claudius. The audience would likewise be affected by their experience with an actor in a current play having performed in a previous play that they had also seen. One example of this link between roles that allows the audience to anticipate the plot comes in *Hamlet,* when Polonius tells us of his having played Caesar. Caesar, of course, was killed by Brutus in Shakespeare's *Julius Caesar.* The actor now playing Polonius had played Caesar previously in *Julius Caesar,* and in that production, he was killed by Brutus, played by Richard Burbage (son of James). In this performance of *Hamlet*, Burbage was playing Hamlet, and he would shortly kill Polonius, in a repeat of history.

The theater is the most collaborative of enterprises. We should think of Shakespeare as a script-writer under considerable pressure to provide material for his colleagues, all of whom viewed the play to come as a fundamentally money-making project. Shakespeare had multiple advantages beyond his inherent verbal and intuitive gifts. Not only did he write for a group of actors whose individual talents he could anticipate in the composition of his characters, but the script that he was creating was often a response to recent successes by rival companies with their own revengers, weak and strong English kings, and disguised lovers.

The performances themselves relied greatly on the power of the audience's imagination to fill in what was missing because of the limitations of the Elizabethan stage, as the self-conscious Prologue in *Henry V* (1599) makes clear by appealing to the audience to imagine whole armies being transported across the sea. Other Elizabethan dramatists did attempt to be "realistic" in ways that are laughable even beyond the well-intended efforts of Quince, Bottom, and the other Mechanicals in *A Midsummer Night's Dream* (1596). Consider, as noted by G. B. Evans, Yarrington's *Two Tragedies in One* (1594–c. 1598), 2.1: "When the boy goeth in to the shop, Merry striketh six blows on his head and, with the seventh, leaves the hammer sticking in his head; the boy groaning must be heard by a maid, who must cry to her master." Three scenes later, a character "Brings him forth in a chair with a hammer sticking in his head" (Evans 71). Such grossly imperfect efforts increasingly gave way to conventional signals expressive of the limitations of the stage. Four or five men with spears and a flag could represent an army, and a single coffin could represent a whole graveyard. While the Globe stage lacked scenery as we know it, it was not lacking in props. Not only were there a trapdoor grave and a bank of flowers, but also a good number of handheld props like swords, torches, chalices, crowns, and skulls, each a real object and potentially a symbol.

Sometimes convention and symbolism gave way to nature in the case of live animals. Men in animal skins are safer, of course, but some animals, like dogs and bears, are trainable. It is certain that Crab, the dog in the *Two Gentlemen of Verona* (1595–96), was "played" by a true canine, and it is quite likely that the bear that pursues Antigonus in *The Winter's Tale* was only sometimes a disguised human being; but at other times, it was a bear, managed but real, possibly even a polar bear reared from the time of its capture as a cub. Further reflection on the known dangers associated with working with bears and our knowledge of the props listed in *Henslowe's Diary* of 'j beares skyne' (Henslowe 319) suggest that Elizabethan actors were more comfortable with artificial bears, thereby avoiding any sudden ursine aggression, revenge for all the suffering their colleagues had endured at the bear-baiting stake.

The authorities whose powers of censorship were real and forceful did not worry much about whether animals were live onstage or not, but they did care about theological issues being discussed explicitly and about urban insurrection, as we know from the strictures applied to *The Book of Sir Thomas More*, a manuscript play in which Shakespeare most probably had a hand. For all their apparent sensitivity to political issues, the government seems not to have interfered with plays that show the removal—or even the murder—of kings, although the scene of the deposing of Richard in *Richard II* (1596) was thought too delicate to be printed during the lifetime of Queen Elizabeth, who recognized Richard as a parallel figure and pointedly said: "I am Richard the Second, know ye not that?" Scholars debate whether some of these potent themes regarding right versus might, illegitimate succession, and successful usurpation were recognized imperfectly by the government and so escaped into performance if not always into print. Another theory is that the authorities allowed the audiences to be excited and then pacified by these entertaining productions, a release of energies that returned the audience at the play's end to an unchanged social and political reality.

While it is now customary to refer to this reality as part of the Early Modern Period, it is still important to remember that the two main cultural forces of the time, the Renaissance and the Reformation, came together in a perfect storm of new ideas about values. The Renaissance brought us the rebirth of classical culture and an emphasis on the dignity of human beings, and the Reformation stripped levels of interpretative authority in favor of the individual's more direct reliance on Scripture. These new ideas, sometimes in concert and sometimes in tension, have led increasingly over four hundred years to our current distant but clearly related theories of skepticism and pragmatism.

It is just as important to remember that when James Burbage built his theater in 1576, he was not so much interested in the idea of the dignity of human beings or in the proper interpretation of Scripture as in the making of money. When his son, Richard, and his son's friend and partner, William Shakespeare, and their fellow shareholders were creating and performing their scripts, they were counting the house above all else. Theater was an essential part of the entertainment industry, and for some, it was especially lucrative. If a man was an actor, he made a little bit of money; if a playwright, a little more; if a shareholder in the company that put on the play, a very great deal more; and if a householder in the building in which the plays were performed, even more still. Shakespeare was all four, and as we read his scripts, we should remember that the artist was also a businessman, interested in the box office as much as or more than any hard-to-imagine immortality. The Elizabethan theater was the forerunner of the multiplex, a collaborative, secular church in which the congregation/audience focused on the service before them, and Shakespeare and his fellows focused on both the service and the collection plate.

And yet with all the primary focus on material gain, Shakespeare and his competitors and collaborators were aware of the cultural importance and historical traditions of drama itself. Their own work continued myths and rituals that had begun in Athens and elsewhere more than two thousand years ago. It may well be true, as Dr. Samuel Johnson famously said, that no man but a blockhead ever wrote for anything but money, and Mozart might have been partially correct when he said that good health and money were the two most important elements in life. Yet we also know that just because a work has been commissioned doesn't rule out the presence of beauty and truth, as indeed Mozart's own works reveal. Michelangelo was paid by Pope Julius II to paint the Sistine Chapel, but nobody thinks of the fee the artist earned when she or he looks at the creation of Adam or the expulsion of Adam and Eve from the Garden of Eden. Shakespeare's career in the Elizabethan theatrical world turned out to be quite lucrative, but given the many profound reasons for which we read and study *A Midsummer Night's Dream, King Lear,* and *The Tempest* today (among so many other plays and poems), we see that the dramatist who created these works and gained so much material success was nevertheless grossly underpaid.

WORKS CITED

Crystal, David and Ben Crystal. *Shakespeare's Words.* London: Penguin, 2002. Print.

Duncan-Jones, Katherine. *Ungentle Shakespeare: Scenes from His Life.* London: Arden Shakespeare-Thomson, 2001. Print.

Evans, G. Blakemore. *Elizabethan-Jacobean Drama.* London: A&C Black, 1988. Print.

Foakes, R. A., ed. *Henslowe's Diary.* 2nd ed. Cambridge: Cambridge UP, 2002. Print.

Greenblatt, Stephen. *Will in the World: How Shakespeare Became Shakespeare.* New York: Norton, 2004. Print.

Gurr, Andrew. *The Shakespearean Stage 1574–1642.* 3rd ed. Cambridge and New York: Cambridge UP, 1992. Print.

Jones, Emrys. *The Origins of Shakespeare.* Oxford: Clarendon, 1977. Print.

Knutson, Rosalyn. *The Repertory of Shakespeare's Company, 1594–1603.* Fayetteville: U of Arkansas P, 1991. Print.

Onions, C. T. *A Shakespeare Glossary.* Oxford: Clarendon, 1911. Print.

Petronella, Vincent F. "Shakespeare's Dramatic Chambers." *In the Company of Shakespeare: Essays on English Renaissance Literature in Honor of G. Blakemore Evans.* Eds. Thomas Moisan and Douglas Bruster. Madison and London: Fairleigh Dickinson and Associated UPs, 2002. 111–38. Print.

Schmidt, Alexander. *Shakespeare Lexicon.* Berlin: Georg Reimer, 1902. Print.

Stern, Tiffany. "'You that walk i' in the Galleries': Standing and Walking in the Galleries of the Globe Theater." *Shakespeare Quarterly* 51 (2000): 211–16. Print.

Thomson, Peter. *Shakespeare's Professional Career.* Cambridge: Cambridge UP, 1992. Print.

Wheeler, Richard P. "Deaths in the Family: The Loss of a Son and the Rise of Shakespearean Comedy." *Shakespeare Quarterly* 51 (2000): 127–54. Print.

INTRODUCTION

Lawrence F. Rhu

HE WINTER'S *Tale* is late Shakespeare, the penultimate play that he composed without collaborating with anyone else. In this final phase of his career, Shakespeare revisited the traumatic plots of his tragedies and revised their unhappy outcomes. Reunion and reconciliation replace death and mourning, and the promise of a new generation's fresh energy imparts hope where despair has previously threatened and often triumphed. Specifically, in Leontes' desperate suspicions and impetuous revenge against his innocent wife, Hermione, *The Winter's Tale* reprises the murderous jealousy of Othello. Leontes, however, requires no demonic tempter, like Iago in *Othello*, to awaken his doubts and fuel his vindictive impulses. Whereas Iago views the courtly familiarities of Cassio's ingratiating manner as a resource to exploit in a calculated scheme to poison Othello's trust in Desdemona, Leontes reaches an extreme of jealousy with no outside help. Moreover, if we appreciate the mores of such a court society as Shakespeare represents in Sicilia, where Leontes reigns, we can see that he has his reasons.

COURTESY AND GRACE

As the play opens, Shakespeare takes pains to show us a world where courtesy itself is a form of competition, and we can hear, in the ceremonious exchanges of gratitude and hospitality between Archidamas and Camillo, an undeclared rivalry. Bohemia could not possibly measure up to the standards of lavish entertainment set by Sicilia during Polixenes' visit there. So, in taking his leave, Archidamas feels obliged to acknowledge the "great difference" between the two kingdoms and the consequent limits to Bohemia's ability to reciprocate. In response, Camillo strikes indirectly one of the keynotes of the play as he lightly chides Archidamas for making too much of his indebtedness to Sicilian hospitality: "You pay a great deal too dear for what's given freely" (1.1.17–8). In the next scene, we will hear three times the word "grace," which is thus given casual emphasis. Because the manifold meanings of this word resonate throughout *The Winter's Tale*, it is wise to mark its earliest and perhaps most oblique appearance.

Theologically, grace is an unmerited reward, a sort of bonus for merely being alive; not even "cheap" (as it is labeled by detractors of some contemporary uses to which this doctrine is put), it is free. European courtiers also esteemed something that they called by this name as an essential attribute of their role in society; but, despite their constant pretense of nonchalance and ease, they often had to work hard for it. Gracious manners required cultivation, although they were meant to appear natural. Likewise, actors on the stage aspired to a quality in their performances whose emotional power and mimetic integrity at their best could earn the tribute of such a term. These three senses of the term "grace"—the courtly, the theatrical, and the theological—overlap and play off one another in *The Winter's Tale*, where all three of these institutions—the court, the stage, and the church—have their words tested by standards of truth and consequentiality that they often seek to evade.

Just as the courtly familiarities of Polixenes and Hermione leave ample room for suspicion, the language of the play's second scene is also laden with possibilities for misunderstanding. If you are in a particular frame of mind, like Leontes, ambiguity easily becomes innuendo, and the absolute power of his sovereignty enables him to act upon imaginary fears—with real consequences. Polixenes' first lines specify the length of his stay as nine months, and Hermione's fully pregnant body serves as an obvious reminder of what has developed during the time of his visit. Ironically, we have heard nothing of the queen's imminent delivery in the opening scene, but only of the promise of her son, Mamillius, whose gallant nature "makes old hearts fresh" (1.1.39). He stands on the brink of a transition from childhood to youth that he will never make, but his name suggests the nursing that Hermione's newborn will soon require. The women's world of pregnancy and childrearing is one in which men take little part, although standing apart, as Leontes does, has its hazards: isolation, misunderstanding, delusion, and paranoia. He succumbs to them all, and he has the power to turn that surrender into a reign of terror.

The memory of Henry VIII was hardly remote under James I, in 1611, when *The Winter's Tale* was probably first staged. In a way, what happens to Perdita in the play happened to Elizabeth Tudor in real life. Declaring her illegitimate, a sexually crazed tyrant tried and executed her mother on fantastic, multiple charges of adultery. What part of this does not sound "torn from the headlines" of our daily newspapers? Perhaps unbridled tyranny takes different forms nowadays, but sexual craziness still abounds in high and low places. This is Shakespeare's great theme from the time Gertrude first makes her appearance in Hamlet's imagination, and the traumatic nature of human sexuality that Shakespeare explores from myriad angles in his great tragic phase remains a deep challenge of our human condition in the twenty-first century, however transformed it has been by uniquely modern circumstances.

We might say, for example, that the contemporary science of DNA testing could resolve Leontes' doubts about the father of his daughter; but that proof would only reveal the charade he's been playing. His doubts are a cover-up and a flight from his own anguish, as he acknowledges obliquely when he remembers an earlier occasion on which he needed grace and Hermione spoke well: "when / Three crabbed months had sour'd themselves to death / Ere I could make thee open thy white hand, / [And] clap thyself my love; then didst thou utter, / 'I am yours forever.'" To which Hermione responds, "'Tis Grace indeed" (1.2.101–5).

Polixenes' fantasy of a boyhood without care or connection to any other person besides a mirror image of himself makes Leontes' denial of his own neediness both clearer and more commonplace. In the masculine mythology of twinship that Polixenes nostalgically dreams up, the agony of sexual dependency amounts to a curse because it brings to an end the idyllic innocence of boyhood friendship (1.2.62–80). Polixenes heretically imagines this stage of life as uncontaminated in its purity and thus free from original sin; the Fall occurs only with the awakening of heterosexual desire, rather than at the very beginning, as the psalmist puts it: "Behold, I was shapen in iniquity; and in sin did my mother conceive me" (Ps. 51.5). Given the courtly style of Polixenes' account, however, the Fall of Man amounts only to tripping, and Original Sin seems a mere peccadillo. Casual though he is in representing this grand casualty, Hermione reads him clearly and deduces the logical implication of his version of this story: women must be devils if they play the part of Satan in occasioning the Fall. As he is drawn into their conversation, Leontes reveals a similar disposition to fantasies of irresponsible boyhood innocence. He claims that the sight of Mamillius, who moments before had been the occasion for harrowing nightmares of cuckoldry, reminds him of his former self at seven:

> Looking on the lines
> Of my boy's face, methoughts I did recoil
> Twenty-three years, and saw myself unbreech'd
> In my green velvet coat, my dagger muzzled,
> Lest it should bite its master, and so prove
> (As [ornament] oft does) too dangerous.

> (1.2.153–8)

Where, then, does evil come from if these worldly men in their earliest years only frisked in the sun like twin lambs? Polixenes attributes their loss of innocence to women, and in so doing, his explanation corresponds with traditional readings of the Genesis story where Eve routinely receives the blame (Kugel, 100–103, 128–29). But the punishment threatened for Adam and Eve's crime of disobedience is not sexual trauma; it is human finitude. In *The Winter's Tale*, though Hermione allegedly dies, Leontes is the one who experiences the most painfully conscious lesson in human mortality. Like the man in the story that Mamillius begins to tell his mother and her attendants, Leontes comes virtually to live beside the churchyard during his sixteen years of daily visits to the graves of his wife and son (3.2.238–42). He most feelingly acknowledges the ravages of loss and time that result from his fit of sexual paranoia and tyrannical vindictiveness. The play tells a version of the story of *Pandosto*, which Shakespeare's early rival, Robert Greene, subtitled *The Triumph of Time*; and Leontes must reckon not only with the catastrophe that he has caused through his denial of sexual dependency and his perverse presumption of certain knowledge about others. He must also experience the slow passage of time (which will ultimately seem just the blink of an eye), fully conscious of the tragic consequences of his headstrong dishonesty with none other than himself.

To put it crudely, Christian theology has a solution for Leontes' problem, and it is expressed most resonantly by St. Paul: "For since by man came death, by a man came also the resurrection of the dead. For as in Adam all die, even so in Christ shall all be made alive" (1 Cor. 15:21–22). Doctrinally, the divine grace of Christ's sacrifice and resurrection answers for the Fall of man in Genesis; but, despite her nominal association with the apostle who penned those words, Paulina's role in Shakespeare's play entails manifold meanings beyond the exclusively theological. Her masculine aggression in defending her victimized friend, Hermione, adds some of the (few) comic touches to the grimly tragic momentum of the first three acts and bespeaks the stock type of the mannish woman or shrew, such as Shakespeare had earlier portrayed in the protagonist of *The Taming of the Shrew*, Katherina. Moreover, Paulina explicitly casts herself in the role of an advisor at court who brings the medicine of honest counsel that heals the malady of princes, however bitter it may taste at first.

In Camillo, the Sicilian court already possesses an inspiring exemplar of key dimensions of what Castiglione calls the perfection of courtiership (Castiglione, 19). Such figures are meant to cultivate courtly graces with public service in mind. However, their attractive behavior can degenerate into flattery and self-seeking when it is not directed to the communal good of keeping the prince mindful of his obligations to the commonwealth. If tyranny balks at all his efforts of persuasion, a good courtier will leave his position at court rather than serve an evil despot (Castiglione, 241). Camillo, clearly but with all due respect, refuses to stand by in silence at the shameful treatment of his queen. Rather, he confronts Leontes about his terrible mistakes, and only when he sees that no sound advice can stop this tyrant does he feign cooperation and seek a way to leave Sicilia. In Bohemia, Camillo continues his good offices in the service of Polixenes until he decides to assist the young lovers in jeopardy and thus becomes, in a way, an agent of Providence. He gives the impetuous runaways a direction and guides them back to Sicilia, and they become the means of reconciliation and reunion for the older generation, whose otherwise irreparable differences would lead only to despair.

According to Leontes, Camillo, though a courtier, has maintained a "priest-like" relationship with his master:

> I have trusted thee, Camillo,
> With all the nearest things to my heart, as well
> My chamber-councils, wherein, priest-like, thou
> Hast cleans'd my bosom: I from thee departed
> Thy penitent reform'd.
>
> (1.2.235–9)

But once Camillo departs from Sicilia, the ultimately "priestess-like" Paulina, who presides over the lawful magic of the statue's awakening in the final scene, forcibly assumes the role of a good courtier. Leontes, in one of the definitive gestures of the tyrant, has informed his advisors bluntly of their irrelevance to his designs—"We need no more of your advice" (2.1.168)—so Paulina takes their place and comes "with words as medicinal as true, / Honest as either, to purge him of that humour / That presses him from sleep" (2.3.37–9).

In such a figure, whose persona cries out for certain stereotypical and confining responses, what the play requires is the patience to appreciate its complexities. Leontes will quickly supply the most predictable of such responses by labeling Paulina with a veritable catalogue of misogynous terms (witch, bawd, Dame Partlet, etc.), and certainly her comportment smacks of the qualities that these clichés pretend to name. Thus, Paulina's conduct tests the boundaries of gender identity. It essays some offices that do not conventionally become a woman best, despite her claim to the contrary, and puts to the test Hermione's assertion that "a lady's 'verily' is / As potent as a lord's" (1.2.50–51). Because the most effective claim she makes—that Hermione is dead—turns out, in fact, to be a lie, we can see how the play complicates matters in ways that require patient reflection. Paulina's lie, like those of Camillo, puts into practice the idea of "salutary deception," explained and commended by Castiglione as the courtier's sometimes necessary means of public service (Castiglione, 213).

An almost rapturous mood pervades the next-to-last scene of the play, as the Sicilian courtiers vie with one another to evoke the moment of revelation when Perdita's true identity came to light. Recalling this event, they appraise it like a painting or some other *objet d'art*, speaking of "the prettiest touches" (5.2.82) in the breathtaking recognition scene that they have just beheld. Laid on with a trowel as it is, their insistent evocation of the sentiment of wonder prepares the audience for an even greater marvel, the (re)animation of Julio Romano's alleged statue of Hermione. Yet, despite the extravagance of feeling and occurrence during these final scenes, the play also strives anxiously after credibility. From the courtiers, we notably learn of the "remov'd house" (5.2.107) whither all the main characters have retreated to view the statue. Paulina, it turns out, has made twice-daily visits there during the past sixteen years. Thus, when Hermione vows at the play's end to explain how she has "preserv'd / [Herself]" (5.3.127–8), it is hard not to think of those visits, lately revealed, as a sort of afterthought, the playwright's awkward backpedaling to address an earlier impression given too unreservedly and now causing unavoidable problems.

The play flirts with heresy. Perdita kneels to the statue in a gesture that would scandalize Jacobean Protestants, and Paulina empties Hermione's grave like a necromancer. Yet we are being somewhat clumsily informed that there is a realistic explanation for this hocus-pocus. This particular magic is "an art / Lawful as eating" (5.3.110–111), and Paulina, like her namesake the apostle Paul, has been testing the boundaries of the law since she first defied an "express commandment" (2.2.8) and retrieved Hermione's newborn baby from prison to bring him to the king, his father. As Northrop Frye remarks, "In several comedies of Shakespeare, including this one [*The Winter's Tale*] and *The Tempest*, the action gets so hard to believe that a central character summons the rest of the cast into—I suppose—the green room afterward, where, it is promised, all the difficulties will be cleared away. Here it looks as though the green room session will be quite prolonged" (Frye, 169).

In Shakespeare's main source, *Pandosto*, the queen's death is irreversibly final, but Shakespeare takes certain liberties with Greene's prose fiction that open up further possibilities and, indeed, other sources. The play's tragicomic mix of genres perhaps takes its cue from Greene's final sentence in which—"to close up the Comedie with a Tragicall stratageme" (Bullough, 199)—we read how the king's guilt-ridden conscience drove him to suicide. Shakespeare, of course, turns his plot's action in the opposite direction. He also reallocates the kingdoms of Bohemia and Sicilia and makes the latter island the site of his tale's transcendental and figurative winter, the barrenness of flesh and spirit that arises from Leontes' murderous rashness. This geo-political revision makes further room for him to draw upon Ovid's *Metamorphoses*, for Sicily is the site of Proserpina's ravishment by Pluto (or Dis), the lord of the underworld, as related by that Roman poet. In Bohemia, before she and Florizel elope to Sicilia, Perdita explicitly evokes this myth of a fall from eternal flourishing and Edenic abundance into unending winter at the sheep-shearing festival over which she presides:

> O Proserpina,
> For the flow'rs now, that, frighted, thou let'st fall
> From Dis's waggon!
>
> (4.4.116–8)

Leontes reminds us of this myth by thus greeting the young lovers upon arrival in Sicilia: "Welcome hither, / As is the spring to th' earth" (5.1.151–2). Indeed, Ovidian tales of transformation dominate the play's second part after the "wide gap" that Time enables the play to skip over. Florizel virtually footnotes this source when he seeks to reassure the worried Perdita about their transgression of the social barrier between royal blood and peasant stock:

> The gods themselves
> (Humbling their deities to love) have taken
> The shapes of beasts upon them. Jupiter
> Became a bull and bellow'd; the green Neptune
> A ram and bleated; and the fire-rob'd god,
> Golden Apollo, a poor humble swain,
> As I seem now. Their transformations
> Were never for a piece of beauty rarer.
>
> (4.4.25–32)

This passage derives directly from a similar moment in *Pandosto*, which invokes the same catalog of lovestruck deities but bespeaks quite different sentiments (Bullough, 184). In Greene's narrative, this inventory of like-minded gods occurs during an interior monologue in which the prince seeks to reassure himself, *not* his beloved, so an attitude of condescension unmistakably defines this moment in *Pandosto*: the prince lowers himself like a god, and that's a comfort.

Such social snobbery can remind us that it was Greene himself, almost two decades earlier, who decried Shakespeare's early success on the stage by labeling him an "upstart crow, beautified with our feathers" (Schoenbaum, 24). The first-person plural here groups Greene, as opposed to Shakespeare, among learned playwrights and so-called University Wits, who wore their educations on their sleeves and readily sneered at those allegedly less erudite than they. John Pitcher finds the memory of Greene's putdown playfully taken up by Shakespeare, who can be understood to fashion a version of himself in the rogue, Autolycus, that "snapper-up of ill-consider'd trifles" (4.3.26) and vendor of broadsides and ballads that contain what amount to popular Ovidian tales of monstrous transformations. This artful pickpocket and cony-catcher, whose name can idiomatically be construed as "lone wolf," also mirrors Leontes' role as a lion among the courtiers by being a wolf among the shepherds. But in the end, his mischief results not only in securing the evidence for Perdita's recognition as a princess and his own return to court, but also in the elevation of the old Shepherd and his son to the status, or at least to the costume, of "gentlemen born" (5.2.127). From the perspective of folklore and mythology, Autolycus is a trickster, like Coyote in Native American folklore or Reynard the Fox in northern European tales. The wily transgressions of such figures bring about good (see Color Plates 1 and 2).

In the second-longest scene he ever wrote, Shakespeare pointedly explores the hottest topic of his culture, a question that was proverbially posed by the same backward glance toward Eden that both Ovid and the Bible facilitate for Shakespeare: "When Adam delved and Eve span, who was then the gentleman?" (Shapin, 42–64, 56). The pastoral mode opens up a space for philosophy in which such revolutionary inquiries can be entertained at a leisurely pace and without insistent pressure for unambiguous answers. Thus, when Polixenes (in disguise) engages Perdita in a discussion about the comparative merits of particular flowers and especially about hybrids and grafting, we should not be surprised if the positions that they reflect in this dialogue precisely contradict the positions that they embody in the action of the play. Perdita, the one character in whom such fastidiousness seems a most unlikely possibility, fusses about the impurity of mixed breeds, while Polixenes, who in the absoluteness of his reaction to his son's marital intentions will soon seem almost a reincarnation of Leontes, adopts a virtually progressive openness to change and experiment and the improvements they might bring. It is not enough simply to say that our horticultural principles need not exactly reflect our views about marriage and family. The terms of this debate require deeper consideration.

ART AND NATURE

The question of the proper relationship between art and nature lies at the heart of *The Winter's Tale*. The controversial business with the statue of Hermione poses it unforgettably. During the frequently hushed attendance on the supposed handiwork of that rare Italian master, Julio Romano, Leontes asks, "What fine chisel / Could ever yet cut breath?" (5.3.78-9). This is itself an artful sentence in which the medial caesura in line 79 mimes the cutting of the breath in the pause that it entails after the word "breath." But that formal accomplishment should not preempt our awareness of the formative work underway throughout the final scenes, which, as we have already noted, echo with cries and evocations of wonder that guide the audience's response to the events that they are beholding. Just as grace is a keynote of the opening scenes, wonder is the major chord of the finale, and it increases apace in the face of an oft-acknowledged skepticism. Indeed, this oscillation between the extremes of skepticism and wonder reveals the dynamics of the response that these scenes seek to elicit. They would not have any significant impact upon a sensibility shut off from such emotions and the lively process of alternation between them.

The philosopher Ludwig Wittgenstein famously averred that the human body is the best picture of the human soul (Wittgenstein, 178), and the petrification of Hermione, her "astonishment" at Leontes' murderous accusations, bears witness to the soul-killing consequences of his aggressive distrust of his wife. When he cynically taunts her with the claim that her actions are his dreams (3.2.82), we can recognize the fully psychotic image of her that he has fashioned and enforced. Because he is the king, he can make it stick; but as a product of his imagination, it also reveals the psychopathology that went into the creation of this "diseas'd opinion" (1.2.297). The cure for this malady takes a long time in coming, although, given the severity of the offense, it is a miracle that it should come at all. Moreover, there lingers in mind irrepressibly the death of Mamillius, who, even at the end, remains unaccounted for (Cavell, 2003, 193).

The power of art provides a cure by imitating nature, but in that process, the line between mimesis and the reality that it would imitate becomes impossible to locate decisively once and for all. Before the statue of Hermione moves and descends from its pedestal, the harsh realism of the artist's hand is fully registered in Leontes' surprise at seeing the wrinkles in her face (5.3.27-9). Time has not stood still; it never does, despite our natural yearnings that it do so. As Florizel rhapsodizes to his beloved Perdita,

> What you do
> Still betters what is done. When you speak, sweet,

I'ld have you do it ever; when you sing,
I'ld have you buy and sell so; so give alms;
Pray so; and for the ord'ring your affairs,
To sing them too. When you do dance, I wish you
A wave o' th' sea, that you might ever do
Nothing but that; move still, still so,
And own no other function.

(4.4.135–43)

It's not so much that Florizel is his father's son, but one of Adam's. Florizel is not abnormally frightened at the power of time to cause change—just frightened enough to take flight in impossible fantasies of permanence. And it is love that makes him fearful.

Normally, the aging process makes its mark little by little. But when we see close friends or family members whom we have not seen in years, the effects of time upon them bring us up short. We have undergone a similar process of aging in the meantime, but we have noted its gradual occurrence on a more regular basis. It does not suddenly dawn upon us after a wide gap of time, with no intermediate stages of development. Unless special circumstances make it apparent, we are not caught off guard by "the unimaginable touch of time," as Wordsworth memorably put it. But Leontes has been out of sync since the play's beginning, caught up in a mad rush to what his warped mind considers justice (Ewbank, 86–87). The destruction thus wreaked upon his world then requires of him sixteen long years of slow penance. When that penitential reformation of his spirit finally seems at an end, he remains (perhaps inevitably) unaware of the full cost of the time that he has wasted. Hermione's wrinkles bring home the impact of the lost years that he can never completely redeem. The statue, before it moves, helps Leontes to a fresh appreciation of human finitude, and it brings us along with him if we are open to the kind of work the play aims to perform upon us.

In a rash moment, before Camillo intervenes with an offer of guidance, Florizel characterizes himself as "heir to his affection," mirroring his father's fateful distemper and echoing Leontes' earlier apostrophe to "affection" (4.4.481; 1.2.138–46). Florizel intends to act on impulse and with complete abandon as "[a slave] of chance" (4.4.540). Ultimately, he yields to the suggestions of Camillo, and heeding his advice, he enters upon a course of action that will make his marriage to Perdita possible and lead to the reunions and resolutions of the conflict between Bohemia and Sicilia with which the play happily concludes. Like the statue of Hermione, these two states, as Shakespeare represents them, hover between allegory and mimetic realism. On the one hand, they reveal in telling detail certain aspects of institutions like the court and kingship in early modern England; on the other, they are not places on a map but rather places in the heart and states of mind. The seacoast in Bohemia is a notorious fiction that has inspired a chorus of scoffers. There, Perdita is found and Antigonus is devoured by a bear as he protests that he is a gentleman to this creature whose appetite must be especially keen upon emerging in the spring from hibernation, like the play itself. The old Shepherd aptly sums up this transitional moment: "thou met'st with things dying, I with things new-born" (3.3.113–4).

In 1610, the year before *The Winter's Tale* was probably first performed, Galileo Galilei published in Venice a pamphlet called *Sidereus Nuncius*, which is translated as "starry" or "sidereal messenger." Using his own enhanced version of the newly invented telescope, Galileo brought his keen powers of observation and induction to bear upon our moon and upon the moons of Jupiter as well, which he named "the Medicean stars" in a clear bid for a position at the court of the Medici in Florence. In this little book of world-historical significance, Galileo defied Aristotelian astronomy's settled convictions that the heavenly planets have smooth surfaces and orbit the earth in perfect circles. To disprove the first of these beliefs, Galileo described the play of light and darkness upon an especially large cavity on the face of the moon: "It offers the same aspect to shadow and illumination as a region similar to Bohemia would offer on Earth, if it were enclosed on all sides by very high mountains, placed around the periphery in a perfect circle" (Galileo, 47). Galileo's Bohemia contrasts starkly with Shakespeare's, as does descriptive analysis with allegorical representation; but both are instruments in a quest for truth rather than symptoms of irreconcilable differences between two inevitably clashing cultures, the arts and sciences.

Understood in this light, the dialogue between Perdita and Polixenes, however conventional and time-bound a Renaissance topos it may first appear to be, can take upon itself considerable contemporary resonance. Moreover, the paradox of behavior that contradicts emphatically expressed principles that we witness in these two interlocutors can thus become more than another commonplace instance of human inconsistency. It can signify a deeply vexing question that regularly returns us to the interrogative mood despite occasional affirmations and answers. It can confront us with an existential predicament that challenges us with the skepticism that we must live rather than decisively answer once and for all. Leontes' skepticism expresses itself in fanatical conviction. He is sure that he has seen through to the bottom of a deception that only the most perceptive could fathom.

The flattery with which he seeks to enlist Camillo in his cause is basically self-congratulation for his own powers of perception:

> Was this taken
> By any understanding pate but thine?
> For thy conceit is soaking, will draw in
> More than the common blocks. Not noted, is't,
> But of the finer natures? By some severals
> Of head-piece extraordinary? Lower messes
> Perchance are to this business purblind? Say.
>
> (1.2.222–8)

Undeniably, Leontes has a problem, and it is a deeply human, perhaps distinctly male, problem at that. Consider the weird turn Paulina's thought takes when she challenges Leontes and imagines the infant Perdita suspecting that her own (future) children are "not her husband's" (2.3.108), as Leontes suspects of Hermione's newborn daughter. There is no realistic symmetry in this comparative proposition. Any woman, including an adulteress, will far more than likely know the father of her children. But such a suspicion often haunts Shakespeare's male characters, and it is not merely their biological destiny. It is a distinctly masculine anxiety, the consequences of a gendered identity that requires of men autonomy and control in areas where such complete mastery is ultimately impossible. One cannot *know* for sure what Leontes claims that he has figured out, the biological paternity of Hermione's child. Indeed, Leontes' turning of his existential dilemma into a problem of knowledge is itself an evasion of the conditions of possibility within which human understanding of this matter must occur. Like Othello before him, Leontes is disappointed in the fact of his limitations and, seeking to deny them, he turns his self-consuming disappointment into a world-destroying revenge (Cavell, 2003, 6).

But if we update the pastoral debate between art and nature, we can see a version of this Shakespearean dilemma in contemporary terms. First of all, nowadays one could know what Leontes claims to have figured out. DNA testing, which is routinely brought to bear as forensic evidence in paternity cases, offers us a solution to the problem of knowledge that Leontes seeks to address. But would such knowledge solve anything of importance that the play seeks to address and explore? Inasmuch as the play is about marriage, it is hard to imagine that a chromosome match could repair the bonds of love that have already been broken by the violence of Leontes' aggressive doubt. In our courts today, such knowledge does not inspire remarriage; it determines who should pay child support. Marriage, in Milton's terms "a meet and happy conversation," could not survive the assault that it weathers in *The Winter's Tale*.

Natural philosophers in Shakespeare's time tried to discover the secrets of nature to use such knowledge for the betterment of humankind. Prospero, the protagonist in *The Tempest*, in some ways fits this description (Mowat, 286–87). Although the debate about art and nature resonates tellingly with questions of aesthetics pertinent to the final scenes of *The Winter's Tale*, it also suggests the problem of boundaries between the given and the manufactured features of our condition, which become more and more deeply intertwined as our knowledge of nature and our consequent ability to manipulate it increase. The boundaries that produce the contradiction between the avowals of Perdita and Polixenes and their conduct are social matters of rank and degree, but the tenacity of such social differences depended in part on myths that naturalized the social order and affirmed it as a just, because given, hierarchy. The egalitarian aplomb with which Perdita later absorbs the denunciation of Florizel's and her marital intentions by Polixenes anticipates revolutionary perspectives that will soon be voiced more audibly during England's mid-century Civil War:

> I was not much afeard; for once or twice
> I was about to speak, and tell him plainly
> The self-same sun that shines upon his court
> Hides not his visage from our cottage, but
> Looks on alike.

(4.4.442–6)

The magic world of Harry Potter not only features the manipulation of nature, such as scientists of all ages aspire to achieve, but also a Hermione who, as a mudblood occasionally exposed to the exclusionary snobbery of purebloods like Draco Malfoy, faces challenges akin to those confronting Perdita as a lowly shepherdess courted by a prince. Like her Shakespearean namesake, Hermione Granger is turned to stone in *Harry Potter and the Chamber of Secrets*. She is petrified by sighting a basilisk in a mirror and spared from death only by the indirection of her vision (Rowling, 190–91, 214–15). If we are curious about Shakespeare as a source in contemporary writing or prone to wonder about the depth at which allusion may function in popular fiction, we should also note how the basilisk initially appears in *The Winter's Tale*, long before the statue of Hermione holds the stage and the gazes of all upon it in the play's final scene. At Polixenes' first acknowledged inkling of Leontes' hostility toward him, he presses the hesitant

Camillo in these terms to divulge anything he may know about Leontes' changed disposition toward him:

Make me not sighted like the basilisk.
I have look'd on thousands who have sped the better
By my regard, but kill'd none so.

(1.2.388–90)

The Shakespearean Hermione informs us that the "Emperor of Russia was [her] father" (3.2.119), the regent of a wintry land where bears famously abound, but such a lineage avails her not at all. The contemporary manipulation of nature by the magic of genetic engineering promises not only therapeutic miracles but also alluring enhancements of nature that trouble many of us as much as grafting disturbs Perdita. Would we produce more of those "natural aristocrats" that Thomas Jefferson and John Adams saw as rising to the top of an increasingly meritocratic society by cloning our foremost athletes, CEOs, and supermodels? Or would we enter a world of restlessness and perpetual dissatisfaction, as well as inhumane rejection of such shortcomings as have forever been a part of human nature and have often elicited the virtues of charity and even the kindness of strangers like the old Shepherd and his son in *The Winter's Tale*?

DESTINATIONS

These traces of *The Winter's Tale* in J. K. Rowling should remind us that works of literature that continue to matter have destinations as well as sources. Just as Ovid undergoes changes to remain vital for Shakespeare's culture, Shakespeare's plays themselves survive via adaptation to new contexts that transform them in the process of keeping them alive for new generations. Ovid himself is a remarkable case when we consider the pervasiveness of erotic wit in his poetry and the constraints that were placed upon such interests by the monastic culture of medieval Christianity, which was responsible for the transmission of classical literature during the European Middle Ages. The need to allegorize Ovid's otherwise lascivious concerns produced an unforeseen *sensus spiritualis* for texts whose literal meanings were more carnally explicit than the ascetic temper of those times would tolerate.

Notably different attitudes animated Renaissance humanism, so Ovid was increasingly stripped of such allegories and became the model for erotic verse by such English poets as Shakespeare and Christopher Marlowe. In *The Winter's Tale*, besides what we have heard of Proserpina's story, several other myths from the *Metamorphoses* come into play, such as Orpheus and Eurydice and, more importantly,

Pygmalion. This latter tale in Ovid contains more than a touch of bawdry, if not kinkiness, which enables Ovid to communicate feelingly both the agony and the comedy of sexual neediness. In Shakespeare's play, the association of Hermione's statue with the artistry of Julio Romano hints at such concerns. Besides his epitaph, which is preserved in Vasari's life of Julio Romano, we have no other indication that Romano was a sculptor (Barkan, 656). His name, however, was commonly associated with *I modi* (*The Positions*), a volume of explicit sexual guidance with verses by the notorious satirist Pietro Aretino and woodcuts as illustrations by Julio Romano (Orgel, 2003, 112–43). As Leontes knowingly informs us, "It is a bawdy planet" (1.2.201).

Recent appropriations of *The Winter's Tale*, or parts thereof, include most notably British playwright Simon Gray's dark comedy, *Butley* (1972), and French filmmaker Eric Rohmer's *Conte d'hiver* (*A Tale of Winter*, 1992), which is the second installment in his tetralogy, *Contes des quatre saisons* (*Tales of the Four Seasons*). In their main characters, both works put an interesting spin on the fanaticism of Leontes.

In *Butley*, Alan Bates memorably interpreted the title role for both stage and screen. Butley is a cynical and perversely disenchanted English professor in a London college that seeks to bring higher education to a diverse urban population, although it somehow manages to offer individual tutorials on the traditional model of elite institutions (Color Plate 3). The play's action occurs against the backdrop of student unrest and violence against such relics of classical culture as the Velium Aristotle, and its central moment features Butley impatiently listening to a student essay on *The Winter's Tale*. The excerpts that we hear read out loud focus on Hermione's "reawakening" and include an unacknowledged borrowing from the final paragraph of an essay on "Shakespeare's Late Plays" by F. R. Leavis, Simon Gray's mentor at Cambridge, whom he once described as "the only great man I have met" (Gray, 1985, 213). Leavis had written of "that effect as of sap rising from the root which *The Winter's Tale* gives us" (Leavis, 181), and Butley's student, Miss Heasman, thus echoes this claim: "As we reach the end of the play we feel our own—spiritual—sap rising" (Gray, 1972, 44). Her words—or are they Leavis's?—elicit this crack from the professor: "Sap. Sap. Yes, I think sap's a better word than some others that spring rhymingly to mind" (Gray, 1972, 45). Mean-spirited as this remark is, it still takes the measure of certain aspirations of our culture. With the political crisis of student protest in the background and the personal crisis of Butley's unraveling ties of family and friendship immediately before us, these words about Shakespeare's words ring hollow and promise no transformation like the one our awakened faith may bring at the end of *The Winter's Tale*.

As a scholar and pedagogue, Butley is the sort of figure that Shakespeare lampoons via Holofernes in *Love's Labor's Lost* or Polonius in *Hamlet*, but as an academic intellectual, he achieves the kind of appalling magnetism that a contemporary playwright like Edward Albee represents in *Who's Afraid of Virginia Woolf?* Butley's destructiveness often exposes hypocrisy and shallowness that deserve no better treatment, but he seems caught in the grip of his own relentless prying and probing, from which he can find no rest. Although once a T. S. Eliot scholar of some promise, Butley's current appetite for verse has fixated upon *Ceciley Parsely's Nursery Rhymes* by Beatrix Potter, and he recites them as a kind of prelinguistic chanting that signals his lost faith in the intelligiblity of any more nuanced literary expression. He seems unable on one occasion even to remember his one-year-old daughter's name, Marina, which calls to mind her namesake in Shakespeare's *Pericles* (a forerunner of Perdita), as well as Eliot's poem of that title. The play's conclusion cites Eliot's citation, in "East Coker," of his Tudor ancestor, Sir Thomas Elyot, who wrote *The Boke Named the Governour* (1531). The aptly named Gardner, who has distinguished himself in the minds of Butley and his colleagues as a "plumed youth" by sporting a hat with feathers in it, reads this passage about dancing and marriage, which calls to mind the sheep-shearing festival in *The Winter's Tale*, before Butley dismisses his new tutee with the following envoi: "Go away, Gardner, and take your plumage with you, I don't want to start again. It's all been a ghastly mistake. I don't find you interesting, any more. You're not what I mean at all, not what I mean at all. I'm too old to play with the likes of you" (Gray, 1972, 77).

The spellbinding morbidity of Butley's disenchantment and cynicism offers us a contemporary version of Leontes' "diseas'd opinion," of which this particular avatar seems incapable of ridding himself. When Miss Heasman identifies the subject of her essay as "*A (sic) Winter's Tale* of a frozen soul," Butley quips, "Bit fish-mongery, that" (Gray, 1972, 43) with his usual perverse misreading of others' words. But she is on to something when she argues that the statue's coming to life represents Leontes' regeneration. That unmoving stone had been the best picture of that human soul prior to his penance and the awakening of his faith under the guidance of Paulina. Its coming to life signals his transformation. There is no resurrection in *The Winter's Tale*, and it would have been tempting the censors to stage such an event. But the play makes us feel what it would be like to witness or experience one; and, of course, such feelings are very much what the Resurrection is about—motions of the heart coming back to life, returning from abysses of loss and despair to a new day as a new person, reborn; something (we had been tempted to believe) that could never happen. If cutting breath means shaping the spirit, guiding it through passages and over thresholds of transformation, Shakespeare's art performs that metaphysical operation upon a responsive audience.

The fanaticism of Leontes reappears in what Stanley Cavell calls the stubbornness of the protagonist of *Conte d'hiver*, Félicie: her unwillingness to settle for less than the person she knows, or rather feels—through what her friend Loic characterizes as her "instinctive science"—to be the true love of her life (Cavell, 2004, 421–43). She recognizes this undeniable depth of her love for Charles first through something she skeptically calls prayer in the Cathedral in Nevers, where their daughter Elise has led her (Color Plate 4). Later, Loic will take Félicie to a performance of *Le conte d'hiver*, as the title of Shakespeare's late play is translated into French on the billboard outside the theater they enter. There, in the statue scene, she will find confirmation of her recognition in the cathedral and the decision that it has inspired. Moved to tears, Félicie takes in, with a similar meditative gaze, a rather stiffly classical rendition of Hermione's reanimation. In it, she finds reassurance of her decision to live without despairing of her lover's return.

Because film, as a medium distinctly different from stage drama, has distinctive means of rendering the effect of the statue scene in *The Winter's Tale*, this Heritage Shakespeare rendition of that moment should not distract us from another, specifically cinematic, way in which Rohmer recounts the return to life of the lost beloved, Charles. What makes movies what they are, motion pictures, is the movement of images that distinguishes them emphatically, if not "magically," from still photography; and it is this feature of film that Rohmer employs to express the "resurrection" of Charles from virtual oblivion. After the prologue-like opening sequence of the film, Charles exists only as a memory and in a snapshot taken on the beach during that "Bohemian" or "pastoral" summer when he and Félicie were lovers, five and a half years ago. That still photo sits on a chest of drawers in their five-year-old daughter Elise's room during the sixteen December days that elapse during the movie. On the last of these days, the subject of that photo comes to life, if you will, on a bus where Elise recognizes and greets her "Papa" seated opposite her and Félicie. Before our eyes (and his alert daughter's), Charles is transformed from a still to a moving picture. The family celebrate their reunion that evening at a dinner which Charles, who is a cook and thus a practitioner of "an art / Lawful as eating" (5.3.110–11), prepares for Félicie's, and now his, entire family.

It is pertinent here to remember that Shakespeare's last plays return to his great tragic cycle to revise their woeful outcomes in wonder and to reprise themes and episodes from the earlier works. For example, the ghost in the first act of *Hamlet* is evoked in the last act of *The Winter's Tale*, when Paulina and Leontes discuss the consequences that they foresee if he were to marry again (Miller, 118–124). Leontes thus speculates about the effect of a second wife, a successor to Hermione:

> One worse,
> And better us'd, would make her sainted spirit
> Again possess her corpse, and on this stage
> (Where we offenders now) appear soul-vex'd,
> And begin, "Why to me—?"
>
> (5.1.56–60)

And Paulina continues this haunting fantasy:

> Were I the ghost that walk'd, I'ld bid you mark
> Her eye, and tell me for what dull part in't
> You chose her; then I'ld shriek, that even your ears
> Should rift to hear me, and the words that follow'd
> Should be "Remember mine."
>
> (5.1.63–7)

Old Hamlet thus walks and cries, "Remember me," but the way Kenneth Branagh represents this figure in the beginning of his 1996 film distinguishes his directorial tactics from those of Rohmer. As Branagh's *Hamlet* opens, the camera pans slowly over a statue of Denmark's heroic late king, and soon it arrives at the pedestal, which announces the name of the figure that it supports. With a different referent, of course, that name also announces the title of the drama about to begin. As the camera then again pans down the statue's length, we briefly glimpse its improbable coming to life: the *statue* begins to draw the sword at its side. The sound occasioned by this gesture gives rise to a sudden flurry of speech and action that decisively interrupts the flow of the camera's initial movements: "Who's there?"

It is easy to miss this filmmaker's trick of animating the bronze effigy of old Hamlet at the start of Branagh's film. We are not prepared for this instant by words such as Paulina's in *The Winter's Tale*, admonishing her audience of Sicilians and their Bohemian visitors and, indirectly, the audience of the play as well: "It is requir'd / You do awake your faith" (5.3.94–5). Only thereafter does the statue of Hermione come to life. Once we comply with Paulina's instructions to become open and receptive, if not credulous, the miracle can occur. The memorial effigy of Hermione can come to life upon that clear condition of our willingness to believe.

The trompe l'oeil at the beginning of Branagh's *Hamlet*, which is so easy to miss, is perhaps usefully conceived of as a "hidden persuader," in Vance Packard's dated phrase: a scarcely noticeable gesture slipped into a sequence of a few frames for the suggestive power it may exert upon an audience's unconscious. Wary as we have become of technological media's capacity to influence indirectly our reception of whatever messages that they seek to impart, our suspicions are far likelier to be fully alert than is our faith to be awakened when we see a movie nowadays. This is especially so when we have an eye upon the prospect of critical discussion of what we have seen onscreen during an epoch notoriously characterized by the hermeneutics of suspicion. Moreover, so much is grandiose about Branagh's *Hamlet* that it only increases our habits of resistance.

Thus, if we turn to his film's final scene and the private conversations between Hamlet and Horatio, some of its "movie business" may strike us as way overdone. Hamlet's serene providentialism, like his secure claim of "perfect conscience" with respect to taking revenge upon Claudius, may trigger more skepticism than conviction. Between his summary assertion, "The readiness is all," and the exhortation, "Let be," the music swells softly. Branagh turns from partial profile and directs his thoughtful gaze nearly straight into the camera. A single tear drops from his right eye and runs slowly down his cheek. If the pathos of this moment affects us, despite the studied resistance that has become almost second nature to practitioners of negative critique and its manifold variants, we might follow Hamlet's advice and, "as a stranger, give it welcome." Perhaps there are "more things in heaven and earth than are dreamed of in your philosophy" (1.5.165–7).

By contrast, Rohmer's film often looks like a home movie, and whatever significance we may find in it will derive from everyday happenings, things that "could happen to anybody," as Maxence puts it in conversation with Félicie. Her achievement of living without despair, which the statue scene in *The Winter's Tale* directly inspires, takes place in contexts whose ordinariness threatens to undermine any sense of consequentiality. Her stubbornness can be construed as fanatic because it denies the obvious lack of a demonstrable basis for the belief she cleaves to, and this characterization of her as a skeptic puts her in the role of Leontes, inasmuch as she insists upon something that others find untenable. The very intensity of her insistence betrays the dubious premise on which she founds her faith. Although what Leontes claimed to know—the paternity of his unborn child—was unknowable to him, the urgency of his need to know is symptomatic both of his maleness and of his sense of masculinity. Thus, finding congruencies between his disposition and that of Félicie nicely complicates our inclination to perceive such skepticism as a gendered trait instead of a condition that can dawn in the mind of any human subject and require an unavoidable reckoning.

The everydayness of the contexts within which Shakespeare becomes a vital resource in Félicie's self-understanding and Rohmer's film puts in perspective the tendency to celebrate this poet's achievement excessively or to challenge it with willful absoluteness. The praise that we automatically lavish upon Shakespeare becomes an occasion for our future revulsion. The tedious oscillation between bardolatry and bardicide that often characterizes the mood swings of our culture's response to Shakespeare makes inaccessible both a precious inheritance and aspects of our everyday experience that we can sometimes make our own through perspectives supplied by the plays.

Félicie comes to understand her situation by witnessing the final scene in *The Winter's Tale* and taking it to heart. Such an awakening becomes intelligible through our interrogation of the play at the place where it is both the most vulnerable and the most compelling. We know that Hermione's return is ultimately a product of human calculation, yet we experience it as a miracle from heaven and the fulfillment of yearnings that the play has aroused—our wish for a happy ending. If we have been tricked, we have also been let in on the trick that's been played upon us, and somehow it holds us nonetheless.

Autolycus is the trickster in the play who gulls the rustics at their festival, and through him, Shakespeare wryly acknowledges the sleights of hand that he sometimes employs in his dramatic art. Autolycus first practices his wiles upon the Shepherd's son and picks his pocket while the Shepherd's son is acting the part of the Good Samaritan and coming to the aid of Autolycus, who pretends that he has been robbed along the road. Autolycus also has a classical lineage that leads us back to the *Metamorphoses* and, beyond that, to the *Odyssey*. "[L]itter'd under Mercury" in Ovid (4.3.25), he is the epic hero's maternal grandfather in Homer. Besides being the patron of thieves, Mercury is also the patron of eloquence, that rhetorical art that Elizabethan schoolboys like Shakespeare trained to acquire and subsequently deployed in their writings of various kinds. Shakespeare's use of *Pandosto* involves an ironically Ovidian return to the rival who had metaphorically accused him, in 1592, of being a literary thief and imposter. Greene echoed a line from *3 Henry VI* to denounce Shakespeare's for his "Tiger's heart wrapt in a player's hide," and John Pitcher explains that this image contains, like a palimpsest, the biblical conceit of a wolf in sheep's clothing (Pitcher, 253). The main root of Autolycus's name means "wolf," as noted before. Thus, Shakespeare seems willing to express a facet of his art as suspect, the machinations of a con artist who gulls his victims mercilessly.

The two most substantial Shakespearean characters without precedent in Greene are Paulina and Autolycus, and both in their different ways are responsible for Ovidian phenomena in the play that express different aspects of Shakespeare's dramatic art. Just as Ovid, by Shakespeare's time, had yielded both high-minded allegories and titillating imitations, so *The Winter's Tale* contains samples of this range of responses to the Roman poet. Paulina presides over a ceremony that recalls the birth of Galatea from the statue that Pygmalion sculpted in so lifelike a manner, which Ovid describes in witty detail. As we have seen, the association of this work with Julio Romano can imply both high and low meanings for the idea of his art, just as this episode evokes both the idea of resurrection and a more worldly view of Pygmalion's experience in an unallegorized Ovid. Among the country bumpkins, Autolycus purveys ballads that recount "how a usurer's wife was brought to bed of twenty money-bags at a burthen" and how a fish "sung . . . against the hard hearts of maids. It was thought she was a woman, and was turn'd into a cold fish for she would not exchange flesh with one that lov'd her. The ballad is very pitiful, and as true" (4.4.262–4, 275–81). The transformation of an unresponsive lover into a "cold fish" seems poetic justice of a distinctly Ovidian kind, and the claim of truth value corresponds to the play's pervasive concern with evidence, or the lack thereof, for convictions of consequence (Lamb, 78).

Paulina echoes a virtual refrain in the play's final scenes when she makes this comment about the statue:

> That she is living,
> Were it but told you, should be hooted at
> Like an old tale.
>
> (5.3.115–7; cf. 5.2.28 and 61)

Mopsa shares her concern with credibility when she gushes over Autolycus's wares: "I love a ballet in print, a-life, for then we are sure they are true" (4.4.260–61). Moreover, such ballads tell tales, or evoke them by the tunes they go to, that apply with considerable precision to the dramatic action of which they are a part. For example, the third of Autolycus's ballads, which he ends up singing with Mopsa and Dorcas, is put to the tune of "Two maids wooing a man" (4.4.289), an apt description of their interactions with the old Shepherd's son at the festival.

But the title to the tale that we watch onstage and to which our response is tested and discussed so persistently in the play itself is registered in an even more self-reflexive moment when Mamillius seeks to entertain his mother and her attendants (2.1.21–32). It is a tale such as Lady Macbeth expresses complete contempt for ["A woman's story at a winter's fire / Authoriz'd by her grandam" (3.4.64–5)] and is nothing like that "summer story" mentioned by Shakespeare in Sonnet 98.7. Mamillius starts to tell it, and his opening lines as a narrator coincide with Leontes' fateful entrance into a scene of tranquil domesticity and playfulness among a world of women which Mamillius, until now, could inhabit safely. Leontes' prompt and open denunciation of Hermione will lead not least to the death of this young prince, upon whose hopes the entire kingdom had rested its confidence. He will be the only unoffending casualty of this outburst and its sequel who is not restored, leaving us to wonder if his sacrifice is not the unacknowledged cost of the reunion and reconciliation that we enjoy as the happy ending of this tragicomedy. Rohmer's *Conte d'hiver* acknowledges a similarly vexing puzzle in its questioning why Félicie made the fateful "lapsus" that misinformed Charles of her address and left them with no way but grace, or good fortune, of ever seeing one another again. She knew she was pregnant, but she told Charles neither that fact nor her right address. Why? Perhaps, if *The Winter's Tale* is any indication of paternal behavior and its consequences, she instinctively (which is her way) meant to spare her child from the dangers of a father's mere presence.

The boy unaccounted for and the silence of Hermione toward Leontes support this sense of patriarchy's murderous entailments, but she does embrace her husband and, according to Camillo, "[hang] about his neck" (5.3.111–12). Moreover, in Rohmer's cinematic telling, we are encouraged to dwell reflectively upon the phrase "tears of joy," which is repeated, as the film's final words, by Félicie and Charles's five-year-old daughter, Elise. At the moment, she has a limited grasp on such an adult expression, no doubt, but that moment, and perhaps that motto as well, should stick with her in what promises to be a happier future for her and her parents. Shakespeare's play makes the same sort of promise and elicits the gratitude that should go along with coming to believe in it despite evidence to the contrary. A grownup can acknowledge painful realities without becoming fixated upon them, learning resilience from the younger generation in the process. Perhaps, in such a moment, we can bridge, however briefly, the widest gap in time of all—that gap "since first / We were dissever'd" (5.3.155).

PERFORMANCE HISTORY

Lawrence F. Rhu

I N   T H E   *Winter's Tale,* anachronisms abound with a sort of grand carelessness about historicity, if not plausibility. We hear about Whitsun pastorals, saintlike sorrows, the emperor of Russia, Julio Romano, and a puritan who sings psalms to hornpipes—all in the pre-Christian world where Apollo presides. Besides historicity, the sequence of events in the plot famously contains a sixteen-year gap and a drastic change of locale—from Sicilia to Bohemia, an ocean away. The plot's structure thus flouts two of the so-called unities that had mounted from one (plot) to three (time, place, and plot) during the European reception of Aristotle's *Poetics* in the sixteenth century. Whether Shakespeare cared much about these matters remains open to question, but Aristotle himself—the Stagirite—sounds dim when, belaboring the obvious, he explains the relative positions in time of the beginning, the middle, and the end. Simplistic as such procedures may sound to the uninitiated, that is how philosophy works, defining its terms before it gets underway. Shakespeare, play by play, demonstrates his mastery of these principles in practice, if not in theory. In *The Tempest,* Shakespeare observes the unities of time, place, and plot that he violated the year before in *The Winter's Tale.*

Nevill Coghill's classic essay, "Six Points of Stagecraft in *The Winter's Tale,*" singles out particular aspects of the play that pose interpretive challenges in performance. As he addresses these so-called problems, he gives a rousing defense of the play's stageworthiness. His approach has influenced the following discussion of what kind of play *The Winter's Tale* is and how it raises issues of interpretation that have been variously addressed in its production and reception over time. Such an approach generally stays close to the text of the play while exploring its afterlife on stage. As a play about resurrection that has frequently achieved dazzling success precisely in that regard, *The Winter's Tale* and its fortunes invite a felicitous application of that grim exchange in Beckett's *Endgame,* when Clov asks Hamm, "Do you believe in the life to come?" and Hamm responds, "Mine always has been" (Beckett, 49). Fraught with sadness and loss though it is, *The Winter's Tale* ultimately provokes laughter and wonder. It inspires the sort of hope in which the promise of tomorrow is present today and we can appreciate what is given because it is no longer taken for granted.

The performance history of *The Winter's Tale* features, like the play itself, some wide gaps in time. Sometimes the play simply went unperformed or, if it was not completely neglected onstage, it was only performed in part. After its earliest recorded production on May 16, 1611, at the Globe in London, court records list five others, at Whitehall, between November 1611 and January 1633. The second of these, in the spring of 1613, was part of a wedding celebration of Princess Elizabeth and Frederick V, the Elector Palatine. He would later become king of Bohemia, and Elizabeth, somewhat like Perdita, would become known as the "winter queen" in Bohemia. Shakespeare could not have foreseen these developments, but he does change the geopolitical arrangements in his primary source, *Pandosto*, in a diplomatic way that suggests his consciousness of England's interest in maintaining Protestant allies on the Continent. Shakespeare removes tyranny from Bohemia, which the Hussite reformation had made Protestant *avant la lettre*, and he relocates it in Sicilia, a securely papistical Italian place in the early modern English imagination. In the process, he loses the traditional association of pastoral poetry with Sicily due to the Syracusan origins of Theocritus, the chief model for Virgil's *Eclogues*. Perdita thus becomes "the queen of curds and cream" in Bohemia (4.4.161).

After 1633, there is no record of any production of *The Winter's Tale* until the mid-eighteenth century, when selective revivals began featuring the play's pastoral scenes. A century is indeed a wide gap in time, but this neglect primarily bespeaks changes in literary taste that are already audible in Ben Jonson's jibe at Shakespearean romance for its willingness "to make nature afraid" (Jonson, 32). Besides the heavy weather of *Tempests* and seacoasts in Bohemia, this inclination would also include the host of improbabilities, excesses, and anachronisms that boldly distinguish *The Winter's Tale* as willfully uninhibited by neoclassical strictures such as the heirs of Jonson's sensibility would express. For Dryden, "poetry was then in its infancy," so we could expect only "some ridiculous, incoherent story... grounded on impossibilities" even from Shakespeare's hand. For Pope, instead of blaming collective naiveté, we can simply forgive Shakespeare for the defects of composition in *The Winter's Tale* because "only some characters, single scenes, or a few particular passages, were of his hand." In Dr. Johnson's assessment of the indirect representation of the reunion of Perdita and Leontes in Act 5, scene 2, the tradition of such exactions continues with this observation: "It was, I suppose, only to spare his own labor that the poet put this whole scene into narrative" (Muir, 24–26). Still, Dr. Johnson concedes that this play "is, with all of its absurdities, very entertaining" (Bronson, 118).

If the earliest record we have is at all representative, neglect and par-
tiality may not be the only sort of inattention that the play has suffered
since its first performances. The recorded stage history of *The Winter's
Tale* begins when Simon Forman enters in his diary a brief account of
his attendance on May 16, 1611, at the Globe. Although he discusses
a performance of *The Winter's Tale*, his few words about it include no
mention of the extraordinary statue scene in Act 5, scene 3, which has
become a signature moment of Shakespeare's late art. This omission
has led some scholars to believe that the scene itself simply was not
yet written in the earliest scripts of the play. Whether or not that is the
case, we may say that, effectively, the scene was not there for Simon
Forman. His absence of a response to its performance indicates either
that it was not performed in the version of the play that he saw or that
somehow Forman did not experience the impact of this momentous
finale. In the latter case, Forman's omission sounds like the account of
somebody who has visited northern Arizona but does not remember
that he saw the Grand Canyon.

Nonetheless, Simon Forman was purposeful in his playgoing that
day, and he did take instruction from his experience in the theater.
Autolycus's larceny and confidence tricks served as a warning to Forman to watch out for such criminals abroad in the land. "Beware," as
he puts it, "of trusting feigned beggars or fawning fellows." Forman
got something out of the play, even though it was not what subsequent
spectators have tended to settle upon as one of the most memorable
aspects of *The Winter's Tale*.

The figure of Autolycus, for example, has come to be seen as a figure of the playwright himself. Shakespeare, thus conceived, becomes
"a snapper up of unconsiderd trifles" (4.3.26) who, in his eclecticism
and resourceful adaptability to a wide range of theatrical opportunities,
makes enduring art out of whatever may come to hand. "Autolycus,"
Louis MacNeice's masterful sketch of the jaunty peddler, artfully
captures in verse something of the audacity in Shakespeare's protean
knack of creatively making do with whatever sources take his fancy,
like works of Robert Greene in various genres. Shakespeare moves
inventively from high to low, from Sicilia to Bohemia, and back again
without any apparent inhibitions such as the University Wits, like
Greene, sought to impose upon him—or at least to die trying.

The Winter's Tale is a play about time in several basic ways. As a generic
hybrid or mixed genre, it mingles the shapes of time that we customarily
expect of the two primary kinds of drama, tragedy and comedy. In
tragedy, time ultimately comes to a halt, and its resumption for those
who survive is hobbled irremediably by the loss of lives that will come
no more except in memory. We experience the tragic waste of these

lives as signs of their worth: Hamlet, Othello, Antony and Cleopatra. Life will go on without them, but it will be a significantly diminished life in consequence. These plays help us mourn human finitude even though they may not teach us any general lesson about our condition except that our limits and our excellences sometimes coincide.

In comedy, the characters must absorb some considerable shocks. For example, the death of Mamillius in *The Winter's Tale* seems to some so irremediable as to undermine any secure sense of recovery and a return to a normally habitable way of life and a shareable sense of community. In most comedies, the characters can take the hard knocks that go with exposing human folly and still come together again in a world reconciled and renewed by the tonic humbling of honest but not fatal reckonings. Marriage, of course, signifies the achievement of this sort of passage through time, just as death leaves its indelible mark on tragic action and thus defines the shape of time that it charts. Once Shakespeare wrote *Hamlet* and entered upon his great tragic phase, he was virtually done with comedy. *Twelfth Night*, which comes a year or so after *Hamlet*, is the last play of this sort whose marriages seem plausible enough to promise some satisfaction and genuine release.

Critics often discuss an apparent paradox in *The Winter's Tale*'s unfolding plot, but they do not usually relate it to the matter of genre and the shapes of time conventionally charted by different kinds of plots. In 4.4.77–108, Polixenes and Perdita disagree ostensibly about gardening but, allegorically, it seems they disagree about intermarriage across ranks in the social hierarchy. The prince is courting a shepherd's daughter and means to marry her without the permission of his father, the king. Perdita's insistence on purity of breeding only like kinds of flowers (original heirloom strains, if you will) apparently contradicts her own intention to marry Florizel, just as King Polixenes' advocacy of grafting, or the cross-breeding of flowers, seems to contradict his disapproval of the betrothal of his son, the heir apparent, to a peasant's daughter. And so they do, if we allegorize along these lines, where horticulture and marriage correspond in the spiritual sense of the purity or impurity of the species combined in reproduction.

The Winter's Tale, however, is a play that memorably talks about itself as a play, as a work of art consciously designed with rare Italianate (if not Italian) mastery. Thus, when we construe hybridity in another figurative sense, it can serve as a sign of *The Winter's Tale*'s mixed genre, tragicomedy, which is frequently characterized in just such terms, as the grafting of one kind of play onto another. That makes it, in Sidney's words, that "mongrel tragicomedy," whose "mingling" of "kings and clowns" and of "horn pipes and funerals" receives such censure from neoclassical purism as Perdita applies to "streak'd gillyvors, / (Which some call Nature's bastards)," in conversation with Polixenes (Gilbert, 451; 4.4.82–3). When Leontes urges Paulina to "afflict" him further, he also echoes a Lucretian commonplace about how poetry works therapeutically, which often served, in Shakespeare's culture, to justify mixed genres and explain other questions of literary theory (Gilbert, 290, 350–51, 380, 427–28, 468, 523):

> Do, Paulina,
> For this affliction has a taste as sweet
> As sweet as any cordial comfort.
>
> (5.3.75–7)

By sweetening the cup of necessarily bitter medicine, such art can please while it instructs, a purpose spectacularly achieved in Paulina's further business with the statue, as well as in Shakespeare's. Despite his sneering at the improbabilities and unnaturalness in *The Winter's Tale*, Ben Jonson reveals a sympathy for the mixed genre of such a play in the frontispiece of his *Works*, which features not only representations of tragedy and comedy but locates the figure of tragicomedy atop the arch whose various niches house the gods and kinds of drama below (Fig. 4). Almost four centuries later, Ingmar Bergman sought to emphasize the play's self-consciousness about such matters by staging *The Winter's Tale* as a play within a play. We can see in the tragic and comic masks sported in the gathering at the beginning of his production that he meant to acknowledge pointedly its metatheatrical understanding of itself (Fig. 5).

The successful return of *The Winter's Tale* to the stage began in the mid-eighteenth century, with performances of excerpts from the play and, especially, with adaptations of the pastoral scenes in Bohemia. This selection enabled performances to focus steadily on the story of Perdita and Florizel as a drama of love impaired by differences of social position. Macnamara Morgan's *The Sheep-Shearing: Or Florizel and Perdita* first appeared in 1754 and was frequently restaged until 1798. Its only real competition was David Garrick's *Florizel and Perdita*, which first appeared in 1756, almost two years after Morgan's play opened. The nearly identical titles can cause confusion, but Garrick's adaptation contained more of the original play, including the statue scene of the last act. It is not hard to understand why a period influenced by neoclassical precepts would thus trim the play of its indecorous mix of genres.

In the play as a whole, the Bohemian scenes make the awkward transition between tragedy and comedy even harder because of the wide gap in time and sentiment that they require the audience to accept; but, on their own, the bulk of these scenes offers material for a drama of star-crossed lovers with a happy ending on the horizon.

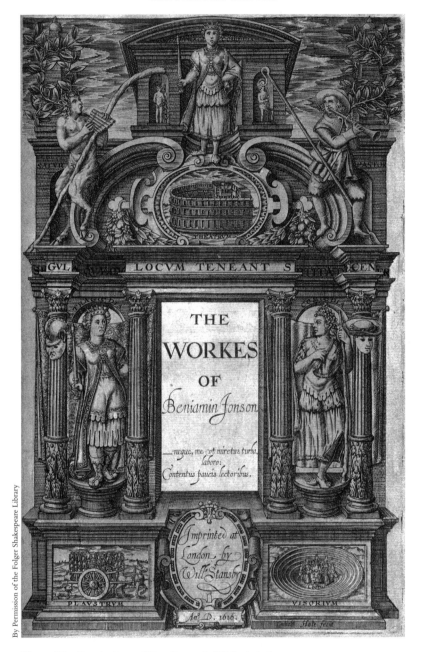

Fig. 4. The frontispiece of Ben Jonson's *Works* (1616).

By permission of Bengt Wanselius

Fig. 5. The masks of tragedy and comedy in Ingmar Bergman's production of *The Winter's Tale* for the Royal Dramatic Theatre of Sweden, Stockholm (1994).

Antigonus's famous *Exit pursued by a bear*, taken straight, can be seen as the culmination of a tyrant's evil deeds and the consequences of a courtier's going along with an evil command. However, immediately thereafter, the Old Shepherd's discovery of the "barne," or infant Perdita, abandoned on the stormstruck coast introduces a drastic change in tone, as does the arrival of his daffy son, the Clown, with his goofy tale of shipwreck and the bear's dinner. From the bear to the "barne," we must traverse a wide range of feelings.

We can see in the terror-stricken Antigonus, dwarfed by such a creature in full attack mode, with flashing teeth, the results of Leontes' tyranny and his courtier's compliance (Fig. 6). However, the infant Perdita, lying behind him in her "bearing-cloth" (3.3.115) on the seacoast of Bohemia, may remind us of another sort of reputation that bears had in Shakespeare's culture. When we look at the emblem that illustrates the origins of the phrase "Licking into shape," we behold a bear mothering her cub with her tongue while a cherub looks on with the town in the background (Fig. 7). He "said his name was Antigonus, a nobleman" (3.3.96–7), says the Clown in his awestruck recounting of this event, whose occurrence he has witnessed firsthand. We can overhear irony in the matter-of-factness of this incidental detail. Antigonus's eleventh-hour claim of nobility did not impress the bear, but the Old Shepherd's sense of the obligations of such a social position can serve as the moral of this moment, which the contrast in these two images sharply illustrates: "We must be gentle, now we are gentlemen" (5.2.152–3). Nature thus teaches culture a lesson; rustics and bears exemplify basic instincts of care and feeding that the artificiality of Sicilian court society cruelly perverts. The bear that devours Antigonus is, like the play, coming out of hibernation. Whether the play can find an art that is as lawful as eating to effect the transition from tragedy to comedy remains to be seen.

The wide gap in time, which the allegorical figure of Time himself soon appears on stage to announce, further complicates the wide gap in feeling that such irony requires us to cross. The pervasive comic pleasures of witnessing these two country bumpkins interact must not be underestimated, but they primarily derive from registers of speech that are precisely the opposite of those consistently heard in Sicilia and from the social differences that such voices signify. The passage of sixteen years mightily compounds this sharp break in the tragic momentum of

Fig. 6. Antigonus (Robert Eddison) and the Bear (Royal Shakespeare Company, 1981).

Reg Wilson ©Royal Shakespeare Company

AMORVM.   57

H

Fig. 7. "Emblemata Amorum." Engraving by Otto Van Veen (1608).

the play that the Old Shepherd and the Clown have already reversed by the complete shift in tone and spirit that their arrival introduces onto the stage. Shakespeare's major source, *Pandosto*, gave Time prominent billing in a subtitle, *The Triumph of Time*, and in an adage that serves as an epigraph, "*Temporis filia veritas*" or "Truth is the daughter of Time" (Fig. 8), but stagecraft cannot so easily gloss over the passage of years as narration can. So Time now asks of us even more indulgence:

Impute it not a crime
To me, or my swift passage, that I slide
O'er sixteen years and leave the growth untried
Of that wide gap, since it is in my pow'r
To o'erthrow law, and in one self-born hour
To plant and o'erwhelm custom. Let me pass
The same I am, ere ancient'st order was,
Or what is now receiv'd. I witness to
The times that brought them in; so shall I do
To th' freshest things now reigning, and make stale
The glistering of this present, as my tale
Now seems to it. Your patience this allowing,

I turn my glass, and give my scene such growing
As you had slept between.

(4.1.4–17)

When Emery Battis appeared as Time in Michael Kahn's 2002 production, he carried neither a sickle nor the hourglass that line 16
seems specifically to assign him as a prop (Fig. 9). Rather, he held a
large snow globe, and one side of his glass displayed in miniature the
play's set of Sicilia, the other that of Bohemia. He turned the globe on
cue from the former locale to the latter, a gesture that deftly illustrates
what philosophers might call a "world-historical event." Time passes,
and we are in a whole new world. In this production, Time's glass thus
represented the moral geography of the play.

Promptly upon his arrival onstage, Autolycus announces the spirit
of this new world. The freshness of springtime triumphs over that
season of sad tales that we are temporarily leaving behind. "For the
red blood reigns in the winter's pale" (4.3.4), as this lawless vagabond
sings during his first appearance in the play. Through him, Bohemia,
now in late summer, will most unrestrainedly come to life, in sharpest
contrast to the claustrophobic frigidities of Leontes' palace and prison

PANDOSTO
The Triumph
of Time.

VVHEREIN IS DISCOVERED
by a pleafant Hiftorie, that although by the
meanes of finifter fortune. Truth may be concealed, yet by Time in fpite of fortune it
is moft manifeftly reuealed.

*Pleafant for age to auoyd drovvfie thoughts, profitable
for youth to efchue other vvanton paftimes, and
bringing to both a defired content.*

Temporis filia veritas.

By Robert Greene Maifter of Artes in Cambridge.

Omne tulit punctum qui mifcuit vtile dulci.

Imprinted at London for I. B. dwelling at the figne of the
Bible, neare vnto the North doore of Paules.
1 5 9 2.

Fig. 8. The title page of
Robert Greene's *Pandosto*
(1592 ed.).

Fig. 9. Emery Battis as Time in Michael Kahn's production of *The Winter's Tale* for The Shakespeare Theatre, Washington, DC (2002).

Photo of Emery Battis in the Shakespeare Theatre Company's 2002 production of The Winter's Tale, photo by Richard Termine.

in Sicilia. In exchange for the grim pallor of tyranny's blanket effect, this splash of color excites the imagination and inspires extravagance, as we can see in two versions of Autolycus—one by the nineteenth-century English painter Charles Robert Leslie and the other from Adrian Noble's 1992 production (Color Plate 1 and Color Plate 2).

In his 1836 painting, Leslie pictures Autolycus at the sheep-shearing festival "puffing his pedlar's wares among the shepherds and shepherdesses outside the old shepherd's cote," as Tom Taylor puts it in his lively introduction to Leslie's autobiography. "The knave, with his box of trinkets and trumpery about his neck, is just twanging off the title of his wonderful ballad 'of a fish that appeared upon the coast, on Wednesday the four-score of April, and sung the ballad against the hard hearts of maids.' Mopsa and Dorcas are scanning the pedlar's toys with greedy eyes, while another shepherdess listens entranced to the tale 'very pitiful and as true,' and the clown, eager for ballads, bids the rogue 'lay it by.'" (Leslie, xxxvi). In the background, sheep graze on the green meadow beneath white clouds of an otherwise blue sky. This Bohemia looks like the Warwickshire countryside of Shakespeare's youth during a sunny moment on a late summer's day. It is impossible to discern if the sheep have been shorn, but, given the occasion, it is a safe bet.

In Noble's production, Autolycus descended from on high, and Robert Smallwood nicely conveys the thrill of this moment. "Against a glorious blue-sky cyclorama, dangling from the end of a huge parachute made of enormous green balloons—like some gigantic bunch of grapes—Richard McCabe's astonishing Autolycus floated down in a battered straw hat and huge-pocketed overcoat, singing with massive enthusiasm and only moderate tunefulness" (Smallwood, 350). Soon he will fleece the Clown—first, of his purse, which is usually of some bright color, like red or gold, to make this theft impossible to miss. Then, in a tour de force of sleight of hand, Autolycus may even dispossess this absent-minded cony of his entire wardrobe, right before our eyes, as he did in Gregory Doran's 1998–99 RSC production. You cannot help but admire this agile felon, whose obliviousness to the stings of conscience can seem an enviable achievement. "For the life to come," he declares, "I sleep out the thought of it" (4.3.30). Our indulgence of this irresistible knave makes us likelier to go easy on Leontes in Act 5 after his long penitential journey.

Even when Leontes has, if you will, paid his dues and performed a saintlike office of repentance, he remains remarkably out of sync with the world as he finds it. The final act begins with Leontes' open acknowledgment that he "kill'd" Hermione. This fact causes him pain when Paulina explicitly names it, but still it is a fact that Leontes now affirms rather than denies once the matter is broached. Hermione is, in Leontes' own words, "her I kill'd." Yet, despite this avowal, Leontes slips a cog and loses track of his own place in time on several notable occasions in what remains of Act 5 after Perdita appears and the mood of wonder starts to prevail. Beholding his own daughter without recognizing her, Leontes expresses his unconsciously incestuous desire for this "most peerless piece of earth . . . / That e're the sun shone bright on" (5.1.94–5), as the Sicilian court poet describes Perdita when he announces the unexpected arrival of the young couple from Bohemia. Later, when Leontes contemplates the statue of Hermione in loving detail, he protests that his deceased wife "was not so much wrinkled, nothing / So aged as this seems" (5.3.28–9). On both of these occasions, Paulina must remind Leontes of time's predictable part in human affairs, including even his own. "Your eye has too much youth in't" (5.1.225), she reminds the king when he suggests that, given the opportunity, he himself may wish to marry Perdita, regardless of the difference of three decades in their ages. Later, when Hermione's wrinkles catch Leontes by surprise, Paulina demonstrates her full appreciation of Julio Romano's excellence as a sculptor who "lets go by some sixteen years, and makes her / As she liv'd now" (5.3.31–2).

Living now is the problem that has stymied Leontes since this play began, and accepting the conditions of possibility for such an accomplishment is the first step toward that goal, which Paulina has been helping Leontes reach. He is, of course, already there, because presence of mind is not a teleological project and the idea of a journey is just a figure of speech. He simply must change by awakening his faith so he can be, as we might put it, *undistractedly* here and now. Or we can swap out the pronouns, which is the play's truest ambition, so that *we* can dwell in the present and participate fully in the transformation of the self that the play's final scene can momentarily accomplish. With all its hokey, Pygmalion-like business about statues coming to life, family reunions and marriages in the nick of time that remains, gentlemen born before their fathers, and so on, this gallimaufry or hodgepodge of a play can, so to speak, make our hearts bleed and then make them fresh. Stones though our hearts have likely become, we can now again breathe through something like artificial respiration performed upon us by this old tale, which Shakespeare keeps telling us that no one in his right mind will ever believe.

During the first decades of the nineteenth century, John Philip Kemble restored most of the Folio text to performance, including the first three acts; and his version of the play was used in major productions for almost half a century. Leontes' passion and Hermione's trial now serve again as a prelude to the action that Morgan and Garrick excerpted to represent their versions of *Florizel and Perdita*. The statue scene thus became more intelligible as the reversal of a tragic sequence of events. The protagonists now enacted again, for virtually the first time in over a century and a half, the major episodes that lead up to that sublime finale.

William Macready and Helena Faucit were especially renowned for their execution of this scene, and she has left accounts of their performances. Macready's intensity and unforeseeable expression of the passions awakened in Leontes by the lifelike statue of Hermione, as it metamorphoses from simulacrum to reality, won him renown. Faucit records her own astonishment at such a performance, as well as her own "personal impersonal quality" in miraculously coming to life (Bartholomuesz, 74). It is as though her body is not her own. Comparison of this inside account with Edwin Morgan's "Advice to an Actor" can remind us that the first actors to perform this role had names like James and John, rather than Helena (Tatspaugh, 799). Either way, it places exceptional demands upon a performer, as Helena Faucit's autobiographical account makes vividly clear and Edwin Morgan's dramatic monologue represents with moving immediacy. A glimpse of Alexandra Gilbreath's performance of this endless moment gives us a moving image of the spiritual stakes in this stillness (Fig. 10).

During the mid-nineteenth century, *The Winter's Tale* went through another remarkable distortion symptomatic of the contemporary *Zeitgeist* when it was being performed. Charles Kean's production relied upon archeological evidence in an effort to supply Shakespeare's fairy tale with a historically accurate version of the Sicilian court of Leontes. By recreating a Syracusan setting from antiquity, Kean amplified the spectacle of his grand production with historically accurate renditions of that ancient tyranny's architecture, dress, and décor. In Castiglione's *The Book of the Courtier*, Plato's experience in Syracuse sets the precedent for conduct in such circumstances as Camillo faces at the play's opening. When Plato realized that Dionysius of Syracuse was of "so evil a nature as to be inveterate in vice," he withdrew from his service, a course of action that Castiglione recommends to all courtiers in similar situations and that Camillo follows (Castiglione, 241). This Renaissance text's paradigmatic illustration of the courtier's dilemma bears more historical pertinence to Camillo's predicament in *The Winter's Tale* than the archeological reconstruction of Kean's *mise-en-scène*, but one era's idea of historicity will not predictably coincide with that of another.

Bob Collier ©Royal Shakespeare Company

Fig. 10. Alexandra Gilbreath as Hermione (Royal Shakespeare Company, 1999).

By the early twentieth century, Harley Granville Barker's production was employing the full Folio text while "eschewing any pretence to the historical," as Stephen Orgel puts it. In this 1912 staging, anachronism "was returned to the heart of the play," and Granville Barker's "revolutionary conception" thus "[reopened] the text to the full range of interpretive possibilities" (Orgel, 1996, 76–77). These interpretations included John Gielgud's 1951 Leontes, whose psychological realism left no doubts about the smoldering jealousy into whose grip Leontes now credibly falls. Almost half a century later, in 1998–99, Anthony Sher would seek out psychiatric advice from numerous experts memorably to conceive of this character as suffering from "morbid jealousy," a condition whose symptoms helpfully corresponded to his understanding of Leontes' character and thus enabled Sher also to achieve psychological realism.

As we can see in the film of this RSC production, Sher portrays the king of Sicilia as a logical lunatic whose insane clarity becomes especially visible in his exchange with Camillo about the queen's infidelity (1.2.210–350) and in his response to the Servant's succinct report about Mamillius's condition (2.3.12–17). In each case, Sher uses his fingers to tick off a list of assertions that effectively embody an orderly itemization of the matter, quite literally, at hand. Here is a king who knows what he is doing, such gestures proclaim, while his derangement only becomes more apparent in the process. The grammar of key passages associated with these gestures nicely suits such an interpretation, whether it is the three topics that organize the dialogue between Camillo and Leontes—cowardice, negligence, and folly—or the sequence of verbs and nouns in parallel structure in Leontes' conversation with the Servant (1.2.239–64; 2.3.12–7). The language invites an actor to build upon these foundations, and Sher aptly bases his Leontes upon them.

Lighting has also been effectively used to set Leontes apart in the prison of his own wild convictions, as Roger Warren observes in discussing Tim Pigott-Smith's performance at Stratford, Ontario (104). I witnessed a similar arrangement in July 2010 at the Courtyard Theatre in Stratford-upon-Avon, where David Farr directed Greg Hicks's finely gauged performance as the jealous king of Sicilia. Leontes seemed something like the title figure in "The Snow Man," a widely anthologized lyric by Wallace Stevens. In conversation with Camillo, Leontes expresses what we may fairly call "a mind of winter," and his line of thought leads him into nothingness, outside and in. His nihilism sounds akin to the emptiness that Stevens conjures up via the same sort of periodic structure dramatically employed by Shakespeare to let Leontes peer into an abyss all his own (1.2.284-96). The Snow Man, however, looks upon a landscape whose appearance mirrors his mind back to him, while Leontes invents the world he inhabits. It is the lens he looks through that creates this panicky Nowhere Man bent on destroying everywhere else, even when the very structure of his crazy argument is, paradoxically, designed to assert the substantiality of "the world and all that's in't" (1.2.293).

In the 2010 English production, the RSC Ensemble was fully engaged with the "entertainment" on stage in Act 1, scene 2, a Christmas party, when a spotlight would single out Leontes and the rest of the stage would go dark. Thus illuminated, Leontes could soliloquize amid the celebrants, whose obliviousness to his mad suspicions seemed absolute while those suspicions themselves had a sort of logical integrity and unitary origin. They were products of an individual source who could reflect in isolation without any special hype to signify the diseased opinion that he was thus expressing.

The theme of enlightenment itself brilliantly complemented such effects with almost manic irony. The thrust stage had a portal at the rear, over which hung a barely discernible painting of Adam and Eve. The mother of humankind was offering our father an apple, or rather *the* apple from the Tree of Knowledge, as became clear when Polixenes casually gestured toward this painting during his speech about the "doctrine of ill-doing" and "the imposition . . . / Hereditary ours" (1.2.67–75). Huge bookshelves, leaning slightly in toward the portal and even a bit out toward the front of the stage, climbed high up the rear walls of the party room. When Antigonus landed on the Bohemian coast, the set had somewhat changed. There was no more festive table colorfully laid out for Christmas dinner. A blustering gale blew out through the portal, announcing a powerful storm. It audibly built in force until the enormous bookshelves, still in the background, suddenly fell forward, flat onto the stage, scattering books and pages everywhere. Amid the wreckage of the Sicilian library, the Old Shepherd would soon sum up his conversation there with his son, the Clown, "Thou met'st with things dying, I with things new-born" (3.3.113–4).

Meanwhile, a bear of sorts, a huge creature manipulated by stagehands, appeared on cue to devour Antigonus. Its "fur" was made of pages like those scattered onstage. Similarly covered persons appeared soon after intermission, which lasted the stage equivalent of sixteen years. They were the Saltiers or Satyrs, "all men of hair," whose arrival so arouses the servant who announces their coming (4.4.326). The pages were their hair, and they sported large clublike phalluses, which the pages scarcely covered and the Saltiers brandished flamboyantly when their fertility dance called for emphasis. So it was that the royal library of Sicilia reappeared in Bohemia, where nature's precedence over culture would fatally and exuberantly make itself felt through death and betrothal and plans for a return trip to Sicilia.

During intermission, it was possible to examine the pages onstage, and I discovered that they were documents of two sorts, abundantly reproduced. One featured Parliamentary debates on both sides—official government records. The other was a facsimile of the title page of the English translation of Immanuel Kant's *Critique of Pure Reason* (1794), with the Preface to the First Edition (1781) on the verso. The stamp of the "Theological Faculty (St. Andrews) Library" indicated the source of this particular copy. The Preface begins with this assertion: "Human reason, in one sphere of its cognition, is called upon to consider questions, which it cannot decline, as they are presented by its own nature, but which it cannot answer, as they transcend every faculty of the mind." Thus, in Bohemia, this flurry of pages and some furry creatures represent the fate of the Enlightenment Project so inauspiciously launched by the mad king of Sicilia. Fortunately, Leontes' designs went far enough awry for his outcast daughter to survive and come of age. Meanwhile, in both countries, good and able servitors at court performed enough salutary deceptions that somehow, with Fortune's connivance, there still was time for a second chance. May we all be so lucky.

WORKS CITED FOR INTRODUCTION AND PERFORMANCE HISTORY

Barkan, Leonard. "'Living Sculptures': Ovid, Michelangelo, and *The Winter's Tale.*" *English Literary History* 48 (1981): 639–67.

Bartholomeusz, Dennis. *"The Winter's Tale" in Performance in England and America, 1611–1976*. Cambridge, UK: Cambridge UP, 1982.

Beckett, Samuel. *Endgame: A Play in One Act*. New York: Grove, 1958.

Bronson, Bertrand H., ed., with Jean M. O'Meara. *Selections from Johnson on Shakespeare*. New Haven: Yale UP, 1986.

Bullough, Geoffrey, ed. *Narrative and Dramatic Sources of Shakespeare*. Vol. VIII. New York: Columbia UP, 1974.

Castiglione, Baldesar. *The Book of the Courtier*. Ed. Daniel Javitch. New York: Norton, 2002.

Cavell, Stanley. *Cities of Words: Pedagogical Letters on a Register of the Moral Life*. Cambridge, MA: Harvard UP, 2004.

———. *Disowning Knowledge in Seven Plays of Shakespeare*. Updated ed. Cambridge, UK: Cambridge UP, 2003.

Coghill, Nevill. "Six Points of Stagecraft in *The Winter's Tale.*" *Shakespeare Survey* 11 (1958): 21–32.

Ewbank, Inga-Stina. "The Triumph of Time in *The Winter's Tale.*" *Review of English Literature* 5 (1964): 83–100.

Frye, Northrop. *Northrop Frye on Shakespeare*. Ed. Robert Sandler. New Haven: Yale UP, 1986.

Galileo, Galilei. *Sidereus Nuncius or The Sidereal Messenger.* Trans. Albert Van Helden. Chicago: U of Chicago P, 1989.

Gilbert, Allan H., Ed. *Literary Criticism: From Plato to Dryden.* Detroit: Wayne State UP, 1962.

Gray, Simon. *An Unatural Pursuit and Other Pieces.* London: Faber, 1985.

———. *Butley.* New York: Viking, 1972.

Jonson, Ben. *Bartholomew Fair.* Ed. Eugene W. Waith. New Haven: Yale UP, 1963.

Kugel, James L. *Traditions of the Bible: A Guide to the Bible as It Was at the Start of the Common Era.* Cambridge, MA: Harvard UP, 1998.

Lamb, Mary Ellen. "Ovid and *The Winter's Tale.*" In *Shakespeare and the Dramatic Tradition: Essays in Honor of S. F. Johnson.* Eds. W. R. Elton and William B. Long. Delaware: U of Delaware P, 1989. 69–87.

Leavis, F. R. *The Common Pursuit.* New York: George W. Stewart, 1952.

Leslie, Charles Robert. *Autobiographical Recollections.* Ed. Tom Taylor. Boston: Ticknor and Fields, 1860.

Miller, David Lee. *Dreams of the Burning Child: Sacrificial Sons and the Father's Witness.* Ithaca, NY: Cornell UP, 2003.

Mowat, Barbara A. "Prospero, Agrippa, and Hocus Pocus." *English Literary Renaissance* 11 (1981): 281–303.

Muir, Kenneth, ed. *"The Winter's Tale." A Casebook.* London: Macmillan, 1969.

Orgel, Stephen. *Imagining Shakespeare: A History of Texts and Visions.* New York: Palgrave Macmillan, 2003.

———, Ed. *The Winter's Tale.* Oxford: Oxford UP, 1996.

Pitcher, John. "Some call him Autolycus." In *In Arden: Editing Shakespeare.* Eds. Ann Thompson and Gordon McMullan. London: Thomson, 2003. 252–68.

Rowling, J. K. *Harry Potter and the Chamber of Secrets.* New York: Arthur A. Levine, 1999.

Schoenbaum, S. *Shakespeare's Lives.* Oxford: Clarendon, 1991.

Shapin, Steven. *A Social History of Truth: Civility and Science in Seventeenth Century England.* Chicago: U of Chicago P, 1994.

Smallwood, Robert. "Shakespeare at Stratford-upon-Avon, 1990." *Shakespeare Quarterly* 44.3 (1993): 343–62.

Stevens, Wallace. "The Snow Man." *The Collected Poems of Wallace Stevens.* New York: Alfred A. Knopf, 1965.

Tatspaugh, Patricia E. "*The Winter's Tale* on Stage: Performances." In *The Winter's Tale: A New Variorum Edition of Shakespeare.* Ed. Robert Kean Turner et al. New York: Modern Languages Association of America, 2003. 708–816.

Warren, Roger. *Staging Shakespeare's Late Plays.* Oxford: Clarendon, 1990.

Wittgenstein, Ludwig. *Philosophical Investigations.* 3d ed. Trans. G. E. M. Anscombe. New York: Macmillan, 1968.

ABBREVIATIONS

F1, F2, etc. First Folio, Second Folio, etc.
conj. conjecture
ed. editor
l(l). line(s)
o.s.d. opening stage direction
s.d(d). stage direction(s)
s.p(p). speech-prefix(es)
subs. substantially

Reference in explanatory and textual notes is in general by last name of editor or author. Not included in the following list of works so cited are editions of the play or special studies referred to in the selected bibliographies appended to the "Note on the Text" following the play.

ALEXANDER, Peter, ed., *Works*, 1951

CAMBRIDGE, *Works*, ed. W. G. Clark and W. A. Wright, 1863-66 (9 vols.); ed. W. A. Wright, 1891-93 (9 vols.)

CAPELL, Edward, ed., *Works*, [1768] (10 vols.)

COLLIER, John P., ed., *Works*, 1842-44 (8 vols.); 1853; 1858 (6 vols.)

CRAIG, William J., ed., *Works*, 1891

DYCE, Alexander, ed., *Works*, 1857 (6 vols.); 1864-67 (9 vols.); 1875-76 (9 vols.)

FURNESS, H. H., ed., New Variorum Edition, 1871-1928 (vols. 1-15; vols. 16-21 by H. H. Furness, Jr.)

HANMER, Thomas, ed., *Works*, 1743-44 (6 vols.); 1745; 1770-71 (6 vols.)

KITTREDGE, George L., ed., *Works*, 1936

JOHNSON, Samuel, ed., *Works*, 1765 (2 eds., 8 vols.); 1768 (8 vols.)

MALONE, Edmond, ed., *Works*, 1790 (10 vols.)

POPE, Alexander, ed., *Works*, 1723-25 (6 vols.); 1728 (8 vols.)

ROWE, Nicholas, ed., *Works*, 1709 (2 eds., 6 vols.); 1714 (8 vols.)

SISSON, Charles, ed., *Works*, [1954]

STAUNTON, Howard, ed., *Works*, 1858-60 (3 vols.)

STEEVENS, George, ed., *Works*, 1773 (with Samuel Johnson, 10 vols.); 1778 (10 vols.); 1793 (15 vols.)

THEOBALD, Lewis, ed., *Works*, 1733 (7 vols.); 1740 (8 vols.); 1757 (8 vols.)

TYRWHITT, Thomas, *Observations and Conjectures upon Some Passages of Shakespeare*, 1766

WALKER, William S., *Critical Examination of the Text of Shakespeare*, 1860 (3 vols.)

WARBURTON, William, ed., *Works*, 1747 (8 vols.)

WHITE, Richard Grant, ed., *Works*, 1857-66 (12 vols.); 1883 (6 vols.)

WILSON, John Dover (with A. Quiller-Couch et al.), ed., *Works* (New Shakespeare), 1921-66 (39 vols.)

THE WINTER'S TALE

THE NAMES OF THE ACTORS

LEONTES, *King of Sicilia*
MAMILLIUS, *young prince of Sicilia*
CAMILLO
ANTIGONUS
CLEOMINES } *four lords of Sicilia*
DION
POLIXENES, *King of Bohemia*
FLORIZEL, *prince of Bohemia*
ARCHIDAMUS, *a lord of Bohemia*
Old SHEPHERD, *reputed father of Perdita*
CLOWN, *his son*
AUTOLYCUS, *a rogue*
[MARINER]
[JAILER]
HERMIONE, *queen to Leontes*
PERDITA, *daughter to Leontes and Hermione*
PAULINA, *wife to Antigonus*
EMILIA, *a lady* [*attending on Hermione*]
[MOPSA
[DORCAS } *shepherdesses*
[TIME, *as Chorus*]
Other LORDS *and* GENTLEMEN, [LADIES, OFFICERS,]
and SERVANTS, SHEPHERDS, *and* SHEPHERDESSES

[SCENE: *Sicilia and Bohemia*]

Act I

SCENE I

Enter CAMILLO *and* ARCHIDAMUS.

ARCHIDAMUS If you shall chance, Camillo, to visit Bohemia on the like occasion whereon my services are
now on foot, you shall see (as I have said) great difference betwixt our Bohemia and your Sicilia.

CAMILLO I think, this coming summer, the King of   5
Sicilia means to pay Bohemia the visitation which he
justly owes him.

ARCHIDAMUS Wherein our entertainment shall shame us:
we will be justified in our loves; for indeed—

CAMILLO Beseech you—   10

ARCHIDAMUS Verily, I speak it in the freedom of my
knowledge: we cannot with such magnificence—in so
rare—I know not what to say—We will give you
sleepy drinks, that your senses (unintelligent of our
insufficience) may, though they cannot praise us, as   15
little accuse us.

CAMILLO You pay a great deal too dear for what's
given freely.

ARCHIDAMUS Believe me, I speak as my understanding instructs me, and as mine honesty puts it to utterance.   20

CAMILLO Sicilia cannot show himself overkind to
Bohemia. They were train'd together in their childhoods; and there rooted betwixt them then such an

---

*Words and passages enclosed in square brackets in the text above are either emendations of
the copy-text or additions to it. The Textual Notes immediately following the play cite the
earliest authority for every such change or insertion and supply the reading of the copy-text
wherever it is emended in this edition.*

1.1. Location: Sicilia. The palace of Leontes. **6. Bohemia:** the King of Bohemia
(a frequent usage). **8. shame us:** i.e. by falling short of your entertainment of us.
9. be . . . loves: make up for it by our affection. **14. unintelligent:** unaware.

71

affection, which cannot choose but branch now. Since
their more mature dignities and royal necessities   25
made separation of their society, their encounters
(though not personal) hath been royally attorney'd
with interchange of gifts, letters, loving embassies,
that they have seem'd to be together, though absent;
shook hands, as over a vast; and embrac'd as it   30
were from the ends of oppos'd winds. The heavens
continue their loves!

ARCHIDAMUS I think there is not in the world either malice
or matter to alter it. You have an unspeakable comfort
of your young prince Mamillius: it is a gentleman of   35
the greatest promise that ever came into my note.

CAMILLO I very well agree with you in the hopes of
him; it is a gallant child; one that, indeed, physics the
subject, makes old hearts fresh. They that went on
crutches ere he was born desire yet their life to see   40
him a man.

ARCHIDAMUS Would they else be content to die?

CAMILLO Yes; if there were no other excuse why they
should desire to live.

ARCHIDAMUS If the King had no son, they would desire to   45
live on crutches till he had one.   *Exeunt.*

SCENE 2

Enter LEONTES, HERMIONE, MAMILLIUS, POLIXENES,
CAMILLO, [*and* ATTENDANTS].

POLIXENES Nine changes of the wat'ry star hath been
The shepherd's note since we have left our throne
Without a burthen. Time as long again
Would be fill'd up, my brother, with our thanks,
And yet we should, for perpetuity,   5
Go hence in debt. And therefore, like a cipher
(Yet standing in rich place), I multiply

24. branch: send out shoots, i.e. flourish. 27. attorney'd: performed by
proxy. 30. vast: wide expanse. 31. ends . . . winds: i.e. opposite corners of the
earth. 36. into my note: under my observation. 38–39. physics the subject:
acts as a restorative medicine to the populace. 1.2. Location: Sicilia. The palace of
Leontes. 1. wat'ry star: moon. 2. we. Royal plural. 3. burthen: burden, i.e.
occupant. 5–6. yet . . . debt: even after that we should depart in your debt forever.
6–7. like . . . place: i.e. having no value in itself, yet capable of multiplying
the value of the numbers that stand before it.

With one "We thank you" many thousands moe
That go before it.

LEONTES   Stay your thanks a while,
And pay them when you part.

POLIXENES   Sir, that's to-morrow.   10
I am question'd by my fears of what may chance
Or breed upon our absence, that may blow
No sneaping winds at home, to make us say,
"This is put forth too truly." Besides, I have stay'd
To tire your royalty.

LEONTES   We are tougher, brother,   15
Than you can put us to't.

POLIXENES   No longer stay.

LEONTES One sev'nnight longer.

POLIXENES   Very sooth, to-morrow.

LEONTES We'll part the time between 's then; and in that
I'll no gainsaying.

POLIXENES   Press me not, beseech you, so.
There is no tongue that moves, none, none i' th' world,   20
So soon as yours could win me. So it should now,
Were there necessity in your request, although
'Twere needful I denied it. My affairs
Do even drag me homeward; which to hinder
Were (in your love) a whip to me; my stay,   25
To you a charge and trouble. To save both,
Farewell, our brother.

LEONTES   Tongue-tied our queen? Speak you.

HERMIONE I had thought, sir, to have held my peace until
You had drawn oaths from him not to stay. You, sir,
Charge him too coldly. Tell him you are sure   30
All in Bohemia's well; this satisfaction
The by-gone day proclaim'd. Say this to him,
He's beat from his best ward.

---

8. moe: more.   **11–14. I . . . truly:** I am concerned about what may happen at
home, by chance or as a direct result of my absence—concerned lest biting (*sneaping*)
winds may blow (i.e. forces hostile to me may be active) to make me say my fears
were well-founded.   **15–16. We . . . to't:** I can withstand your extremest pressure,
i.e. you couldn't stay long enough to tire me.   **18. part the time:** i.e. split the difference (of one week).   **19. I'll no gainsaying:** I'll take no denial.   **22–23. although . . .
it:** even if I had pressing reason to refuse it.   **25. in . . . whip:** though a sign of
your love, a punishment.   **26. charge:** expense.   **31–32. this . . . proclaim'd:** this
reassuring news was heard from Bohemia yesterday.   **33. beat . . . ward:** forced
from his best defensive position. The combat imagery goes back to *Charge* (line 30).

LEONTES   Well said, Hermione.

HERMIONE To tell he longs to see his son were strong;
But let him say so then, and let him go;   35
But let him swear so, and he shall not stay,
We'll thwack him hence with distaffs.
Yet of your royal presence I'll adventure
The borrow of a week. When at Bohemia
You take my lord, I'll give him my commission   40
To let him there a month behind the gest
Prefix'd for 's parting; yet, good deed, Leontes,
I love thee not a jar o' th' clock behind
What lady she her lord. You'll stay?

POLIXENES   No, madam.

HERMIONE Nay, but you will?

POLIXENES   I may not, verily.   45

HERMIONE Verily?
You put me off with limber vows; but I,
Though you would seek t' unsphere the stars with oaths,
Should yet say, "Sir, no going." Verily,
You shall not go; a lady's "verily" is   50
As potent as a lord's. Will you go yet?
Force me to keep you as a prisoner,
Not like a guest: so you shall pay your fees
When you depart, and save your thanks. How say you?
My prisoner? or my guest? By your dread "verily,"   55
One of them you shall be.

POLIXENES   Your guest then, madam.
To be your prisoner should import offending,
Which is for me less easy to commit
Than you to punish.

HERMIONE   Not your jailer then,
But your kind hostess. Come, I'll question you   60
Of my lord's tricks and yours when you were boys.
You were pretty lordings then?

POLIXENES   We were, fair queen,
Two lads that thought there was no more behind

---

34. tell: tell us.   **38. adventure:** risk (since she must stand ready to repay the loan with interest).   **40. take:** charm. **commission:** authorization.   **41. let him:** permit him to remain. **gest:** a stop on a royal journey; here, appointed day. **42. Prefix'd:** set in advance. **good deed:** in truth.   **43. jar:** tick.   **44. What lady she:** any lady whatever.   **47. limber:** limp, flabby.   **53. fees.** Jailers claimed a fee from prisoners upon their release.   **57. import offending:** imply that I had committed some offense.   **63. behind:** beyond, to come.

But such a day to-morrow as to-day,
And to be boy eternal.

HERMIONE   Was not my lord   65
  The verier wag o' th' two?

POLIXENES We were as twinn'd lambs that did frisk i' th' sun,
  And bleat the one at th' other. What we chang'd
  Was innocence for innocence; we knew not
  The doctrine of ill-doing, nor dream'd   70
  That any did. Had we pursu'd that life,
  And our weak spirits ne'er been higher rear'd
  With stronger blood, we should have answer'd heaven
  Boldly, "Not guilty"; the imposition clear'd,
  Hereditary ours.

HERMIONE   By this we gather   75
  You have tripp'd since.

POLIXENES   O my most sacred lady,
  Temptations have since then been born to 's: for
  In those unfledg'd days was my wife a girl;
  Your precious self had then not cross'd the eyes
  Of my young playfellow.

HERMIONE   Grace to boot!   80
  Of this make no conclusion, lest you say
  Your queen and I are devils. Yet go on,
  Th' offenses we have made you do we'll answer,
  If you first sinn'd with us, and that with us
  You did continue fault, and that you slipp'd not   85
  With any but with us.

LEONTES   Is he won yet?

HERMIONE He'll stay, my lord.

LEONTES   At my request he would not.
  Hermione, my dearest, thou never spok'st
  To better purpose.

HERMIONE   Never?

LEONTES   Never, but once.

HERMIONE What? have I twice said well? When was't before?   90
  I prithee tell me; cram 's with praise, and make 's

66. **verier wag:** greater rascal. 67. **twinn'd:** exactly alike. 68. **chang'd:** exchanged. 73. **stronger blood:** i.e. the passions of maturity. 74–75. **the imposition . . . ours:** even original sin being remitted (because our wills would never have been corrupted). 78. **unfledg'd:** immature. 80. **Grace to boot:** heavenly grace help me. 81. **Of . . . conclusion:** don't follow out that line of reasoning to its logical end. 83. **answer:** answer for. 84, 85. **that.** Takes on the sense of *If* (line 84); a common usage in Elizabethan English. 85. **fault:** offense, sin. 91. **cram 's:** cram us. Hermione speaks for herself and all women.

As fat as tame things. One good deed dying tongueless
Slaughters a thousand waiting upon that.
Our praises are our wages. You may ride 's
With one soft kiss a thousand furlongs ere   95
With spur we heat an acre. But to th' goal:
My last good deed was to entreat his stay;
What was my first? It has an elder sister,
Or I mistake you. O, would her name were Grace!
But once before I spoke to th' purpose? when?   100
Nay, let me have't; I long.
LEONTES   Why, that was when
Three crabbed months had sour'd themselves to death,
Ere I could make thee open thy white hand,
[And] clap thyself my love; then didst thou utter,
"I am yours for ever."
HERMIONE   'Tis Grace indeed.   105
Why, lo you now! I have spoke to th' purpose twice:
The one for ever earn'd a royal husband;
Th' other for some while a friend.
                            [*Gives her hand to Polixenes.*]
LEONTES   [*Aside.*] Too hot, too hot!
To mingle friendship far is mingling bloods.
I have *tremor cordis* on me; my heart dances,   110
But not for joy; not joy. This entertainment
May a free face put on, derive a liberty
From heartiness, from bounty, fertile bosom,
And well become the agent; 't may—I grant.
But to be paddling palms and pinching fingers,   115
As now they are, and making practic'd smiles,
As in a looking-glass; and then to sigh, as 'twere
The mort o' th' deer—O, that is entertainment
My bosom likes not, nor my brows! Mamillius,
Art thou my boy?
MAMILLIUS   Ay, my good lord.
LEONTES   I' fecks!   120

---

92. tongueless: without praise.   **93. waiting upon that:** i.e. which would have
followed that if it had been praised.   **96. heat:** race over. **goal:** point aimed at, purpose.   **99. would . . . Grace:** i.e. may it prove to have been a virtuous action (with
a backward glance at lines 76–86).   **104. clap:** pledge by handclasp.   **110. tremor
cordis:** fluttering of the heart.   **111. entertainment:** courtesy to a guest.   **112.
free:** innocent.   **113. heartiness:** warmheartedness. **fertile bosom:** generous affection.   **118. mort . . . deer:** horn blast announcing the death of the hunted
deer.   **119. brows.** Alluding to the common Elizabethan notion that a cuckold
grew horns.   **120. I' fecks:** in faith.

Why, that's my bawcock. What? [hast] smutch'd thy nose?
They say it is a copy out of mine. Come, captain,
We must be neat; not neat, but cleanly, captain:
And yet the steer, the heckfer, and the calf
Are all call'd neat.—Still virginalling   125
Upon his palm?—How now, you wanton calf,
Art thou my calf?
MAMILLIUS   Yes, if you will, my lord.
LEONTES Thou want'st a rough pash and the shoots that I have,
To be full like me; yet they say we are
Almost as like as eggs; women say so—   130
That will say any thing. But were they false
As o'er-dy'd blacks, as wind, as waters, false
As dice are to be wish'd by one that fixes
No bourn 'twixt his and mine, yet were it true
To say this boy were like me. Come, sir page,   135
Look on me with your welkin eye. Sweet villain!
Most dear'st! my collop! Can thy dam?—may't be?—
Affection! thy intention stabs the centre.
Thou dost make possible things not so held,
Communicat'st with dreams (how can this be?),   140
With what's unreal thou co-active art,
And fellow'st nothing. Then 'tis very credent
Thou mayst co-join with something, and thou dost
(And that beyond commission), and I find it
(And that to the infection of my brains   145
And hard'ning of my brows).
POLIXENES   What means Sicilia?
HERMIONE He something seems unsettled.
POLIXENES   How? my lord?
LEONTES What cheer? How is't with you, best brother?

---

121. bawcock: fine fellow (French *beau coq*). **123. not neat.** Leontes' mind leaps
from the sense "tidy" to the sense "cattle," and he rejects the term because cattle
have horns. **124. heckfer:** heifer. **125. virginalling:** fingering, as when playing
the virginals. **126. wanton:** sportive. **128. rough pash:** shaggy head. **shoots:**
horns. **129. full:** entirely. **132. o'er-dy'd blacks:** black things painted over
with another color. **134. bourn:** boundary. **136. welkin:** like the sky, i.e. blue.
137. collop: bit of meat cut from a larger piece, i.e. portion of my own flesh.
138. Affection: *affectio*, a sudden, unexplained change in mind and body; here,
jealousy. **intention:** intensity. **centre:** heart (?) or core of existence (?). **139. not so
held:** not supposed possible. **142. fellow'st nothing:** you associate yourself with
what is nonexistent. **credent:** credible. **144. commission:** what is authorized.
find: experience. **147. something seems:** seems somewhat. **148. What . . .
brother.** Many editors assign this speech to Polixenes.

HERMIONE   You look
    As if you held a brow of much distraction.
    Are you mov'd, my lord?
LEONTES   No, in good earnest.   150
    How sometimes nature will betray its folly!
    Its tenderness! and make itself a pastime
    To harder bosoms! Looking on the lines
    Of my boy's face, methoughts I did recoil
    Twenty-three years, and saw myself unbreech'd   155
    In my green velvet coat, my dagger muzzled,
    Lest it should bite its master, and so prove
    (As [ornament] oft does) too dangerous.
    How like (methought) I then was to this kernel,
    This squash, this gentleman. Mine honest friend,   160
    Will you take eggs for money?
MAMILLIUS No, my lord, I'll fight.
LEONTES You will? Why, happy man be 's dole! My brother,
    Are you so fond of your young prince as we
    Do seem to be of ours?
POLIXENES   If at home, sir,   165
    He's all my exercise, my mirth, my matter;
    Now my sworn friend, and then mine enemy;
    My parasite, my soldier, statesman, all.
    He makes a July's day short as December,
    And with his varying childness cures in me   170
    Thoughts that would thick my blood.
LEONTES   So stands this squire
    Offic'd with me. We two will walk, my lord,
    And leave you to your graver steps. Hermione,
    How thou lov'st us, show in our brother's welcome;
    Let what is dear in Sicily be cheap.   175
    Next to thyself and my young rover, he's
    Apparent to my heart.
HERMIONE   If you would seek us,
    We are yours i' th' garden. Shall 's attend you there?

---

150. mov'd: angry. **152. pastime:** source of mirth. **154. methoughts:** it seemed to me (a variant of *methought*). **recoil:** go back. **155–56. unbreech'd . . . coat:** i.e. not old enough to wear men's clothes. **159. kernel:** seed. **160. squash:** unripe pea pod. **honest:** worthy. **161. take . . . money:** allow yourself to be imposed upon. **163. happy . . . dole:** may his lot be that of a happy man (proverbial). **166. matter:** interest. **170. childness:** childish ways. **171. thick my blood:** make me melancholy. **171–72. So . . . Offic'd:** this boy holds the same position. **177. Apparent:** heir apparent, i.e. closest.

LEONTES To your own bents dispose you; you'll be found,
  Be you beneath the sky. [*Aside.*] I am angling now,   180
  Though you perceive me not how I give line.
  Go to, go to!
  How she holds up the neb! the bill to him!
  And arms her with the boldness of a wife
  To her allowing husband!
                [*Exeunt Polixenes, Hermione, and Attendants.*]
              Gone already!   185
  Inch-thick, knee-deep, o'er head and ears a fork'd one!
  Go play, boy, play. Thy mother plays, and I
  Play too, but so disgrac'd a part, whose issue
  Will hiss me to my grave: contempt and clamor
  Will be my knell. Go play, boy, play. There have been   190
  (Or I am much deceiv'd) cuckolds ere now,
  And many a man there is (even at this present,
  Now, while I speak this) holds his wife by th' arm,
  That little thinks she has been sluic'd in 's absence,
  And his pond fish'd by his next neighbor—by   195
  Sir Smile, his neighbor. Nay, there's comfort in't,
  Whiles other men have gates, and those gates open'd,
  As mine, against their will. Should all despair
  That have revolted wives, the tenth of mankind
  Would hang themselves. Physic for't there's none.   200
  It is a bawdy planet, that will strike
  Where 'tis predominant; and 'tis pow'rful—think it—
  From east, west, north, and south. Be it concluded,
  No barricado for a belly. Know't,
  It will let in and out the enemy,   205
  With bag and baggage. Many thousand on 's
  Have the disease, and feel't not. How now, boy?
MAMILLIUS I am like you, [they] say.
LEONTES   Why, that's some comfort.
  What? Camillo there?
CAMILLO Ay, my good lord.   210
LEONTES Go play, Mamillius, thou'rt an honest man.
                    [*Exit Mamillius.*]

179. found. With pun on the sense "found out." **182. Go to:** a common expression of reproof or admonition. **183. neb:** mouth. **185. allowing:** approving. **186. fork'd:** horned. **187–89. Go . . . grave.** Leontes puns on three senses of *play*: (1) amuse yourself, (2) engage in sexual dalliance, (3) act a part; and on three senses of *issue*: (1) outcome, (2) offspring, (3) exit. **195. next:** nearest. **199. revolted:** unfaithful. **201–2. strike . . . predominant:** exercise a harmful influence when it is in the ascendant. **204. barricado:** fortification. **206. on 's:** of us.

Camillo, this great sir will yet stay longer.

CAMILLO You had much ado to make his anchor hold,
When you cast out, it still came home.

LEONTES   Didst note it?

CAMILLO He would not stay at your petitions, made   215
His business more material.

LEONTES   Didst perceive it?
[*Aside.*] They're here with me already, whisp'ring, rounding:
"Sicilia is a so-forth." 'Tis far gone,
When I shall gust it last.—How came't, Camillo,
That he did stay?

CAMILLO   At the good Queen's entreaty.   220

LEONTES At the Queen's be't; "good" should be pertinent,
But so it is, it is not. Was this taken
By any understanding pate but thine?
For thy conceit is soaking, will draw in
More than the common blocks. Not noted, is't,   225
But of the finer natures? By some severals
Of head-piece extraordinary? Lower messes
Perchance are to this business purblind? Say.

CAMILLO Business, my lord? I think most understand
Bohemia stays here longer.   230

LEONTES   Ha?

CAMILLO   Stays here longer.

LEONTES Ay, but why?

CAMILLO To satisfy your Highness and the entreaties
Of our most gracious mistress.

LEONTES   Satisfy?
Th' entreaties of your mistress? Satisfy?
Let that suffice. I have trusted thee, Camillo,   235
With all the nearest things to my heart, as well
My chamber-counsels, wherein, priest-like, thou
Hast cleans'd my bosom: I from thee departed
Thy penitent reform'd. But we have been

---

214. still came home: always failed to hold. **217. They're . . . me:** people are aware of my situation. **rounding:** whispering. **218. so-forth:** you-know-what. **219. gust:** taste, i.e. perceive. Leontes means, "Everybody must know it, for I know it, and the husband is always the last to find out." **222. so it is:** as things stand. **taken:** perceived. **224. conceit is soaking:** intelligence is highly absorbent. **225. blocks:** blockheads. **226. severals:** individuals. **227. Lower messes:** those lower at the dining table, i.e. lower in rank. A mess was originally a group of four served from the same dishes. **228. purblind:** completely blind. **233. Satisfy.** Leontes interprets the word in a sexual sense. **237. chamber-counsels:** private concerns.

Deceiv'd in thy integrity, deceiv'd   240
In that which seems so.

CAMILLO   Be it forbid, my lord!

LEONTES To bide upon't: thou art not honest; or
If thou inclin'st that way, thou art a coward,
Which hoxes honesty behind, restraining
From course requir'd; or else thou must be counted   245
A servant grafted in my serious trust
And therein negligent; or else a fool,
That seest a game play'd home, the rich stake drawn,
And tak'st it all for jest.

CAMILLO   My gracious lord,
I may be negligent, foolish, and fearful: 250
In every one of these no man is free
But that his negligence, his folly, fear,
Among the infinite doings of the world,
Sometime puts forth. In your affairs, my lord,
If ever I were willful-negligent,   255
It was my folly; if industriously
I play'd the fool, it was my negligence,
Not weighing well the end; if ever fearful
To do a thing, where I the issue doubted,
Whereof the execution did cry out   260
Against the non-performance, 'twas a fear
Which oft infects the wisest: these, my lord,
Are such allow'd infirmities that honesty
Is never free of. But beseech your Grace
Be plainer with me, let me know my trespass   265
By its own visage. If I then deny it,
'Tis none of mine.

LEONTES   Ha' not you seen, Camillo
(But that's past doubt; you have, or your eye-glass
Is thicker than a cuckold's horn), or heard
(For to a vision so apparent rumor   270
Cannot be mute), or thought (for cogitation
Resides not in that man that does not think)

---

242. bide: dwell, insist.   **244. hoxes:** hamstrings.   **248. home:** i.e. in dead
seriousness.   **drawn:** won.   **251. free:** guiltless.   **254. puts forth:** shows itself.
256. industriously: deliberately.   **263. allow'd:** acknowledged. **that:** as.   **266. By . . .
visage:** i.e. in such a fashion that I can recognize it.   **267. Ha':** have.   **268. eye-
glass:** lens of the eye.   **269. thicker:** more opaque. **cuckold's horn.** Horn, which
in thin sheets is nearly transparent, offers a natural comparison, but in Leontes'
mind *horn* is immediately equated with *cuckold's horn.*   **270. vision so apparent:**
sight so plain.   **272. think:** think so.

My wife is slippery? If thou wilt confess,
Or else be impudently negative,
To have nor eyes nor ears nor thought, then say   275
My wife's a [hobby]-horse, deserves a name
As rank as any flax-wench that puts to
Before her troth-plight: say't and justify't.
CAMILLO I would not be a stander-by to hear
My sovereign mistress clouded so, without   280
My present vengeance taken. 'Shrew my heart,
You never spoke what did become you less
Than this; which to reiterate were sin
As deep as that, though true.
LEONTES   Is whispering nothing?
Is leaning cheek to cheek? is meeting noses?   285
Kissing with inside lip? stopping the career
Of laughter with a sigh (a note infallible
Of breaking honesty)? horsing foot on foot?
Skulking in corners? wishing clocks more swift?
Hours, minutes? noon, midnight? and all eyes   290
Blind with the pin and web but theirs, theirs only,
That would unseen be wicked? Is this nothing?
Why then the world and all that's in't is nothing,
The covering sky is nothing, Bohemia nothing,
My wife is nothing, nor nothing have these nothings,   295
If this be nothing.
CAMILLO   Good my lord, be cur'd
Of this diseas'd opinion, and betimes,
For 'tis most dangerous.
LEONTES   Say it be, 'tis true.
CAMILLO No, no, my lord.
LEONTES   It is: you lie, you lie!
I say thou liest, Camillo, and I hate thee,   300
Pronounce thee a gross lout, a mindless slave,
Or else a hovering temporizer, that
Canst with thine eyes at once see good and evil,
Inclining to them both. Were my wive's liver

---

274. impudently: shamelessly. 275. nor eyes: neither eyes. 276. hobby-horse: loose woman. 277. puts to: copulates. 281. present: instant. 'Shrew: beshrew, curse. 283–84. which . . . true: repeating this would be as sinful as her adultery if it were a fact, which it isn't. 286. career: full gallop. 288. honesty: chastity. horsing: mounting and moving up and down. 291. pin and web: cataract. 297. betimes: quickly. 298. Say it be: suppose it is (dangerous). 302. hovering: wavering.

Infected as her life, she would not live   305
  The running of one glass.
CAMILLO   Who does infect her?
LEONTES Why, he that wears her like her medal hanging
  About his neck, Bohemia—who, if I
  Had servants true about me, that bare eyes
  To see alike mine honor as their profits   310
  (Their own particular thrifts), they would do that
  Which should undo more doing; ay, and thou,
  His cupbearer—whom I from meaner form
  Have bench'd and rear'd to worship, who mayst see
  Plainly as heaven sees earth and earth sees heaven,   315
  How I am gall'd—mightst bespice a cup,
  To give mine enemy a lasting wink;
  Which draught to me were cordial.
CAMILLO   Sir, my lord,
  I could do this, and that with no rash potion,
  But with a ling'ring dram that should not work   320
  Maliciously, like poison; but I cannot
  Believe this crack to be in my dread mistress
  (So sovereignly being honorable).
  I have lov'd thee—
LEONTES   Make that thy question, and go rot!
  Dost think I am so muddy, so unsettled,   325
  To appoint myself in this vexation, sully
  The purity and whiteness of my sheets
  (Which to preserve is sleep, which being spotted
  Is goads, thorns, nettles, tails of wasps),
  Give scandal to the blood o' th' Prince my son   330
  (Who I do think is mine and love as mine),
  Without ripe moving to't? Would I do this?
  Could man so blench?

304–5. liver ... life. Some editors read *life ... liver*, arguing that her liver (regarded as the seat of the passions) *was* fatally infected. But the sense may be "If her body were as seriously diseased as her behavior is." **306. glass:** hourglass. **307. like her medal:** i.e. as he might wear her medallion portrait. **309. bare:** bore. **311. particular thrifts:** personal gains. **313. meaner form:** lower degree. **314. bench'd:** given official status. **rear'd to worship:** raised to a position of dignity. **316. gall'd:** rubbed sore. **318. were cordial:** would be curative. **319. rash:** quick-acting. **321. Maliciously:** violently. **322. crack:** flaw. **dread:** revered. **323. So ... honorable:** who is so supremely honorable. **324. Make ... rot:** if you're going to take that line, go and be damned. **325. muddy:** i.e. disturbed in mind (synonymous with *unsettled*). **326. appoint:** place. **332. ripe:** full, ample. **333. blench:** swerve (from rational behavior).

CAMILLO   I must believe you, sir.
  I do, and will fetch off Bohemia for't;
  Provided that, when he's remov'd, your Highness   335
  Will take again your queen as yours at first,
  Even for your son's sake, and thereby for sealing
  The injury of tongues in courts and kingdoms
  Known and allied to yours.
LEONTES   Thou dost advise me
  Even so as I mine own course have set down.   340
  I'll give no blemish to her honor, none.
CAMILLO My lord,
  Go then; and with a countenance as clear
  As friendship wears at feasts, keep with Bohemia
  And with your queen. I am his cupbearer: 345
  If from me he have wholesome beverage,
  Account me not your servant.
LEONTES   This is all:
  Do't, and thou hast the one half of my heart;
  Do't not, thou split'st thine own.
CAMILLO   I'll do't, my lord.
LEONTES I will seem friendly, as thou hast advis'd me. 350
                                                    Exit.

CAMILLO O miserable lady! But for me,
  What case stand I in? I must be the poisoner
  Of good Polixenes, and my ground to do't
  Is the obedience to a master; one
  Who, in rebellion with himself, will have   355
  All that are his so too. To do this deed,
  Promotion follows. If I could find example
  Of thousands that had struck anointed kings
  And flourish'd after, I'ld not do't; but since
  Nor brass nor stone nor parchment bears not one,   360
  Let villainy itself forswear't. I must
  Forsake the court. To do't, or no, is certain
  To me a break-neck. Happy star reign now!
  Here comes Bohemia.

---

334. fetch off: Perhaps deliberately ambiguous: (1) kill; (2) bear off, rescue (cf. *bear'st . . . off,* line 462). So also *remov'd,* line 335; and see lines 346–47.   **337. sealing:** silencing.   **344. keep:** keep company.   **351. for:** as for.   **355–56. Who . . . too:** who, because he has turned against his better nature, would have all his subjects do so too.   **357. If:** even if.   **362. To . . . no:** either to kill Polixenes, or not to kill him.   **363. a break-neck:** i.e. fatal. **Happy:** propitious.

Enter POLIXENES.

POLIXENES This is strange; methinks
My favor here begins to warp. Not speak?   365
Good day, Camillo.
CAMILLO   Hail, most royal sir!
POLIXENES What is the news i' th' court?
CAMILLO   None rare, my lord.
POLIXENES The King hath on him such a countenance
As he had lost some province and a region
Lov'd as he loves himself. Even now I met him   370
With customary compliment, when he,
Wafting his eyes to th' contrary and falling
A lip of much contempt, speeds from me, and
So leaves me to consider what is breeding
That changes thus his manners.   375
CAMILLO I dare not know, my lord.
POLIXENES How, dare not? Do not? Do you know, and dare not?
Be intelligent to me, 'tis thereabouts:
For to yourself, what you do know, you must,
And cannot say you dare not. Good Camillo,   380
Your chang'd complexions are to me a mirror
Which shows me mine chang'd too; for I must be
A party in this alteration, finding
Myself thus alter'd with't.
CAMILLO   There is a sickness
Which puts some of us in distemper, but   385
I cannot name the disease, and it is caught
Of you that yet are well.
POLIXENES   How caught of me?
Make me not sighted like the basilisk.
I have look'd on thousands, who have sped the better
By my regard, but kill'd none so. Camillo,   390
As you are certainly a gentleman, thereto
Clerk-like experienc'd, which no less adorns

---

365. warp: change for the worse. **367. rare:** remarkable. **369. As:** as if.
372. Wafting . . . contrary: averting his eyes. **falling:** letting droop. **374. breeding:** hatching. **377. Do not:** i.e. do you mean you do not. **378. intelligent:**
communicative, informative. **'Tis thereabouts:** that's getting near it, i.e. telling
me is probably what you dare not do. **379–80. what . . . not:** what you know,
you know perforce; daring doesn't enter into it. **388. basilisk:** fabulous serpent
whose glance killed. **389–90. sped . . . regard:** fared the better for my look.
391. gentleman: man of gentle birth. **thereto:** in addition to that. **392. Clerk-
like experienc'd:** having the experience of an educated man.

Our gentry than our parents' noble names,
In whose success we are gentle, I beseech you,
If you know aught which does behove my knowledge   395
Thereof to be inform'd, imprison't not
In ignorant concealment.

CAMILLO   I may not answer.

POLIXENES A sickness caught of me, and yet I well?
I must be answer'd. Dost thou hear, Camillo,
I conjure thee, by all the parts of man   400
Which honor does acknowledge, whereof the least
Is not this suit of mine, that thou declare
What incidency thou dost guess of harm
Is creeping toward me; how far off, how near,
Which way to be prevented, if to be;   405
If not, how best to bear it.

CAMILLO   Sir, I will tell you,
Since I am charg'd in honor and by him
That I think honorable. Therefore mark my counsel,
Which must be ev'n as swiftly followed as
I mean to utter it; or both yourself and me   410
Cry lost, and so good night!

POLIXENES   On, good Camillo.

CAMILLO I am appointed him to murther you.

POLIXENES By whom, Camillo?

CAMILLO   By the King.

POLIXENES   For what?

CAMILLO He thinks, nay, with all confidence he swears,
As he had seen't or been an instrument   415
To vice you to't, that you have touch'd his queen
Forbiddenly.

POLIXENES   O then, my best blood turn
To an infected jelly, and my name
Be yok'd with his that did betray the Best!
Turn then my freshest reputation to   420
A savor that may strike the dullest nostril
Where I arrive, and my approach be shunn'd,

---

393. gentry: status as gentlemen. **394. In whose success:** in succession from
whom. **395–96. does . . . inform'd:** would be advantageous for me to learn.
397. ignorant concealment: concealment in pretended ignorance (?) or concealment which would keep me ignorant (?). **400. parts:** duties. **403. incidency:**
likelihood. **405. if to be:** if it can be prevented. **411. good night:** farewell
forever. **412. him:** the person. **416. vice:** screw or force, as with the carpenter's
tool; with implication of evil arising from the sense "wrongdoing." **419. his . . .
Best:** that of Judas, the betrayer of Jesus.

Nay, hated too, worse than the great'st infection
That e'er was heard or read!
CAMILLO   Swear his thought over
By each particular star in heaven, and   425
By all their influences, you may as well
Forbid the sea for to obey the moon
As or by oath remove or counsel shake
The fabric of his folly, whose foundation
Is pil'd upon his faith, and will continue   430
The standing of his body.
POLIXENES   How should this grow?
CAMILLO I know not; but I am sure 'tis safer to
Avoid what's grown than question how 'tis born.
If therefore you dare trust my honesty,
That lies enclosed in this trunk which you   435
Shall bear along impawn'd, away to-night!
Your followers I will whisper to the business,
And will by twos and threes at several posterns
Clear them o' th' city. For myself, I'll put
My fortunes to your service, which are here   440
By this discovery lost. Be not uncertain,
For by the honor of my parents, I
Have utt'red truth; which if you seek to prove,
I dare not stand by; nor shall you be safer
Than one condemn'd by the King's own mouth—thereon 445
His execution sworn.
POLIXENES   I do believe thee:
I saw his heart in 's face. Give me thy hand,
Be pilot to me, and thy places shall
Still neighbor mine. My ships are ready, and
My people did expect my hence departure   450
Two days ago. This jealousy
Is for a precious creature: as she's rare,
Must it be great; and as his person's mighty,
Must it be violent; and as he does conceive
He is dishonor'd by a man which ever   455

---

424. Swear . . . over: swear that his suspicion is false.   **428. or by. . . or:** either by . . . or by.   **429. fabric:** construction.   **430. pil'd . . . faith:** based upon his firm conviction.   **430–31. continue . . . body:** last as long as his body does.   **431. How . . . grow:** how can this have come about.   **435. trunk:** (1) body; (2) container.   **436. impawn'd:** as a pledge (of my good faith).   **438. posterns:** back gates.   **441. discovery:** disclosure.   **443. prove:** test.   **448–49. thy . . . mine:** your position will always be close to the throne.

Profess'd to him, why, his revenges must
In that be made more bitter. Fear o'ershades me.
Good expedition be my friend, and comfort
The gracious queen, part of his theme, but nothing
Of his ill-ta'en suspicion! Come, Camillo,   460
I will respect thee as a father, if
Thou bear'st my life off. Hence! Let us avoid.
CAMILLO It is in mine authority to command
  The keys of all the posterns. Please your Highness
  To take the urgent hour. Come, sir, away.   *Exeunt.*

---

456. Profess'd: professed friendship.   **458. expedition:** speed.   **458–60. comfort
. . . suspicion:** (may my speedy departure) ease the situation of the Queen, who
is involved in the King's misconception but is entirely innocent of what he suspects.   **462. avoid:** be off.   **465. take . . . hour:** seize this critical moment.

Act 2

SCENE I

Enter HERMIONE, MAMILLIUS, LADIES.

HERMIONE Take the boy to you; he so troubles me,
　'Tis past enduring.
[1.] LADY　　　　　Come, my gracious lord,
　Shall I be your playfellow?
MAMILLIUS　　　　　No, I'll none of you.
[1.] LADY Why, my sweet lord?
MAMILLIUS You'll kiss me hard and speak to me as if　　5
　I were a baby still.—I love you better.
2. LADY And why so, my lord?
MAMILLIUS　　　　　Not for because
　Your brows are blacker, yet black brows they say
　Become some women best, so that there be not
　Too much hair there, but in a semicircle,　　10
　Or a half-moon made with a pen.
2. LADY　　　　　Who taught' this?
MAMILLIUS I learn'd it out of women's faces. Pray now
　What color are your eyebrows?
[1.] LADY　　　　　Blue, my lord.
MAMILLIUS Nay, that's a mock. I have seen a lady's nose
　That has been blue, but not her eyebrows.
[1.] LADY　　　　　Hark ye,　　15
　The Queen your mother rounds apace: we shall
　Present our services to a fine new prince
　One of these days, and then you'ld wanton with us,
　If we would have you.
2. LADY　　　　　She is spread of late
　Into a goodly bulk. Good time encounter her!　　20
HERMIONE What wisdom stirs amongst you? Come, sir, now
　I am for you again. Pray you sit by us,
　And tell 's a tale.

2.1. Location: Sicilia. The palace of Leontes.　**11. taught':** taught you.　**18. wanton:** play.

MAMILLIUS   Merry, or sad, shall't be?

HERMIONE As merry as you will.

MAMILLIUS A sad tale's best for winter. I have one   25
  Of sprites and goblins.

HERMIONE   Let's have that, good sir.
  Come on, sit down, come on, and do your best
  To fright me with your sprites; you're pow'rful at it.

MAMILLIUS There was a man—

HERMIONE   Nay, come sit down; then on.

MAMILLIUS Dwelt by a churchyard. I will tell it softly,
  Yond crickets shall not hear it.   30

HERMIONE   Come on then,
  And give't me in mine ear.

        [*Enter*] LEONTES, ANTIGONUS, LORDS, [*and others*].

LEONTES Was he met there? his train? Camillo with him?

[1.] LORD Behind the tuft of pines I met them; never
  Saw I men scour so on their way. I ey'd them   35
  Even to their ships.

LEONTES   How blest am I
  In my just censure! in my true opinion!
  Alack, for lesser knowledge! how accurs'd
  In being so blest! There may be in the cup
  A spider steep'd, and one may drink; depart,   40
  And yet partake no venom (for his knowledge
  Is not infected), but if one present
  Th' abhorr'd ingredient to his eye, make known
  How he hath drunk, he cracks his gorge, his sides,
  With violent hefts. I have drunk, and seen the spider.   45
  Camillo was his help in this, his pandar.
  There is a plot against my life, my crown;
  All's true that is mistrusted. That false villain
  Whom I employ'd was pre-employ'd by him:
  He has discover'd my design, and I   50
  Remain a pinch'd thing; yea, a very trick
  For them to play at will. How came the posterns
  So easily open?

[1.] LORD   By his great authority,

---

31. crickets: i.e. the chattering ladies. **35. scour:** hurry. **37. censure:** judgment. **38. for lesser knowledge:** would that I knew less. **39–45. There . . . hefts.** An old superstition about spiders. **44. gorge:** throat. **45. hefts:** heavings, retchings. **48. mistrusted:** suspected. **50. discover'd:** disclosed. **51. pinch'd:** tormented (?) or manipulated (?).

Which often hath no less prevail'd than so
On your command.

LEONTES   I know't too well.   55
Give me the boy. I am glad you did not nurse him.
Though he does bear some signs of me, yet you
Have too much blood in him.

HERMIONE   What is this? Sport?

LEONTES Bear the boy hence, he shall not come about her.
Away with him! and let her sport herself   60
With that she's big with, for 'tis Polixenes
Has made thee swell thus.

HERMIONE   But I'ld say he had not;
And I'll be sworn you would believe my saying,
Howe'er you lean to th' nayward.

LEONTES   You, my lords,
Look on her, mark her well; be but about   65
To say she is a goodly lady, and
The justice of your hearts will thereto add
'Tis pity she's not honest—honorable.
Praise her but for this her without-door form
(Which on my faith deserves high speech) and straight   70
The shrug, the hum or ha (these petty brands
That calumny doth use—O, I am out—
That mercy does, for calumny will sear
Virtue itself), these shrugs, these hums and ha's,
When you have said she's goodly, come between   75
Ere you can say she's honest: but be't known
(From him that has most cause to grieve it should be)
She's an adult'ress.

HERMIONE   Should a villain say so,
The most replenish'd villain in the world,
He were as much more villain: you, my lord,   80
Do but mistake.

LEONTES   You have mistook, my lady,
Polixenes for Leontes. O thou thing!
Which I'll not call a creature of thy place,
Lest barbarism (making me the precedent)
Should a like language use to all degrees,   85
And mannerly distinguishment leave out

---

64. to th' nayward: in the opposite direction. **66. goodly:** beautiful.
68. honest: chaste. **69. without-door:** external. **72. out:** in error. **75. come
between:** interrupt, i.e. break off. **79. replenish'd:** complete. **83. Which . . .
place:** a name I will not apply to anyone of your rank.

Betwixt the prince and beggar. I have said
She's an adult'ress, I have said with whom:
More—she's a traitor, and Camillo is
A federary with her, and one that knows   90
What she should shame to know herself,
But with her most vild principal—that she's
A bed-swerver, even as bad as those
That vulgars give bold'st titles; ay, and privy
To this their late escape.
HERMIONE   No, by my life,   95
Privy to none of this. How will this grieve you,
When you shall come to clearer knowledge, that
You thus have publish'd me! Gentle my lord,
You scarce can right me throughly, then, to say
You did mistake.
LEONTES   No; if I mistake   100
In those foundations which I build upon,
The centre is not big enough to bear
A schoolboy's top. Away with her, to prison!
He who shall speak for her is afar off guilty
But that he speaks.
HERMIONE   There's some ill planet reigns;   105
I must be patient, till the heavens look
With an aspect more favorable. Good my lords,
I am not prone to weeping, as our sex
Commonly are, the want of which vain dew
Perchance shall dry your pities; but I have   110
That honorable grief lodg'd here which burns
Worse than tears drown. Beseech you all, my lords,
With thoughts so qualified as your charities
Shall best instruct you, measure me; and so
The King's will be perform'd!
LEONTES   Shall I be heard?   115
HERMIONE Who is't that goes with me? Beseech your Highness
My women may be with me, for you see
My plight requires it. Do not weep, good fools,
There is no cause. When you shall know your mistress

---

90. **federary:** confederate.   92. **vild principal:** vile partner.   94. **vulgars . . . titles:** common people call by the bluntest names.   98. **publish'd:** publicly proclaimed. **Gentle my:** my noble.   99. **throughly:** thoroughly, fully. **to say:** by saying.   102. **centre:** earth.   104–5. **afar . . . speaks:** indirectly guilty merely for speaking.   113. **qualified:** tempered.   114. **measure:** judge.   115. **heard:** obeyed.   118. **fools.** Often, as here, a term of affection and pity.

Has deserv'd prison, then abound in tears 120
As I come out; this action I now go on
Is for my better grace. Adieu, my lord,
I never wish'd to see you sorry, now
I trust I shall. My women, come, you have leave.

LEONTES Go, do our bidding; hence! 125

[*Exit Queen guarded, with Ladies.*]

[1.] LORD Beseech your Highness call the Queen again.

ANTIGONUS Be certain what you do, sir, lest your justice
Prove violence, in the which three great ones suffer,
Yourself, your queen, your son.

[1.] LORD   For her, my lord,
I dare my life lay down—and will do't, sir, 130
Please you t' accept it—that the Queen is spotless
I' th' eyes of heaven and to you—I mean,
In this which you accuse her.

ANTIGONUS   If it prove
She's otherwise, I'll keep my stables where
I lodge my wife; I'll go in couples with her; 135
Than when I feel and see her no farther trust her;
For every inch of woman in the world,
Ay, every dram of woman's flesh is false,
If she be.

LEONTES   Hold your peaces.

[1.] LORD   Good my lord—

ANTIGONUS It is for you we speak, not for ourselves. 140
You are abus'd, and by some putter-on
That will be damn'd for't. Would I knew the villain,
I would land-damn him. Be she honor-flaw'd,
I have three daughters: the eldest is eleven;
The second and the third, nine, and some five; 145
If this prove true, they'll pay for't. By mine honor,
I'll geld 'em all; fourteen they shall not see
To bring false generations. They are co-heirs,
And I had rather glib myself than they
Should not produce fair issue.

---

122. better grace: greater honor (when I am vindicated). **134–35. I'll . . . wife.**
Meaning uncertain; perhaps "I'll guard (*keep*) my wife as I guard my horses" or
"I'll keep my wife away from men as watchfully as I keep my mares from my
stallions." **135. in . . . her:** i.e. constantly beside her, as if we were two dogs
leashed together. **139. she:** i.e. Hermione. **141. abus'd:** deceived. **putter-on:**
inciter. **143. land-damn.** The word occurs only here and has not been satisfacto-
rily explained. **148. false generations:** illegitimate children. **149. glib:** castrate.

LEONTES   Cease, no more.   150
  You smell this business with a sense as cold
  As is a dead man's nose; but I do see't, and feel't,
  As you feel doing thus [*grasps his arm*]—and see withal
  The instruments that feel.
ANTIGONUS   If it be so,
  We need no grave to bury honesty,   155
  There's not a grain of it the face to sweeten
  Of the whole dungy earth.
LEONTES   What? lack I credit?
[1.] LORD I had rather you did lack than I, my lord,
  Upon this ground; and more it would content me
  To have her honor true than your suspicion,   160
  Be blam'd for't how you might.
LEONTES   Why, what need we
  Commune with you of this, but rather follow
  Our forceful instigation? Our prerogative
  Calls not your counsels, but our natural goodness
  Imparts this; which if you—or stupefied   165
  Or seeming so in skill—cannot, or will not,
  Relish a truth like us, inform yourselves
  We need no more of your advice. The matter,
  The loss, the gain, the ord'ring on't, is all
  Properly ours.
ANTIGONUS   And I wish, my liege,   170
  You had only in your silent judgment tried it,
  Without more overture.
LEONTES   How could that be?
  Either thou art most ignorant by age,
  Or thou wert born a fool. Camillo's flight,
  Added to their familiarity   175
  (Which was as gross as ever touch'd conjecture,
  That lack'd sight only, nought for approbation
  But only seeing, all other circumstances
  Made up to th' deed), doth push on this proceeding.
  Yet, for a greater confirmation   180

---

154. instruments: (1) Leontes' fingers; (2) Hermione and Polixenes.   **159. Upon this ground:** in this matter.   **163. instigation:** motive for action.   **163–64. Our prerogative … counsels:** I am under no obligation to consult you.   **166. seeming … skill:** cunningly pretending to be so.   **167. Relish:** taste, i.e. perceive.   **169. on't:** of it.   **170. liege:** sovereign.   **172. overture:** public disclosure.   **176. gross:** palpable, manifest. **touch'd conjecture:** conjecture reached to.   **177. approbation:** proof.   **179. Made up:** added up.

(For in an act of this importance 'twere
Most piteous to be wild), I have dispatch'd in post
To sacred Delphos, to Apollo's temple,
Cleomines and Dion, whom you know
Of stuff'd sufficiency. Now, from the oracle   185
They will bring all, whose spiritual counsel had,
Shall stop or spur me. Have I done well?
[1.] LORD Well done, my lord.
LEONTES Though I am satisfied, and need no more
Than what I know, yet shall the oracle   190
Give rest to th' minds of others—such as he,

                                          [*Points at Antigonus.*]

Whose ignorant credulity will not
Come up to th' truth. So have we thought it good
From our free person she should be confin'd,
Lest that the treachery of the two fled hence   195
Be left her to perform. Come follow us,
We are to speak in public; for this business
Will raise us all.
ANTIGONUS   [*Aside.*] To laughter, as I take it,
If the good truth were known.   *Exeunt.*

SCENE 2

Enter PAULINA, *a* GENTLEMAN, [*and* ATTENDANTS].

PAULINA The keeper of the prison, call to him;
Let him have knowledge who I am. [*Exit Gentleman.*] Good lady,
No court in Europe is too good for thee,
What dost thou then in prison?

         [*Enter* GENTLEMAN *with the*] JAILER.

                    Now, good sir,
You know me, do you not?
JAILER   For a worthy lady,   5
And one who much I honor.
PAULINA   Pray you then,
Conduct me to the Queen.

---

182. wild: rash. **post:** haste. **183. Delphos.** See note on 3.1.2. **185. stuff'd
sufficiency:** full competence. **189. satisfied:** free from doubt. **193. we.** Note
the shift to the royal plural. **194. From:** away from. **free:** freely accessible.
195. treachery: i.e. the "plot against my life" (line 45). **198. raise:** rouse.
2.2. Location: Sicilia. A prison.

JAILER   I may not, madam:
  To the contrary I have express commandment.
PAULINA Here's ado, to lock up honesty
  And honor from th' access of gentle visitors.   10
  Is't lawful, pray you, to see her women?
  Any of them? Emilia?
JAILER   So please you, madam,
  To put apart these your attendants, I
  Shall bring Emilia forth.
PAULINA   I pray now call her.—
  Withdraw yourselves.

                             [Exeunt Gentleman and Attendants.]
JAILER   And, madam, I must   15
  Be present at your conference.
PAULINA   Well; be't so; prithee.   *[Exit Jailer.]*
  Here's such ado to make no stain a stain
  As passes coloring.

                [Enter JAILER with] EMILIA.

          Dear gentlewoman,
  How fares our gracious lady?
EMILIA As well as one so great and so forlorn   20
  May hold together. On her frights and griefs
  (Which never tender lady hath borne greater)
  She is, something before her time, deliver'd.
PAULINA A boy?
EMILIA   A daughter, and a goodly babe,
  Lusty and like to live. The Queen receives   25
  Much comfort in't; says, "My poor prisoner,
  I am innocent as you."
PAULINA   I dare be sworn.
  These dangerous, unsafe lunes i' th' King, beshrew them!
  He must be told on't, and he shall. The office
  Becomes a woman best. I'll take't upon me.   30
  If I prove honey-mouth'd, let my tongue blister;
  And never to my red-look'd anger be
  The trumpet any more. Pray you, Emilia,
  Commend my best obedience to the Queen.
  If she dares trust me with her little babe,   35

18. coloring: (1) dyeing; (2) excusing.   **21. On:** in consequence of.   **28. lunes:** fits
of lunacy.   **29. The office:** i.e. that duty.   **30. Becomes:** befits.   **31. my tongue
blister.** Lying was supposed to blister the tongue.   **32. red-look'd:** flushing.
34. Commend: deliver.

I'll show't the King, and undertake to be
Her advocate to th' loud'st. We do not know
How he may soften at the sight o' th' child:
The silence often of pure innocence
Persuades when speaking fails.

EMILIA   Most worthy madam,   40
Your honor and your goodness is so evident
That your free undertaking cannot miss
A thriving issue. There is no lady living
So meet for this great errand. Please your ladyship
To visit the next room, I'll presently   45
Acquaint the Queen of your most noble offer,
Who but to-day hammered of this design,
But durst not tempt a minister of honor,
Lest she should be denied.

PAULINA   Tell her, Emilia,
I'll use that tongue I have. If wit flow from't   50
As boldness from my bosom, let't not be doubted
I shall do good.

EMILIA   Now be you blest for it!
I'll to the Queen.—Please you, come something nearer.

JAILER Madam, if't please the Queen to send the babe,
I know not what I shall incur to pass it,   55
Having no warrant.

PAULINA   You need not fear it, sir.
This child was prisoner to the womb, and is
By law and process of great Nature thence
Freed and enfranchis'd, not a party to
The anger of the King, nor guilty of   60
(If any be) the trespass of the Queen.

JAILER I do believe it.

PAULINA Do not you fear. Upon mine honor, I
Will stand betwixt you and danger.   *Exeunt.*

SCENE 3

Enter LEONTES; SERVANTS [*keeping the door*].

LEONTES Nor night, nor day, no rest. It is but weakness
To bear the matter thus—mere weakness. If

---

37. to th' loud'st: at the top of my voice.   **42. free:** generous.   **43. thriving issue:** successful result.   **45. presently:** immediately.   **47. hammered of:** shaped, worked out.   **48. tempt . . . honor:** i.e. solicit any person of standing to undertake it. **50. wit:** wisdom.   **2.3. Location:** Sicilia. The palace of Leontes.

The cause were not in being—part o' th' cause,
She th' adult'ress; for the harlot king
Is quite beyond mine arm, out of the blank   5
And level of my brain, plot-proof; but she
I can hook to me—say that she were gone,
Given to the fire, a moi'ty of my rest
Might come to me again. Who's there?
[1.] SERVANT [*Advancing.*]   My lord?
LEONTES How does the boy?
[1.] SERVANT   He took good rest to-night;   10
'Tis hop'd his sickness is discharg'd.
LEONTES To see his nobleness,
Conceiving the dishonor of his mother!
He straight declin'd, droop'd, took it deeply,
Fasten'd and fix'd the shame on't in himself,   15
Threw off his spirit, his appetite, his sleep,
And downright languish'd. Leave me solely; go,
See how he fares. [*Exit First Servant.*] Fie, fie, no thought of him;
The very thought of my revenges that way
Recoil upon me: in himself too mighty,   20
And in his parties, his alliance. Let him be,
Until a time may serve. For present vengeance,
Take it on her. Camillo and Polixenes
Laugh at me; make their pastime at my sorrow:
They should not laugh if I could reach them, nor   25
Shall she, within my pow'r.

>   *Enter* PAULINA [*with a child*]; ANTIGONUS *and* LORDS
>   [*endeavoring to hold her back*].

[1.] LORD   You must not enter.
PAULINA Nay, rather, good my lords, be second to me.
Fear you his tyrannous passion more, alas,
Than the Queen's life? A gracious innocent soul,
More free than he is jealous.
ANTIGONUS   That's enough.   30
[2.] SERVANT Madam—he hath not slept to-night, commanded
None should come at him.

---

4. **harlot:** lewd (formerly used of either sex).   5–6. **blank And level.** Both nouns mean "aim"; literally, *blank* = bull's-eye of a target.   8. **Given . . . fire.** The punishment for treason, which a queen's adultery would amount to. **moi'ty:** portion.   15. **on't:** of it.   17. **solely:** alone.   18. **him:** i.e. Polixenes.   27. **be second to:** support.   30. **free:** innocent.

PAULINA   Not so hot, good sir,
  I come to bring him sleep. 'Tis such as you,
  That creep like shadows by him, and do sigh
  At each his needless heavings, such as you   35
  Nourish the cause of his awaking. I
  Do come with words as medicinal as true,
  Honest as either, to purge him of that humor
  That presses him from sleep.
LEONTES   [What] noise there, ho?
PAULINA No noise, my lord, but needful conference   40
  About some gossips for your Highness.
LEONTES   How?
  Away with that audacious lady! Antigonus,
  I charg'd thee that she should not come about me:
  I knew she would.
ANTIGONUS   I told her so, my lord,
  On your displeasure's peril and on mine,   45
  She should not visit you.
LEONTES   What? canst not rule her?
PAULINA From all dishonesty he can. In this,
  Unless he take the course that you have done—
  Commit me for committing honor—trust it,
  He shall not rule me.
ANTIGONUS   La you now, you hear!   50
  When she will take the rein I let her run,
  [*Aside.*] But she'll not stumble.
PAULINA   Good my liege, I come—
  And I beseech you hear me, who professes
  Myself your loyal servant, your physician,
  Your most obedient counsellor; yet that dares   55
  Less appear so, in comforting your evils,
  Than such as most seem yours—I say, I come
  From your good queen.
LEONTES Good queen?
PAULINA Good queen, my lord, good queen, I say good queen,   60
  And would by combat make her good, so were I
  A man, the worst about you.

---

36. awaking: wakefulness. **38. humor:** distemper. **41. gossips:** baptismal sponsors (for the baby). **49. Commit:** imprison. **for committing honor:** i.e. for honorable behavior which you misjudge as a crime, just as in Hermione's case. **56. comforting:** condoning. **57. yours:** i.e. your loyal servants. **61. by combat.** A reference to trial by combat as a means of proving innocence or guilt. **make her good:** make good her assertion of innocence. **62. worst:** least worthy.

LEONTES   Force her hence.
PAULINA Let him that makes but trifles of his eyes
First hand me. On mine own accord I'll off,
But first I'll do my errand. The good queen   65
(For she is good) hath brought you forth a daughter—
Here 'tis—commends it to your blessing.

                              [*Laying down the child.*]
LEONTES   Out!
A mankind witch! Hence with her, out o' door!
A most intelligencing bawd!
PAULINA   Not so.
I am as ignorant in that, as you   70
In so entit'ling me; and no less honest
Than you are mad; which is enough, I'll warrant
(As this world goes), to pass for honest.
LEONTES   Traitors!
Will you not push her out? [*To Antigonus.*] Give her the bastard,
Thou dotard, thou art woman-tir'd; unroosted   75
By thy Dame Partlet here. Take up the bastard,
Take't up, I say; give't to thy crone.
PAULINA   For ever
Unvenerable be thy hands, if thou
Tak'st up the Princess by that forced baseness
Which he has put upon't!
LEONTES   He dreads his wife.   80
PAULINA So I would you did; then 'twere past all doubt
You'ld call your children yours.
LEONTES   A nest of traitors!
ANTIGONUS I am none, by this good light.
PAULINA   Nor I, nor any
But one that's here—and that's himself; for he
The sacred honor of himself, his queen's,   85
His hopeful son's, his babe's, betrays to slander,
Whose sting is sharper than the sword's, and will not
(For as the case now stands, it is a curse
He cannot be compell'd to't) once remove

---

68. mankind: masculine, i.e. behaving with unwomanly violence.
69. intelligencing bawd: spying go-between (for the Queen and Polixenes).
71. entit'ling. A contraction of the old spelling *entituling.* **honest:** chaste.
75. woman-tir'd: henpecked. *Tire* = tear with the beak (a term from falconry).
unroosted: pushed off the roost. **76. Partlet:** traditional name for a hen.
79. forced baseness: wrongfully imposed name of bastard. **83. by . . . light:** by
my eyesight (a common oath).

The root of his opinion, which is rotten   90
As ever oak or stone was sound.
LEONTES   A callat
Of boundless tongue, who late hath beat her husband,
And now baits me! This brat is none of mine,
It is the issue of Polixenes.
Hence with it, and together with the dam   95
Commit them to the fire!
PAULINA   It is yours:
And might we lay th' old proverb to your charge,
So like you, 'tis the worse. Behold, my lords,
Although the print be little, the whole matter
And copy of the father—eye, nose, lip,   100
The trick of 's frown, his forehead, nay, the valley,
The pretty dimples of his chin and cheek, his smiles,
The very mould and frame of hand, nail, finger.
And thou, good goddess Nature, which hast made it
So like to him that got it, if thou hast   105
The ordering of the mind too, 'mongst all colors
No yellow in 't, lest she suspect, as he does,
Her children not her husband's!
LEONTES   A gross hag!
And, lozel, thou art worthy to be hang'd,
That wilt not stay her tongue.
ANTIGONUS   Hang all the husbands   110
That cannot do that feat, you'll leave yourself
Hardly one subject.
LEONTES   Once more, take her hence.
PAULINA A most unworthy and unnatural lord
Can do no more.
LEONTES   I'll ha' thee burnt.
PAULINA   I care not:
It is an heretic that makes the fire,   115
Not she which burns in 't. I'll not call you tyrant;
But this most cruel usage of your queen
(Not able to produce more accusation

---

91. callat: scold.   **93. baits:** harasses, as dogs do bears; with a pun on *beat* (line 92), then pronounced *bait*.   **101. trick:** characteristic expression. **valley:** cleft of the chin (?).   **105. got:** begot.   **107. yellow.** Symbolic of jealousy.   **107–8. lest . . . hus-band's.** It has been pointed out that this would be an odd effect of suspicion of one's husband. Perhaps the wording reflects Paulina's excitement.   **109. lozel:** scoundrel (addressed to Antigonus).   **115–16. It . . . in't:** i.e. it is the guilt of the condemned that makes the fire an act of justice, not the mere fact that a woman is burned.

Than your own weak-hing'd fancy) something savors
Of tyranny, and will ignoble make you,   120
Yea, scandalous to the world.
LEONTES   On your allegiance,
   Out of the chamber with her! Were I a tyrant,
   Where were her life? She durst not call me so,
   If she did know me one. Away with her!
PAULINA I pray you do not push me, I'll be gone.   125
   Look to your babe, my lord, 'tis yours. Jove send her
   A better guiding spirit! What needs these hands?
   You, that are thus so tender o'er his follies,
   Will never do him good, not one of you.
   So, so. Farewell, we are gone.   *Exit.* 130
LEONTES Thou, traitor, hast set on thy wife to this.
   My child? Away with't! Even thou, that hast
   A heart so tender o'er it, take it hence,
   And see it instantly consum'd with fire.
   Even thou, and none but thou. Take it up straight.   135
   Within this hour bring me word 'tis done
   (And by good testimony), or I'll seize thy life,
   With what thou else call'st thine. If thou refuse
   And wilt encounter with my wrath, say so;
   The bastard brains with these my proper hands   140
   Shall I dash out. Go, take it to the fire,
   For thou set'st on thy wife.
ANTIGONUS   I did not, sir.
   These lords, my noble fellows, if they please,
   Can clear me in't.
LORDS   We can. My royal liege,
   He is not guilty of her coming hither.   145
LEONTES You're liars all.
[1.] LORD Beseech your Highness, give us better credit.
   We have always truly serv'd you, and beseech'
   So to esteem of us; and on our knees we beg
   (As recompense of our dear services   150
   Past and to come) that you do change this purpose,
   Which being so horrible, so bloody, must
   Lead on to some foul issue. We all kneel.
LEONTES I am a feather for each wind that blows.
   Shall I live on to see this bastard kneel   155

---

127. What . . . hands: no need to push me. **140. proper:** own. **147. credit:**
belief. **148. beseech':** beseech you. **150. dear:** heartfelt, deeply loyal.

And call me father? Better burn it now
Than curse it then. But be it; let it live.
It shall not neither. [*To Antigonus.*] You, sir, come you hither:
You that have been so tenderly officious
With Lady Margery, your midwife there,   160
To save this bastard's life—for 'tis a bastard,
So sure as this beard's grey—what will you adventure
To save this brat's life?
ANTIGONUS   Any thing, my lord,
That my ability may undergo
And nobleness impose; at least thus much: 165
I'll pawn the little blood which I have left
To save the innocent—any thing possible.
LEONTES It shall be possible. Swear by this sword
Thou wilt perform my bidding.
ANTIGONUS   I will, my lord.
LEONTES Mark and perform it—seest thou? for the fail   170
Of any point in't shall not only be
Death to thyself but to thy lewd-tongu'd wife,
Whom for this time we pardon. We enjoin thee,
As thou art liegeman to us, that thou carry
This female bastard hence, and that thou bear it   175
To some remote and desert place quite out
Of our dominions, and that there thou leave it
(Without more mercy) to it own protection,
And favor of the climate. As by strange fortune
It came to us, I do in justice charge thee,   180
On thy soul's peril, and thy body's torture,
That thou commend it strangely to some place
Where chance may nurse or end it. Take it up.
ANTIGONUS I swear to do this—though a present death
Had been more merciful. Come on, poor babe.   185
Some powerful spirit instruct the kites and ravens
To be thy nurses! Wolves and bears, they say,
Casting their savageness aside, have done
Like offices of pity. Sir, be prosperous

---

160. Lady Margery. Perhaps equivalent to *Dame Partlet* (line 76), since *margery-prater* is recorded as a slang term for "hen." **162. this beard.** Probably Antigonus'. **adventure:** risk. **170. fail:** failure (the regular Elizabethan form). **174. liege-man:** loyal subject. **178. it:** its. **182. commend:** commit. **strangely . . . place:** i.e. to some foreign place. The same sense of *strange* is present in *strange fortune* (line 179), where Leontes must intend not only "extraordinary" but also "brought about by a foreigner."

In more than this deed does require! And blessing 190
Against this cruelty fight on thy side,
Poor thing, condemn'd to loss! *Exit [with the child].*
LEONTES   No! I'll not rear
Another's issue.

Enter a SERVANT.

SERVANT   Please' your Highness, posts
From those you sent to th' oracle are come
An hour since. Cleomines and Dion, 195
Being well arriv'd from Delphos, are both landed,
Hasting to th' court.
[1.] LORD   So please you, sir, their speed
Hath been beyond accompt.
LEONTES   Twenty-three days
They have been absent. 'Tis good speed; foretells
The great Apollo suddenly will have 200
The truth of this appear. Prepare you, lords,
Summon a session, that we may arraign
Our most disloyal lady; for as she hath
Been publicly accus'd, so shall she have
A just and open trial. While she lives 205
My heart will be a burthen to me. Leave me,
And think upon my bidding. *Exeunt.*

---

190. **In more:** in more ways (?) or to a greater degree (?). **require:** deserve.
192. **loss:** destruction.   193. **Please':** please it, i.e. may it please. **posts:** speedy
messengers.   198. **accompt:** record, i.e. precedent.   200. **suddenly:** at once.
202. **session:** trial.

Act 3

SCENE I

Enter CLEOMINES *and* DION.

CLEOMINES The climate's delicate, the air most sweet,
    Fertile the isle, the temple much surpassing
    The common praise it bears.
DION   I shall report,
    For most it caught me, the celestial habits
    (Methinks I so should term them) and the reverence   5
    Of the grave wearers. O, the sacrifice!
    How ceremonious, solemn, and unearthly
    It was i' th' off'ring!
CLEOMINES   But of all, the burst
    And the ear-deaf'ning voice o' th' oracle,
    Kin to Jove's thunder, so surpris'd my sense,   10
    That I was nothing.
DION   If th' event o' th' journey
    Prove as successful to the Queen (O be't so!)
    As it hath been to us rare, pleasant, speedy,
    The time is worth the use on't.
CLEOMINES   Great Apollo
    Turn all to th' best! These proclamations,   15
    So forcing faults upon Hermione,
    I little like.
DION   The violent carriage of it
    Will clear or end the business. When the oracle
    (Thus by Apollo's great divine seal'd up)
    Shall the contents discover, something rare   20
    Even then will rush to knowledge. Go; fresh horses!
    And gracious be the issue!   *Exeunt.*

3.1. Location: Sicilia. On the road.   **2. isle.** Shakespeare follows his source *Pandosto* in locating Apollo's oracle on "the isle of Delphos"—perhaps a confusion of Delphi with the island of Delos, the god's reputed birthplace.   **4. caught:** charmed. **habits:** garments.   **10. surpris'd:** overwhelmed.   **11. event:** outcome.   **17. carriage:** handling.   **19. great divine:** chief priest.   **20. discover:** reveal.

SCENE 2

Enter LEONTES, LORDS, OFFICERS.

LEONTES This sessions (to our great grief we pronounce)
Even pushes 'gainst our heart—the party tried,
The daughter of a king, our wife, and one
Of us too much belov'd. Let us be clear'd
Of being tyrannous, since we so openly   5
Proceed in justice, which shall have due course,
Even to the guilt or the purgation.
Produce the prisoner.
OFFICERS It is his Highness' pleasure that the Queen
Appear in person here in court.

  [*Enter*] HERMIONE (*as to her trial*) , [PAULINA, *and*]
  LADIES [*attending*].

                        Silence!   10
LEONTES Read the indictment.
OFFICERS [*Reads.*] "Hermione, queen to the worthy
Leontes, King of Sicilia, thou art here accused and
arraigned of high treason, in committing adultery with
Polixenes, King of Bohemia, and conspiring with   15
Camillo to take away the life of our sovereign lord the
King, thy royal husband: the pretense whereof being
by circumstances partly laid open, thou, Hermione,
contrary to the faith and allegiance of a true subject,
didst counsel and aid them, for their better safety, to   20
fly away by night."
HERMIONE Since what I am to say must be but that
Which contradicts my accusation, and
The testimony on my part no other
But what comes from myself, it shall scarce boot me   25
To say "Not guilty." Mine integrity,
Being counted falsehood, shall (as I express it)
Be so receiv'd. But thus, if pow'rs divine
Behold our human actions (as they do),
I doubt not then but innocence shall make   30
False accusation blush, and tyranny
Tremble at patience. You, my lord, best know
([Who] least will seem to do so) my past life

3.2. Location: Sicilia. A court of justice. **4. Of:** by. **7. purgation:** exculpation.
17. pretense: design. **25. boot:** profit.

Hath been as continent, as chaste, as true,
As I am now unhappy; which is more   35
Than history can pattern, though devis'd
And play'd to take spectators. For behold me,
A fellow of the royal bed, which owe
A moi'ty of the throne, a great king's daughter,
The mother to a hopeful prince, here standing   40
To prate and talk for life and honor 'fore
Who please to come and hear. For life, I prize it
As I weigh grief, which I would spare; for honor,
'Tis a derivative from me to mine,
And only that I stand for. I appeal   45
To your own conscience, sir, before Polixenes
Came to your court, how I was in your grace,
How merited to be so; since he came,
With what encounter so uncurrent I
Have strain'd t' appear thus; if one jot beyond   50
The bound of honor, or in act or will
That way inclining, hard'ned be the hearts
Of all that hear me, and my near'st of kin
Cry fie upon my grave!

LEONTES   I ne'er heard yet
That any of these bolder vices wanted   55
Less impudence to gainsay what they did
Than to perform it first.

HERMIONE   That's true enough,
Though 'tis a saying, sir, not due to me.

LEONTES You will not own it.

HERMIONE   More than mistress of
Which comes to me in name of fault, I must not   60
At all acknowledge. For Polixenes
(With whom I am accus'd), I do confess
I lov'd him as in honor he requir'd;
With such a kind of love as might become

---

35. which: which unhappiness. **36. history:** story. **pattern:** show a precedent
for. **37. take:** charm. **38. which owe:** who own. **39. moi'ty:** share (?) or half (?)
42–43. For . . . spare: as for life, I rate it as I rate grief, and would as willingly
give it up. **44. a derivative:** something to be handed on. **mine:** my children.
45. stand: make a stand, fight. **46. conscience:** consideration, judgment. **49. encounter so uncurrent:** conduct so unlawful. **50. strain'd:** transgressed. **thus:** i.e.
on trial for adultery. **55–56. wanted Less:** i.e. were more wanting in. *Less* (where
a modern ear expects *More*) intensifies the idea of deficiency in *wanted*. **58. due:**
applicable. **59. mistress:** possessor. **60. fault:** ordinary human failings (not any
of the "bolder vices" of line 56). **63. he requir'd:** was his due.

A lady like me; with a love even such,   65
So, and no other, as yourself commanded;
Which not to have done I think had been in me
Both disobedience and ingratitude
To you and toward your friend, whose love had spoke,
Even since it could speak, from an infant, freely,   70
That it was yours. Now for conspiracy,
I know not how it tastes, though it be dish'd
For me to try how. All I know of it
Is that Camillo was an honest man;
And why he left your court, the gods themselves   75
(Wotting no more than I) are ignorant.
LEONTES You knew of his departure, as you know
     What you have underta'en to do in 's absence.
HERMIONE Sir,
     You speak a language that I understand not.   80
     My life stands in the level of your dreams,
     Which I'll lay down.
LEONTES   Your actions are my dreams.
     You had a bastard by Polixenes,
     And I but dream'd it. As you were past all shame
     (Those of your fact are so), so past all truth;   85
     Which to deny concerns more than avails; for as
     Thy brat hath been cast out, like to itself,
     No father owning it (which is indeed
     More criminal in thee than it), so thou
     Shalt feel our justice; in whose easiest passage   90
     Look for no less than death.
HERMIONE   Sir, spare your threats.
     The bug which you would fright me with, I seek.
     To me can life be no commodity;
     The crown and comfort of my life, your favor,
     I do give lost, for I do feel it gone,   95
     But know not how it went. My second joy
     And first-fruits of my body, from his presence
     I am barr'd, like one infectious. My third comfort
     (Starr'd most unluckily) is from my breast

72. **dish'd:** served up, placed before me. 76. **Wotting:** knowing, i.e. if they know. 81. **level:** aim. **dreams:** fantasies, delusions. 85. **Those . . . fact:** those who commit the crime that you have committed. 86. **concerns . . . avails:** costs more effort than it will repay. 87. **like to itself:** i.e. appropriately for a bastard. 90–91. **in . . . death.** A threat of torture in addition to death. 92. **bug:** bugbear, bogey. 93. **commodity:** benefit. 95. **give:** account.

(The innocent milk in it most innocent mouth)   100
Hal'd out to murther; myself on every post
Proclaim'd a strumpet; with immodest hatred
The child-bed privilege denied, which 'longs
To women of all fashion; lastly, hurried
Here to this place, i' th' open air, before   105
I have got strength of limit. Now, my liege,
Tell me what blessings I have here alive,
That I should fear to die? Therefore proceed.
But yet hear this—mistake me not; no life
(I prize it not a straw), but for mine honor,   110
Which I would free—if I shall be condemn'd
Upon surmises (all proofs sleeping else
But what your jealousies awake), I tell you
'Tis rigor and not law. Your honors all,
I do refer me to the oracle: 115
Apollo be my judge!
[1.] LORD   This your request
Is altogether just; therefore bring forth,
And in Apollo's name, his oracle.

                                    [*Exeunt certain Officers.*]

HERMIONE The Emperor of Russia was my father.
  O that he were alive, and here beholding   120
His daughter's trial! that he did but see
The flatness of my misery, yet with eyes
Of pity, not revenge!

         [*Enter* OFFICERS *with*] CLEOMINES, DION.

OFFICER You here shall swear upon this sword of justice,
  That you, Cleomines and Dion, have   125
Been both at Delphos, and from thence have brought
This seal'd-up oracle, by the hand deliver'd
Of great Apollo's priest; and that since then
You have not dar'd to break the holy seal
Nor read the secrets in't.
CLEOMINES, DION   All this we swear.   130
LEONTES Break up the seals, and read.
OFFICER [*Reads.*] "Hermione is chaste, Polixenes

99. **Starr'd most unluckily:** born under unlucky stars.   100. **it:** its.   101. **post.** Public notices were placed on posts.   102. **immodest:** immoderate.   103. **'longs:** belongs.   104. **all fashion:** every rank.   106. **got . . . limit:** i.e. regained customary strength following childbirth.   111. **free:** clear.   114. **rigor:** tyranny. 122. **flatness:** completeness.

blameless, Camillo a true subject, Leontes a jealous
tyrant, his innocent babe truly begotten, and the King
shall live without an heir, if that which is lost be not   135
found."
LORDS Now blessed be the great Apollo!
HERMIONE   Praised!
LEONTES Hast thou read truth?
OFFICER   Ay, my lord, even so
As it is here set down.
LEONTES There is no truth at all i' th' oracle.   140
The sessions shall proceed; this is mere falsehood.

[*Enter a* SERVANT.]

SERVANT My lord the King! the King!
LEONTES   What is the business?
SERVANT O sir, I shall be hated to report it!
The Prince your son, with mere conceit and fear
Of the Queen's speed, is gone.
LEONTES   How? gone?
SERVANT   Is dead.   145
LEONTES Apollo's angry, and the heavens themselves
Do strike at my injustice. [*Hermione swoons.*] How now there?
PAULINA This news is mortal to the Queen. Look down
And see what death is doing.
LEONTES   Take her hence;
Her heart is but o'ercharg'd; she will recover.   150
I have too much believ'd mine own suspicion.
Beseech you tenderly apply to her
Some remedies for life.
                    [*Exeunt Paulina and Ladies with Hermione.*]
                    Apollo, pardon
My great profaneness 'gainst thine oracle!
I'll reconcile me to Polixenes,   155
New woo my queen, recall the good Camillo,
Whom I proclaim a man of truth, of mercy;
For being transported by my jealousies
To bloody thoughts, and to revenge, I chose
Camillo for the minister to poison   160
My friend Polixenes; which had been done,
But that the good mind of Camillo tardied
My swift command, though I with death and with

141. mere: utter. **144. conceit and fear:** anxious thoughts. **145. speed:** fortune.

Reward did threaten and encourage him,
Not doing it and being done. He (most humane   165
And fill'd with honor) to my kingly guest
Unclasp'd my practice, quit his fortunes here
(Which you knew great), and to the hazard of
All incertainties himself commended,
No richer than his honor. How he glisters   170
Through my rust! and how his piety
Does my deeds make the blacker!

[*Enter* PAULINA.]

PAULINA   Woe the while!
O, cut my lace, lest my heart, cracking it,
Break too!
[1.] LORD   What fit is this, good lady?
PAULINA What studied torments, tyrant, hast for me?   175
What wheels? racks? fires? What flaying? boiling
In leads or oils? What old or newer torture
Must I receive, whose every word deserves
To taste of thy most worst? Thy tyranny,
Together working with thy jealousies   180
(Fancies too weak for boys, too green and idle
For girls of nine), O, think what they have done,
And then run mad indeed—stark mad! for all
Thy by-gone fooleries were but spices of it.
That thou betrayedst Polixenes, 'twas nothing—   185
That did but show thee, of a fool, inconstant,
And damnable ingrateful; nor was't much
Thou wouldst have poison'd good Camillo's honor,
To have him kill a king—poor trespasses,
More monstrous standing by; whereof I reckon   190
The casting forth to crows thy baby-daughter
To be or none or little—though a devil
Would have shed water out of fire ere done't;
Nor is't directly laid to thee, the death
Of the young Prince, whose honorable thoughts   195
(Thoughts high for one so tender) cleft the heart
That could conceive a gross and foolish sire

---

167. Unclasp'd my practice: disclosed my plot.   **169. commended:** committed.
170. No richer than: taking nothing with him except. **glisters:** shines.
184. spices: slight foretastes. **186. of:** for. **189. poor:** trivial. **190. standing
by:** to follow (?) or standing beside them for comparison (?)   **196. tender:** young.

Blemish'd his gracious dam; this is not, no,
Laid to thy answer: but the last—O lords,
When I have said, cry "Woe!"—the Queen, the Queen,   200
The sweet'st, dear'st creature's dead, and vengeance for't
Not dropp'd down yet.
[1.] LORD   The higher pow'rs forbid!
PAULINA I say she's dead; I'll swear't. If word nor oath
    Prevail not, go and see. If you can bring
    Tincture or lustre in her lip, her eye,   205
    Heat outwardly or breath within, I'll serve you
    As I would do the gods. But, O thou tyrant!
    Do not repent these things, for they are heavier
    Than all thy woes can stir; therefore betake thee
    To nothing but despair. A thousand knees,   210
    Ten thousand years together, naked, fasting,
    Upon a barren mountain, and still winter
    In storm perpetual, could not move the gods
    To look that way thou wert.
LEONTES   Go on, go on;
    Thou canst not speak too much, I have deserv'd   215
    All tongues to talk their bitt'rest.
[1.] LORD   Say no more.
    Howe'er the business goes, you have made fault
    I' th' boldness of your speech.
PAULINA   I am sorry for't.
    All faults I make, when I shall come to know them,
    I do repent. Alas, I have show'd too much   220
    The rashness of a woman; he is touch'd
    To th' noble heart. What's gone and what's past help
    Should be past grief. Do not receive affliction
    At my petition; I beseech you, rather
    Let me be punish'd, that have minded you   225
    Of what you should forget. Now, good my liege,
    Sir, royal sir, forgive a foolish woman.
    The love I bore your queen—lo, fool again!—
    I'll speak of her no more, nor of your children;
    I'll not remember you of my own lord,   230
    Who is lost too. Take your patience to you,
    And I'll say nothing.

---

200. said: i.e. said what I have to say.   **209. woes:** lamentations. **stir:** move.
212. still: always.   **214. that . . . wert:** in your direction.   **223–24. Do . . .
petition:** let not my prayer for vengeance bring down suffering upon you.
225. minded: reminded.   **230. remember:** remind.

LEONTES   Thou didst speak but well
When most the truth; which I receive much better
Than to be pitied of thee. Prithee bring me
To the dead bodies of my queen and son.   235
One grave shall be for both; upon them shall
The causes of their death appear (unto
Our shame perpetual). Once a day I'll visit
The chapel where they lie, and tears shed there
Shall be my recreation. So long as nature   240
Will bear up with this exercise, so long
I daily vow to use it. Come, and lead me
To these sorrows.   *Exeunt.*

SCENE 3

Enter ANTIGONUS [*and*] *a* MARINER [*with the*] *babe.*

ANTIGONUS Thou art perfect then, our ship hath touch'd upon
The deserts of Bohemia?
MARINER   Ay, my lord, and fear
We have landed in ill time: the skies look grimly,
And threaten present blusters. In my conscience,
The heavens with that we have in hand are angry,   5
And frown upon 's.
ANTIGONUS Their sacred wills be done! Go get aboard;
Look to thy bark, I'll not be long before
I call upon thee.
MARINER Make your best haste, and go not   10
Too far i' th' land; 'tis like to be loud weather.
Besides, this place is famous for the creatures
Of prey that keep upon 't.
ANTIGONUS   Go thou away,
I'll follow instantly.
MARINER   I am glad at heart
To be so rid o' th' business.   *Exit.*
ANTIGONUS   Come, poor babe.   15
I have heard (but not believ'd) the spirits o' th' dead
May walk again. If such thing be, thy mother
Appear'd to me last night; for ne'er was dream

3.3. Location: Bohemia. The sea-coast. **1. perfect:** certain. **4. present:** immediate.
conscience: opinion. **5. that . . . hand:** what we are doing. **13. keep upon't:**
inhabit it.

So like a waking. To me comes a creature,
Sometimes her head on one side, some another—   20
I never saw a vessel of like sorrow,
So fill'd, and so becoming; in pure white robes,
Like very sanctity, she did approach
My cabin where I lay; thrice bow'd before me,
And (gasping to begin some speech) her eyes   25
Became two spouts; the fury spent, anon
Did this break from her: "Good Antigonus,
Since fate (against thy better disposition)
Hath made thy person for the thrower-out
Of my poor babe, according to thine oath,   30
Places remote enough are in Bohemia,
There weep and leave it crying; and for the babe
Is counted lost for ever, Perdita
I prithee call't. For this ungentle business,
Put on thee by my lord, thou ne'er shalt see   35
Thy wife Paulina more." And so, with shrieks,
She melted into air. Affrighted much,
I did in time collect myself and thought
This was so, and no slumber. Dreams are toys,
Yet for this once, yea, superstitiously,   40
I will be squar'd by this. I do believe
Hermione hath suffer'd death, and that
Apollo would (this being indeed the issue
Of King Polixenes) it should here be laid,
Either for life or death, upon the earth   45
Of its right father. Blossom, speed thee well!
                    [*Laying down the child, with a scroll.*]
There lie, and there thy character; there these,
                    [*Placing a bundle beside it.*]
Which may, if Fortune please, both breed thee, pretty,
And still rest thine. [*Thunder.*] The storm begins. Poor wretch,
That for thy mother's fault art thus expos'd   50
To loss, and what may follow! Weep I cannot,
But my heart bleeds; and most accurs'd am I
To be by oath enjoin'd to this. Farewell!
The day frowns more and more; thou'rt like to have

---

22. becoming: i.e. beautiful in sorrow.   **32. for:** because.   **33. Perdita:** i.e. the lost
one.   **34. ungentle:** ignoble.   **39. toys:** trifles.   **41. squar'd:** ruled.   **47. character:**
writing, i.e. written statement which will later prove her identity (see 5.2.33–35).
these: i.e. gold and jewels.   **48–49. breed . . . thine:** pay for your bringing up and
still leave something over.   **51. Weep I cannot.** See line 32.

Pl. 1 In this 1836 painting of Autolycus, hawking ballads and various baubles, Charles Robert Leslie colorfully illustrates the fresh life that this character injects into the play during its Bohemian interlude. The eyes of his rustic beholders reveal the fascination that Autolycus exerts upon his potential victims, and the landscape in the background situates this pastoral scene in the Warwickshire countryside of Shakespeare's youth. On the meadow in the distance, there are sheep aplenty, but it is impossible to discern whether or not they have recently been shorn.

Pl. 2 The play announces the first appearance of Autolycus singing about the triumph of both spring and fresh energy over "the winter's pale" (4.3.4). That last phrase rhymingly suggests the play's title, and the arrival of Autolycus makes it conspicuously clear that *The Winter's Tale* is about to become another sort of story. In Adrian Noble's 1992 RSC production Richard McCabe sang this song during his descent via an enormous balloon parachute, making this dramatic change of genre all the more spectacular and vividly complementing the devil-may-care exuberance of Shakespeare's late art.

Pl. 3 In Simon Gray's vitriolic comedy, *Butley* (1971), Alan Bates performed the title role to great acclaim. Butley, an alchoholic English professor, disintegrates in the shadow of T. S. Eliot and in the words of F. R. Leavis, who sought to recuperate late Shakespeare and successfully advocated the Great Tradition in British schools. For Butley, "success" is a relative term, and the reanimation of Hermione leaves this Leontes figure cold. The bottle he holds has unfortunately become the only company he seems able to keep.

Pl. 4 Finally, this couple is reunited at the end of Eric Rohmer's *Conte d'hiver* (1992). Their reunion causes what both mother and daughter call "tears of joy," as Charles (Frédéric Van Den Driessche) and Félicie (Charlotte Véry) find one another again. That repeated phrase sounds like Leontes telling Paulina that his "affliction has a taste as sweet / As any cordial comfort," when Julio Romano's statue of Hermione astonishes Leontes with its uncannily lifelike appearance in *The Winter's Tale* (5.3.76-7). In both cases the incredibility of such endings challenges skeptics to consult their feelings before further doubts distance them once again from an awareness of their hearts' desires.

A lullaby too rough. I never saw   55
The heavens so dim by day. A savage clamor!
Well may I get aboard! This is the chase;
I am gone for ever.   *Exit pursued by a bear.*

[Enter] SHEPHERD.

SHEPHERD I would there were no age between ten and
three-and-twenty, or that youth would sleep out   60
the rest; for there is nothing in the between but getting
wenches with child, wronging the ancientry, stealing,
fighting— *[Horns.]* Hark you now! Would any but
these boil'd-brains of nineteen and two-and-twenty
hunt this weather? They have scar'd away two   65
of my best sheep, which I fear the wolf will sooner
find than the master. If any where I have them, 'tis
by the sea-side, browsing of ivy. Good luck, and't
be thy will! What have we here? Mercy on 's, a
barne? A very pretty barne! A boy, or a child,   70
I wonder? A pretty one, a very pretty one: sure
some scape. Though I am not bookish, yet I can read
waiting-gentlewoman in the scape. This has been
some stair-work, some trunk-work, some behind-
door-work. They were warmer that got this than   75
the poor thing is here. I'll take it up for pity, yet
I'll tarry till my son come; he hallow'd but even now.
Whoa-ho-hoa!

Enter CLOWN.

CLOWN Hilloa, loa!
SHEPHERD What? art so near? If thou'lt see a thing to   80
talk on when thou art dead and rotten, come hither.
What ail'st thou, man?
CLOWN I have seen two such sights, by sea and by
land! But I am not to say it is a sea, for it is now the
sky, betwixt the firmament and it you cannot thrust a   85
bodkin's point.
SHEPHERD Why, boy, how is it?
CLOWN I would you did but see how it chafes, how it
rages, how it takes up the shore! But that's not to the

---

62. ancientry: old people. **64. boil'd-brains:** senseless creatures. **70. barne:**
bairn, child. **child:** girl. **72. scape:** sexual escapade. **74. trunk-work:** secret
affair involving a trunk (perhaps with play on *trunk* = body). **75. got:** begot.
78 s.d. **Clown:** rustic. **86. bodkin's:** needle's. **89. takes up:** rebukes.

point. O, the most piteous cry of the poor souls! 90
Sometimes to see 'em, and not to see 'em; now the
ship boring the moon with her mainmast, and anon
swallow'd with yest and froth, as you'ld thrust a
cork into a hogshead. And then for the land-service,
to see how the bear tore out his shoulder-bone, 95
how he cried to me for help, and said his name was
Antigonus, a nobleman. But to make an end of the
ship, to see how the sea flap-dragon'd it; but, first,
how the poor souls roar'd, and the sea mock'd
them; and how the poor gentleman roar'd, and the 100
bear mock'd him, both roaring louder than the sea or
weather.

SHEPHERD Name of mercy, when was this, boy?

CLOWN Now, now; I have not wink'd since I saw
these sights. The men are not yet cold under water, nor 105
the bear half din'd on the gentleman. He's at it now.

SHEPHERD Would I had been by, to have help'd the old
man!

CLOWN I would you had been by the ship side, to have
help'd her; there your charity would have lack'd 110
footing.

SHEPHERD Heavy matters, heavy matters! But look
thee here, boy. Now bless thyself: thou met'st with
things dying, I with things new-born. Here's a
sight for thee; look thee, a bearing-cloth for a squire's 115
child! Look thee here, take up, take up, boy; open't.
So, let's see—it was told me I should be rich by the
fairies. This is some changeling; open't; what's
within, boy?

CLOWN You're a [made] old man; if the sins of your 120
youth are forgiven you, you're well to live. Gold,
all gold!

SHEPHERD This is fairy gold, boy, and 'twill prove so.
Up with't, keep it close. Home, home, the next

---

93. yest: yeast, foam.   **94. the land-service:** (1) what was taking place ashore
(literally, military service on land, in contrast to naval service); (2) the dish that
was being served up ashore.   **98. flap-dragon'd:** swallowed as if it had been a
flap-dragon (a raisin floating on burning brandy).   **110–11. would . . . footing:**
would have lacked a firm foothold (such as the land would provide), with pun
on the sense "would not have founded a charitable institution."   **115. bearing-
cloth:** rich cloth in which an infant was borne to its baptism.   **118. changeling:**
child left by fairies.   **121. well to live:** well-to-do, with pun on the sense "living
in virtue."   **124. close:** secret. It was bad luck to talk about gifts from the fairies.

way. We are lucky, boy, and to be so still requires   125
    nothing but secrecy. Let my sheep go. Come, good
    boy, the next way home.
CLOWN Go you the next way with your findings; I'll
    go see if the bear be gone from the gentleman and
    how much he hath eaten. They are never curst but   130
    when they are hungry. If there be any of him left, I'll
    bury it.
SHEPHERD That's a good deed. If thou mayest discern
    by that which is left of him what he is, fetch me to th'
    sight of him.   135
CLOWN Marry, will I; and you shall help to put him i'
    th' ground.
SHEPHERD 'Tis a lucky day, boy, and we'll do good
    deeds on't.   *Exeunt.*

---

125. be so still: go on being so.   **127. next:** nearest, shortest.   **130. curst:** fierce.
136. Marry: indeed (originally the name of the Virgin Mary used as an oath).

Act 4

SCENE I

Enter TIME, *the Chorus.*

TIME I, that please some, try all, both joy and terror
   Of good and bad, that makes and unfolds error,
   Now take upon me, in the name of Time,
   To use my wings. Impute it not a crime
   To me, or my swift passage, that I slide   5
   O'er sixteen years and leave the growth untried
   Of that wide gap, since it is in my pow'r
   To o'erthrow law, and in one self-born hour
   To plant and o'erwhelm custom. Let me pass
   The same I am, ere ancient'st order was,   10
   Or what is now receiv'd. I witness to
   The times that brought them in; so shall I do
   To th' freshest things now reigning, and make stale
   The glistering of this present, as my tale
   Now seems to it. Your patience this allowing,   15
   I turn my glass, and give my scene such growing
   As you had slept between. Leontes leaving—
   Th' effects of his fond jealousies so grieving
   That he shuts up himself—imagine me,
   Gentle spectators, that I now may be   20
   In fair Bohemia, and remember well,
   I mentioned a son o' th' King's, which Florizel
   I now name to you; and with speed so pace
   To speak of Perdita, now grown in grace
   Equal with wond'ring. What of her ensues   25

4.1.1. **Try:** test. **6. leave . . . untried:** leave unexamined the developments.
8. self-born: self-same. **9–11. Let . . . receiv'd:** i.e. accept me as the same before
civilization began and right now. **14. glistering:** brightness, freshness.
15. seems to it: i.e. seems stale in comparison with the present. **16. glass:** hour-
glass (regularly carried by Time in conventional representations). **17. As:** as
if. **18. fond:** foolish. **22. I . . . King's.** The mention of Polixenes' son in 1.2 is
part of "Time's news"(line 26). **23. pace:** proceed. **25. Equal with wond'ring:**
to a degree that creates admiring wonderment.

I list not prophesy; but let Time's news
Be known when 'tis brought forth. A shepherd's daughter,
And what to her adheres, which follows after,
Is th' argument of Time. Of this allow,
If ever you have spent time worse ere now;   30
If never, yet that Time himself doth say,
He wishes earnestly you never may.   *Exit.*

SCENE 2

Enter POLIXENES *and* CAMILLO.

POLIXENES I pray thee, good Camillo, be no more im-
portunate. 'Tis a sickness denying thee any thing; a
death to grant this.

CAMILLO It is fifteen years since I saw my country;
though I have for the most part been air'd abroad,   5
I desire to lay my bones there. Besides, the penitent
King, my master, hath sent for me, to whose feeling
sorrows I might be some allay (or I o'erween to think
so), which is another spur to my departure.

POLIXENES As thou lov'st me, Camillo, wipe not out the   10
rest of thy services by leaving me now. The need I
have of thee, thine own goodness hath made. Better
not to have had thee than thus to want thee. Thou,
having made me businesses which none without thee can
sufficiently manage, must either stay to execute   15
them thyself, or take away with thee the very services
thou hast done; which if I have not enough consider'd
(as too much I cannot), to be more thankful to thee
shall be my study, and my profit therein the heaping
friendships. Of that fatal country Sicilia, prithee   20
speak no more, whose very naming punishes me with
the remembrance of that penitent (as thou call'st him)
and reconcil'd king, my brother, whose loss of his
most precious queen and children are even now to be
afresh lamented. Say to me, when saw'st thou the   25
Prince Florizel, my son? Kings are no less unhappy,

---

26. list not: do not wish to. **28. adheres:** relates. **29. argument:** subject matter.
4.2. Location: Bohemia. The palace of Polixenes. **5. been air'd:** lived.
8. o'erween: am conceited enough. **13. want:** lack, i.e. lose. **17. consider'd:**
rewarded. **19–20. heaping friendships:** piling up of kind services. **22. as . . .
him:** to use your own word (no implication of doubt is intended).

their issue not being gracious, than they are in losing
them when they have approv'd their virtues.

CAMILLO Sir, it is three days since I saw the Prince.
What his happier affairs may be, are to me un-   30
known; but I have (missingly) noted, he is of late much
retir'd from court, and is less frequent to his princely
exercises than formerly he hath appear'd.

POLIXENES I have consider'd so much, Camillo, and with
some care, so far that I have eyes under my service   35
which look upon his removedness; from whom I have
this intelligence, that he is seldom from the house of a
most homely shepherd, a man, they say, that from very
nothing, and beyond the imagination of his neighbors, is
grown into an unspeakable estate.   40

CAMILLO I have heard, sir, of such a man, who hath a
daughter of most rare note. The report of her is
extended more than can be thought to begin from such
a cottage.

POLIXENES That's likewise part of my intelligence; but   45
(I fear) the angle that plucks our son thither. Thou
shalt accompany us to the place, where we will (not
appearing what we are) have some question with the
shepherd; from whose simplicity I think it not uneasy
to get the cause of my son's resort thither. Prithee   50
be my present partner in this business, and lay aside
the thoughts of Sicilia.

CAMILLO I willingly obey your command.

POLIXENES My best Camillo! We must disguise our-
selves.   *Exeunt.*

SCENE 3

Enter AUTOLYCUS *singing.*

[AUTOLYCUS] When daffadils begin to peer,
With heigh, the doxy over the dale!

---

27. being gracious: having princely qualities. **28. approv'd:** proved. **31. missingly:** aware of missing him. **35–36. eyes . . . removedness:** spies who watch
him in his retirement from court. **37. intelligence:** news. **from:** away from.
38. homely: plain, simple. **40. unspeakable:** unutterable, i.e. beyond reckoning.
42. note: distinction. **46. angle:** baited hook. **48. question:** conversation.
49. uneasy: difficult. **4.3. Location:** Bohemia. A road near the Shepherd's
cottage. **1. daffadils:** daffodils. **peer:** peep out. **2. doxy:** beggar's wench.

Why, then comes in the sweet o' the year,
    For the red blood reigns in the winter's pale.

The white sheet bleaching on the hedge,   5
    With hey, the sweet birds, O how they sing!
Doth set my pugging tooth an edge,
    For a quart of ale is a dish for a king.

The lark, that tirra-lyra chaunts,
    With heigh, [with heigh,] the thrush and the jay!   10
Are summer songs for me and my aunts,
    While we lie tumbling in the hay.

I have serv'd Prince Florizel, and in my time wore
three-pile, but now I am out of service.

But shall I go mourn for that, my dear?   15
    The pale moon shines by night;
And when I wander here and there,
    I then do most go right.

If tinkers may have leave to live,
    And bear the sow-skin bouget,   20
Then my account I well may give,
    And in the stocks avouch it.

My traffic is sheets; when the kite builds, look to
lesser linen. My father nam'd me Autolycus, who
being, as I am, litter'd under Mercury, was like-   25
wise a snapper-up of unconsider'd trifles. With die
and drab I purchas'd this caparison, and my revenue
is the silly cheat. Gallows and knock are too powerful
on the highway. Beating and hanging are terrors to
me. For the life to come, I sleep out the thought of it.   30
A prize, a prize!

---

4. pale: (1) paleness; (2) area of royal authority.   **7. pugging:** thieving. **set . . . an edge:** set . . . on edge, i.e. sharpen make keen.   **11. aunts:** i.e. whores.   **14. three-pile:** costly velvet.   **20. bouget:** budget, i.e. wallet or bag.   **22. avouch it:** testify to my thieving trade.   **23–24. My . . . linen.** Autolycus steals sheets which have been left to dry on hedges; the kite at nesting-time steals smaller pieces of linen.   **24. Autolycus.** The ancient Autolycus, Ulysses' grandfather, was the son of Mercury, god of thieves, and was himself an expert thief.   **25. litter'd under Mercury:** (1) begotten by Mercury; (2) born when the planet Mercury was in the ascendant.   **26–27. With . . . caparison:** dice and women have reduced me to these rags.   **27. revenue:** source of income.   **28. silly cheat:** petty swindle (?) or cheating the simple (?). **knock:** beating.   **30. For:** as for.   **31. A prize:** booty, something for the taking.

Enter CLOWN.

CLOWN Let me see: every 'leven wether tods, every
tod yields pound and odd shilling; fifteen hundred
shorn, what comes the wool to?

AUTOLYCUS [*Aside.*] If the springe hold, the cock's mine.   35

CLOWN I cannot do't without compters. Let me see:
what am I to buy for our sheep-shearing feast? Three
pound of sugar, five pound of currants, rice—what will
this sister of mine do with rice? But my father hath
made her mistress of the feast, and she lays it on.   40
She hath made me four and twenty nosegays for the
shearers (three-man song-men all, and very good ones),
but they are most of them means and bases; but one
Puritan amongst them, and he sings psalms to horn-
pipes. I must have saffron to color the warden   45
pies; mace; dates, none—that's out of my note; nut-
megs, seven; a race or two of ginger, but that I may
beg; four pounds of pruins, and as many of raisins o'
th' sun.

AUTOLYCUS O that ever I was born!   50

[*Grovelling on the ground.*]

CLOWN I' th' name of me—

AUTOLYCUS O, help me, help me! Pluck but off these
rags; and then, death, death!

CLOWN Alack, poor soul, thou hast need of more rags
to lay on thee, rather than have these off.   55

AUTOLYCUS O sir, the loathsomeness of them offend me
more than the stripes I have receiv'd, which are mighty
ones and millions.

CLOWN Alas, poor man, a million of beating may come
to a great matter.   60

AUTOLYCUS I am robb'd, sir, and beaten; my money and
apparel ta'en from me, and these detestable things put
upon me.

CLOWN What, by a horseman, or a footman?

---

32. every . . . tods: every eleven sheep produce a tod (28 pounds) of wool. The Clown and his father will get over £143 at this shearing; they are very prosperous shepherds. **35. springe:** snare. **cock:** woodcock, a proverbially silly bird. **36. compters:** counters, metal disks used in calculating. **42. three-man song-men:** singers of catches or rounds for three voices. **43. means:** tenors. **44–45. hornpipes:** dance tunes. **45–46. warden pies:** pies made of winter pears. **46. out . . . note:** crossed off my list. **47. race:** root. **48. pruins:** prunes. **48–49. o' th' sun:** sun-dried.

AUTOLYCUS A footman, sweet sir, a footman.   65
CLOWN Indeed, he should be a footman by the gar-
   ments he has left with thee. If this be a horseman's
   coat, it hath seen very hot service. Lend me thy hand,
   I'll help thee. Come, lend me thy hand.
AUTOLYCUS O good sir, tenderly, O!   70
CLOWN Alas, poor soul!
AUTOLYCUS O good sir, softly, good sir! I fear, sir, my
   shoulder-blade is out.
CLOWN How now? canst stand?
AUTOLYCUS Softly, dear sir; [*picking his pocket*] good sir,   75
   softly. You ha' done me a charitable office.
CLOWN Dost lack any money? I have a little money
   for thee.
AUTOLYCUS No, good sweet sir; no, I beseech you, sir.
   I have a kinsman not past three quarters of a mile   80
   hence, unto whom I was going. I shall there have
   money, or any thing I want. Offer me no money, I
   pray you, that kills my heart.
CLOWN What manner of fellow was he that robb'd
   you?   85
AUTOLYCUS A fellow, sir, that I have known to go about
   with troll-my-dames. I knew him once a servant of
   the Prince. I cannot tell, good sir, for which of his
   virtues it was, but he was certainly whipt out of the
   court.   90
CLOWN His vices, you would say; there's no virtue
   whipt out of the court. They cherish it to make it
   stay there; and yet it will no more but abide.
AUTOLYCUS Vices, I would say, sir. I know this man
   well; he hath been since an ape-bearer, then a   95
   process-server, a bailiff, then he compass'd a motion
   of the Prodigal Son, and married a tinker's wife within
   a mile where my land and living lies; and, having
   flown over many knavish professions, he settled only
   in rogue. Some call him Autolycus.   100
CLOWN Out upon him! prig, for my life, prig! He
   haunts wakes, fairs, and bear-baitings.

---

72. softly: gently.   **87. troll-my-dames:** a game resembling bagatelle.   **93. abide:**
stay briefly.   **95. ape-bearer:** exhibitor of a tame monkey.   **96. compass'd:**
got possession of (?) or contrived (?) or took on tour (?). **motion:** puppet show.
101. prig: thief.   **102. wakes:** village festivals.

AUTOLYCUS Very true, sir; he, sir, he. That's the rogue
   that put me into this apparel.

CLOWN Not a more cowardly rogue in all Bohemia. If   105
   you had but look'd big, and spit at him, he'ld have run.

AUTOLYCUS I must confess to you, sir, I am no fighter. I
   am false of heart that way, and that he knew, I warrant
   him.

CLOWN How do you now?   110

AUTOLYCUS Sweet sir, much better than I was: I can stand
   and walk. I will even take my leave of you, and pace
   softly towards my kinsman's.

CLOWN Shall I bring thee on the way?

AUTOLYCUS No, good-fac'd sir, no, sweet sir.   115

CLOWN Then fare thee well, I must go buy spices for
   our sheep-shearing.   *Exit.*

AUTOLYCUS Prosper you, sweet sir! Your purse is not
   hot enough to purchase your spice. I'll be with you at
   your sheep-shearing too. If I make not this cheat   120
   bring out another, and the shearers prove sheep, let me
   be unroll'd, and my name put in the book of virtue!

SONG

Jog on, jog on, the foot-path way,
And merrily hent the stile-a;
A merry heart goes all the day,   125
Your sad tires in a mile-a.   *Exit.*

SCENE 4

Enter FLORIZEL, PERDITA.

FLORIZEL These your unusual weeds to each part of you
   Does give a life; no shepherdess, but Flora
   Peering in April's front. This your sheep-shearing
   Is as a meeting of the petty gods,
   And you the queen on't.

PERDITA   Sir, my gracious lord,   5
   To chide at your extremes it not becomes me.

---

106. look'd big: put on a bold front.   **114. bring ... way:** go part of the way with
you.   **122. unroll'd:** struck from the roll of thieves.   **124. hent:** grasp (in order to
leap over).   **4.4. Location:** Bohemia. Before the Shepherd's cottage.   **1. unusual
weeds:** unaccustomed garments.   **2. Flora:** goddess of flowers.   **3. Peering ...
front:** peeping out in early April.   **6. extremes:** exaggerations.

O, pardon, that I name them! Your high self,
The gracious mark o' th' land, you have obscur'd
With a swain's wearing, and me, poor lowly maid,
Most goddess-like prank'd up. But that our feasts   10
In every mess have folly, and the feeders
Digest['t] with a custom, I should blush
To see you so attir'd—sworn, I think,
To show myself a glass.

FLORIZEL   I bless the time
When my good falcon made her flight across   15
Thy father's ground.

PERDITA   Now Jove afford you cause!
To me the difference forges dread; your greatness
Hath not been us'd to fear. Even now I tremble
To think your father, by some accident,
Should pass this way as you did. O, the Fates!   20
How would he look to see his work, so noble,
Vildly bound up? What would he say? Or how
Should I, in these my borrowed flaunts, behold
The sternness of his presence?

FLORIZEL   Apprehend
Nothing but jollity. The gods themselves   25
(Humbling their deities to love) have taken
The shapes of beasts upon them. Jupiter
Became a bull and bellow'd; the green Neptune
A ram and bleated; and the fire-rob'd god,
Golden Apollo, a poor humble swain,   30
As I seem now. Their transformations
Were never for a piece of beauty rarer,
Nor in a way so chaste, since my desires
Run not before mine honor, nor my lusts
Burn hotter than my faith.

---

8. gracious . . . land: one whose graces cause him to be noted by everybody (like Hamlet, "Th' observ'd of all observers"). **9. swain's wearing:** country youth's garb. **10. prank'd up:** bedecked. **11. mess:** group (see note on 1.2.227). **12. Digest't . . . custom:** i.e. accept it because they have become used to it. **13–14. sworn . . . glass:** i.e. dedicated to showing me what I ought to see if I looked in a mirror—one dressed in rustic attire. Many editors follow Theobald in emending *sworn* to *swoon*, which makes easy sense: "faint if I were to see myself in a mirror." **17. difference:** i.e. disparity in rank. **22. bound up:** i.e. clothed (a metaphor from bookbinding). **23. flaunts:** bits of finery. **27–30. Jupiter . . . swain.** The references are to Jupiter's wooing of Europa, Neptune's wooing of Theophane, and Apollo's role in the wooing of Alcestis by Admetus. **32. a piece . . . rarer:** a woman more beautiful than you. **33. Nor . . . chaste:** nor for a purpose so chaste (since he intends marriage).

PERDITA   O but, sir,   35
  Your resolution cannot hold when 'tis
  Oppos'd (as it must be) by th' pow'r of the King.
  One of these two must be necessities,
  Which then will speak, that you must change this purpose,
  Or I my life.
FLORIZEL   Thou dear'st Perdita,   40
  With these forc'd thoughts I prithee darken not
  The mirth o' th' feast. Or I'll be thine, my fair,
  Or not my father's; for I cannot be
  Mine own, nor any thing to any, if
  I be not thine. To this I am most constant,   45
  Though destiny say no. Be merry, gentle!
  Strangle such thoughts as these with any thing
  That you behold the while. Your guests are coming:
  Lift up your countenance, as it were the day
  Of celebration of that nuptial, which   50
  We two have sworn shall come.
PERDITA   O Lady Fortune,
  Stand you auspicious!
FLORIZEL   See, your guests approach,
  Address yourself to entertain them sprightly,
  And let's be red with mirth.

  [Enter] SHEPHERD, CLOWN, POLIXENES [and] CAMILLO
    [disguised], MOPSA, DORCAS, SERVANTS.

SHEPHERD Fie, daughter, when my old wife liv'd, upon   55
  This day she was both pantler, butler, cook,
  Both dame and servant; welcom'd all, serv'd all;
  Would sing her song, and dance her turn; now here,
  At upper end o' th' table, now i' th' middle;
  On his shoulder, and his; her face o' fire   60
  With labor, and the thing she took to quench it
  She would to each one sip. You are retired,
  As if you were a feasted one and not
  The hostess of the meeting. Pray you bid
  These unknown friends to 's welcome, for it is   65
  A way to make us better friends, more known.
  Come, quench your blushes, and present yourself

40. Or . . . life: i.e. or I will have to undergo some harsh change in my life.
41. forc'd: farfetched. 42. Or: either. 49. as: as if. 53. Address: prepare.
entertain: receive. 54. red: flushed. 56. pantler: pantry servant. 60. On his . . .
his: at one man's . . . another man's.

That which you are, mistress o' th' feast. Come on,
And bid us welcome to your sheep-shearing,
As your good flock shall prosper.
PERDITA [*To Polixenes.*]   Sir, welcome.   70
It is my father's will I should take on me
The hostess-ship o' th' day. [*To Camillo.*] You're welcome, sir.
Give me those flow'rs there, Dorcas. Reverend sirs,
For you there's rosemary and rue; these keep
Seeming and savor all the winter long.   75
Grace and remembrance be to you both,
And welcome to our shearing!
POLIXENES   Shepherdess
(A fair one are you!), well you fit our ages
With flow'rs of winter.
PERDITA   Sir, the year growing ancient,
Not yet on summer's death, nor on the birth   80
Of trembling winter, the fairest flow'rs o' th' season
Are our carnations and streak'd gillyvors
(Which some call Nature's bastards). Of that kind
Our rustic garden's barren, and I care not
To get slips of them.
POLIXENES   Wherefore, gentle maiden,   85
Do you neglect them?
PERDITA   For I have heard it said,
There is an art which in their piedness shares
With great creating Nature.
POLIXENES   Say there be;
Yet Nature is made better by no mean
But Nature makes that mean; so over that art   90
Which you say adds to Nature, is an art
That Nature makes. You see, sweet maid, we marry
A gentler scion to the wildest stock,
And make conceive a bark of baser kind
By bud of nobler race. This is an art   95
Which does mend Nature—change it rather; but
The art itself is Nature.
PERDITA   So it is.
POLIXENES Then make [your] garden rich in gillyvors,
And do not call them bastards.

---

75. Seeming and savor: color and scent.   **76. Grace and remembrance.** Symbolized by rue and rosemary respectively.   **82. gillyvors:** gillyflowers, pinks.
85. slips: cuttings.   **86. For:** because.   **87. art:** i.e. the gardener's skill in crossbreeding. **piedness:** variegated color.   **89. mean:** means.

PERDITA   I'll not put
The dibble in earth to set one slip of them;   100
No more than were I painted I would wish
This youth should say 'twere well, and only therefore
Desire to breed by me. Here's flow'rs for you:
Hot lavender, mints, savory, marjorum,
The marigold, that goes to bed wi' th' sun,   105
And with him rises weeping. These are flow'rs
Of middle summer, and I think they are given
To men of middle age. Y' are very welcome.
CAMILLO I should leave grazing, were I of your flock,
And only live by gazing.
PERDITA   Out, alas!   110
You'ld be so lean, that blasts of January
Would blow you through and through. Now, my fair'st friend,
I would I had some flow'rs o' th' spring that might
Become your time of day—and yours, and yours,
That wear upon your virgin branches yet   115
Your maidenheads growing. O Proserpina,
For the flow'rs now, that, frighted, thou let'st fall
From Dis's waggon! daffadils,
That come before the swallow dares, and take
The winds of March with beauty; violets, dim,   120
But sweeter than the lids of Juno's eyes,
Or Cytherea's breath; pale primeroses,
That die unmarried, ere they can behold
Bright Phoebus in his strength (a malady
Most incident to maids); bold oxlips, and   125
The crown imperial; lilies of all kinds
(The flow'r-de-luce being one). O, these I lack,
To make you garlands of, and my sweet friend,
To strew him o'er and o'er!
FLORIZEL   What? like a corse?
PERDITA No, like a bank, for love to lie and play on;   130
Not like a corse; or if—not to be buried,
But quick and in mine arms. Come, take your flow'rs.

---

100. dibble: small implement used to make holes in the soil for planting.
104. Hot. Meaning here uncertain. Contemporary herbalists classified some herbs
as hot, others as cold. **marjorum:** marjoram.   **116–18. Proserpina . . . waggon.**
Proserpina, Ceres' daughter, was gathering flowers when Pluto (Dis) saw her and carried her in his chariot to the underworld to become his queen.   **119. take:** bewitch.
122. Cytherea's: Venus'. **primeroses:** primroses.   **124. Phoebus:** the sun-
god.   **127. flow'r-de-luce:** fleur-de-lis.   **129. corse:** corpse.   **132. quick:** alive.

Methinks I play as I have seen them do
In Whitsun pastorals. Sure this robe of mine
Does change my disposition.
FLORIZEL   What you do   135
Still betters what is done. When you speak, sweet,
I'd have you do it ever; when you sing,
I'd have you buy and sell so; so give alms;
Pray so; and for the ord'ring your affairs,
To sing them too. When you do dance, I wish you   140
A wave o' th' sea, that you might ever do
Nothing but that; move still, still so,
And own no other function. Each your doing
(So singular in each particular)
Crowns what you are doing in the present deeds,   145
That all your acts are queens.
PERDITA   O Doricles,
Your praises are too large. But that your youth,
And the true blood which peeps fairly through't,
Do plainly give you out an unstain'd shepherd,
With wisdom I might fear, my Doricles,   150
You woo'd me the false way.
FLORIZEL   I think you have
As little skill to fear as I have purpose
To put you to't. But come, our dance, I pray.
Your hand, my Perdita. So turtles pair
That never mean to part.
PERDITA   I'll swear for 'em.   155
POLIXENES This is the prettiest low-born lass that ever
Ran on the green-sord. Nothing she does, or seems,
But smacks of something greater than herself,
Too noble for this place.
CAMILLO   He tells her something
That makes her blood look on't. Good sooth, she is   160
The queen of curds and cream.
CLOWN   Come on. Strike up.

---

134. Whitsun pastorals: May games and dances, with Robin Hood and Maid
Marian as leading characters. Perdita thinks of them as somewhat indecent and is
surprised at herself, a modest girl, for talking in their vein.   **143. Each your doing:**
the manner in which you perform each act.   **144. singular:** distinctively yours.
146. Doricles: Florizel's assumed name.   **152. skill:** reason.   **154. turtles:** turtledoves
(symbolic of constancy in love).   **157. green-sord:** greensward.   **160. makes . . .
on't:** makes her blush. Most editors emend *on't* to *out*. **Good sooth:** in truth.

DORCAS Mopsa must be your mistress; marry, garlic,
  To mend her kissing with!
MOPSA   Now in good time!
CLOWN Not a word, a word, we stand upon our manners.
  Come, strike up.   [*Music.*] 165

  Here a dance of Shepherds and Shepherdesses.

POLIXENES Pray, good shepherd, what fair swain is this
  Which dances with your daughter?
SHEPHERD They call him Doricles, and boasts himself
  To have a worthy feeding; but I have it
  Upon his own report, and I believe it.   170
  He looks like sooth. He says he loves my daughter.
  I think so too; for never gaz'd the moon
  Upon the water as he'll stand and read
  As 'twere my daughter's eyes; and to be plain,
  I think there is not half a kiss to choose   175
  Who loves another best.
POLIXENES   She dances featly.
SHEPHERD So she does any thing, though I report it
  That should be silent. If young Doricles
  Do light upon her, she shall bring him that
  Which he not dreams of.   180

  Enter SERVANT.

SERVANT O master! if you did but hear the pedlar at
  the door, you would never dance again after a tabor and
  pipe; no, the bagpipe could not move you. He sings
  several tunes faster than you'll tell money; he utters
  them as he had eaten ballads and all men's ears grew   185
  to his tunes.
CLOWN He could never come better; he shall come in.
  I love a ballad but even too well, if it be doleful matter
  merrily set down, or a very pleasant thing indeed and
  sung lamentably.   190
SERVANT He hath songs for man or woman, of all
  sizes; no milliner can so fit his customers with gloves.
  He has the prettiest love-songs for maids, so without

---

163. Now . . . time: an expression of indignation. **168. boasts:** he boasts.
169. feeding: pasture lands, i.e. landed estate. **171. looks like sooth:** gives the
impression of being an honest man. **176. another:** the other. **featly:** grace-
fully. **179. light upon:** choose. **182. tabor:** small drum. **184. tell:** count.
185. ballads: here, the individual sheets on which ballads were printed and offered
for sale. On Autolycus' stock of these "broadsides" see lines 259ff. below.

bawdry, which is strange; with such delicate burthens
of dildos and fadings, "jump her and thump her";   195
and where some stretch-mouth'd rascal would (as it
were) mean mischief, and break a foul gap into the
matter, he makes the maid to answer, "Whoop, do me
no harm, good man"—puts him off, slights him, with
"Whoop, do me no harm, good man."   200
POLIXENES This is a brave fellow.
CLOWN Believe me, thou talkest of an admirable conceited fellow. Has he any unbraided wares?
SERVANT He hath ribbons of all the colors i' th' rainbow; points more than all the lawyers in Bohemia   205
can learnedly handle, though they come to him by th'
gross; inkles, caddises, cambrics, lawns. Why, he
sings 'em over as they were gods or goddesses: you
would think a smock were a she-angel, he so chaunts to
the sleeve-hand and the work about the square on't.   210
CLOWN Prithee bring him in, and let him approach
singing.
PERDITA Forewarn him that he use no scurrilous words
in 's tunes.   [*Exit Servant.*]
CLOWN You have of these pedlars, that have more in   215
them than you'ld think, sister.
PERDITA Ay, good brother, or go about to think.

Enter AUTOLYCUS *singing.*

[AUTOLYCUS] Lawn as white as driven snow,
Cypress black as e'er was crow,
Gloves as sweet as damask roses,   220
Masks for faces and for noses;
Bugle-bracelet, necklace amber,
Perfume for a lady's chamber;

194–95. burthens . . . thump her: ballad refrains. Actually, those commended by
the servant allude to male sex organs, orgasms, and erotic play, so that his examples
absurdly contradict his "so without bawdry." **196. stretch-mouth'd:** foul-
mouthed. **197–98. break . . . matter:** introduce obscenity. **198–99. Whoop . . .
man.** A line from a popular ballad. The original words are lost, but the tune
survives, along with several later ballads set to it. **201. brave:** splendid.
202–3. admirable conceited: wonderfully clever. **203. unbraided:** fresh.
205. points: laces to fasten hose to doublet (with a pun on the sense
"arguments"). **207. inkles:** linen tapes. **caddises:** worsted tapes for garters.
210. sleeve-hand: wrist-band. **square on't:** yoke of it. **215. You have:** there
are some. **217. go about:** intend. s.d. **Autolycus.** He is disguised with a beard
(see lines 713–14, where he removes it). **219. Cypress:** filmy crepe. **220. sweet.**
Gloves were often perfumed. **222. Bugle-bracelet:** bracelet made of black beads.

Golden quoifs and stomachers
For my lads to give their dears;   225
Pins and poking-sticks of steel;
What maids lack from head to heel:
Come buy of me, come; come buy, come buy,
Buy, lads, or else your lasses cry:
Come buy.   230

CLOWN If I were not in love with Mopsa, thou
shouldst take no money of me, but being enthrall'd as I
am, it will also be the bondage of certain ribbons and
gloves.

MOPSA I was promis'd them against the feast, but   235
they come not too late now.

DORCAS He hath promis'd you more than that, or
there be liars.

MOPSA He hath paid you all he promis'd you. May
be he has paid you more, which will shame you to give   240
him again.

CLOWN Is there no manners left among maids? Will
they wear their plackets where they should bear their
faces? Is there not milking-time? when you are going
to bed? or kill-hole? to whistle [off] these secrets,   245
but you must be tittle-tattling before all our guests?
'Tis well they are whisp'ring. Clamor your tongues,
and not a word more.

MOPSA I have done. Come, you promis'd me a
tawdry-lace and a pair of sweet gloves.   250

CLOWN Have I not told thee how I was cozen'd by the
way, and lost all my money?

AUTOLYCUS And indeed, sir, there are cozeners abroad,
therefore it behooves men to be wary.

---

224. quoifs: coifs, tight caps. **stomachers:** ornamental chest-coverings worn to fill in the front opening of the bodice. **226. poking-sticks:** metal rods used to iron fluted ruffs. **232–34. being . . . gloves:** since I have been taken prisoner by love, certain ribbons and gloves must also be taken prisoner, i.e. be bought and bound up in a parcel. **235. against:** before, in readiness for. **237–38. He . . . liars:** i.e. the rumor is that he has promised to marry you. **240–41. more . . . again:** i.e. an illegitimate child. **243–44. wear . . . faces:** i.e. disclose their most private affairs (?). *Plackets* = slits in petticoats. **245. kill-hole:** kiln-hole, fireplace. **whistle off:** release (term from falconry). **247. Clamor.** The sense must be "silence." The word has been connected by some with *clammer*, a term in bell-ringing. Others emend to *Charm a'* or *Clam a'*. **250. tawdry-lace:** bright neckerchief. *Tawdry* is a corruption of the name of Saint Audrey, whose feast day was celebrated with a fair at which showy articles of dress were sold. **251. cozen'd:** cheated.

CLOWN Fear not thou, man, thou shalt lose nothing   255
here.

AUTOLYCUS I hope so, sir, for I have about me many
parcels of charge.

CLOWN What hast here? Ballads?

MOPSA Pray now buy some. I love a ballet in print,   260
a-life, for then we are sure they are true.

AUTOLYCUS Here's one to a very doleful tune, how a
usurer's wife was brought to bed of twenty money-
bags at a burthen, and how she long'd to eat adders'
heads, and toads carbonado'd.   265

MOPSA Is it true, think you?

AUTOLYCUS Very true, and but a month old.

DORCAS Bless me from marrying a usurer!

AUTOLYCUS Here's the midwive's name to't, one Mistress
Tale-porter, and five or six honest wives that were   270
present. Why should I carry lies abroad?

MOPSA Pray you now buy it.

CLOWN Come on, lay it by; and let's first see moe
ballads. We'll buy the other things anon.

AUTOLYCUS Here's another ballad, of a fish that appear'd   275
upon the coast on We'n'sday the fourscore of April,
forty thousand fadom above water, and sung this ballad
against the hard hearts of maids. It was thought she
was a woman, and was turn'd into a cold fish for she
would not exchange flesh with one that lov'd her.   280
The ballad is very pitiful, and as true.

DORCAS Is it true too, think you?

AUTOLYCUS Five justices' hands at it, and witnesses more
than my pack will hold.

CLOWN Lay it by too. Another.   285

AUTOLYCUS This is a merry ballad, but a very pretty one.

MOPSA Let's have some merry ones.

AUTOLYCUS Why, this is a passing merry one and goes to
the tune of "Two maids wooing a man." There's
scarce a maid westward but she sings it. 'Tis in re-   290
quest, I can tell you.

MOPSA We can both sing it. If thou'lt bear a part,
thou shalt hear; 'tis in three parts.

---

257. hope so: i.e. hope you are right.   **258. parcels of charge:** valuable articles.
260. ballet: ballad.   **261. a-life:** on my life.   **265. carbonado'd:** sliced and scored
across for broiling.   **273. moe:** more.

DORCAS We had the tune on't a month ago.

AUTOLYCUS I can bear my part, you must know 'tis my   295
    occupation. Have at it with you.

SONG

AUTOLYCUS Get you hence, for I must go
        Where it fits not you to know.
DORCAS   Whither?   MOPSA O, whither?
         DORCAS Whither?
MOPSA   It becomes thy oath full well,   300
         Thou to me thy secrets tell.
DORCAS   Me too; let me go thither.
MOPSA   Or thou goest to th' grange, or mill.
DORCAS   If to either, thou dost ill.
AUTOLYCUS   Neither.   DORCAS What, neither?   305
         AUTOLYCUS Neither.
DORCAS   Thou hast sworn my love to be.
MOPSA   Thou hast sworn it more to me:
         Then whither goest? say, whither?

CLOWN We'll have this song out anon by ourselves.
    My father and the gentlemen are in sad talk, and   310
    we'll not trouble them. Come bring away thy pack
    after me. Wenches, I'll buy for you both. Pedlar, let's
    have the first choice. Follow me, girls.
                 [Exit with Dorcas and Mopsa.]

AUTOLYCUS And you shall pay well for 'em.

SONG

       Will you buy any tape,   315
         Or lace for your cape,
     My dainty duck, my dear-a?
         Any silk, any thread,
         Any toys for your head
    Of the new'st and fin'st, fin'st wear-a?   320
         Come to the pedlar,
         Money's a meddler,
    That doth utter all men's ware-a.   *Exit.*

[Enter SERVANT.*]*

SERVANT Master, there is three carters, three shep-
    herds, three neat-herds, three swine-herds, that   325

303. grange: farm.   **310. sad:** serious.   **319. toys:** trifling ornaments.   **323. utter:**
put to sale.

have made themselves all men of hair. They call themselves Saltiers, and they have a dance which the
wenches say is a gallimaufry of gambols, because they
are not in't; but they themselves are o' th' mind (if it
be not too rough for some that know little but bowling)   330
it will please plentifully.

SHEPHERD Away! we'll none on't. Here has been too
    much homely foolery already. I know, sir, we weary
    you.

POLIXENES You weary those that refresh us. Pray let's   335
    see these four threes of herdsmen.

SERVANT One three of them, by their own report, sir,
    hath danc'd before the King; and not the worst of the
    three but jumps twelve foot and a half by th' squier.

SHEPHERD Leave your prating. Since these good men   340
    are pleas'd, let them come in; but quickly now.

SERVANT Why, they stay at door, sir.   [Exit.]

                Here a dance of twelve Satyrs.

POLIXENES O, father, you'll know more of that hereafter.
    [*To Camillo.*] Is it not too far gone? 'Tis time to part them.
    He's simple, and tells much. [*To Florizel.*] How now,
            fair shepherd?   345
    Your heart is full of something that does take
    Your mind from feasting. Sooth, when I was young,
    And handed love as you do, I was wont
    To load my she with knacks. I would have ransack'd
    The pedlar's silken treasury, and have pour'd it   350
    To her acceptance; you have let him go,
    And nothing marted with him. If your lass
    Interpretation should abuse, and call this
    Your lack of love or bounty, you were straited
    For a reply, at least if you make a care   355
    Of happy holding her.

FLORIZEL   Old sir, I know
    She prizes not such trifles as these are.
    The gifts she looks from me are pack'd and lock'd
    Up in my heart, which I have given already,

---

326. of hair: wearing skins of animals. **327. Saltiers:** i.e. satyrs (but probably
with additional sense "leapers"; *sault* = jump, as in *somersault*). **328. gallimaufry:** jumble, hodgepodge. **339. squier:** square, foot-rule. **348. handed:** was involved in. **352. nothing marted:** done no business. **353. Interpretation should
abuse:** should misinterpret. **354. were straited:** would be hard pressed. **355–56.
make . . . her:** are seriously concerned to keep her happy. **358. looks:** looks for.

But not deliver'd. O, hear me breathe my life   360
Before this ancient sir, whom, it should seem,
Hath sometime lov'd! I take thy hand, this hand,
As soft as dove's down and as white as it,
Or Ethiopian's tooth, or the fann'd snow that's bolted
By th' northern blasts twice o'er.

POLIXENES   What follows this?   365
How prettily th' young swain seems to wash
The hand was fair before! I have put you out.
But to your protestation; let me hear
What you profess.

FLORIZEL   Do, and be witness to't.

POLIXENES And this my neighbor too?

FLORIZEL   And he, and more   370
Than he, and men—the earth, the heavens, and all:
That were I crown'd the most imperial monarch,
Thereof most worthy, were I the fairest youth
That ever made eye swerve, had force and knowledge
More than was ever man's, I would not prize them   375
Without her love; for her, employ them all,
Commend them and condemn them to her service,
Or to their own perdition.

POLIXENES   Fairly offer'd.

CAMILLO This shows a sound affection.

SHEPHERD   But, my daughter,
Say you the like to him?

PERDITA   I cannot speak   380
So well, nothing so well; no, nor mean better.
By th' pattern of mine own thoughts I cut out
The purity of his.

SHEPHERD   Take hands, a bargain!
And, friends unknown, you shall bear witness to't:
I give my daughter to him, and will make   385
Her portion equal his.

FLORIZEL   O, that must be
I' th' virtue of your daughter. One being dead,
I shall have more than you can dream of yet,
Enough then for your wonder. But come on,
Contract us 'fore these witnesses.

---

364. bolted: sifted. **367. was:** which was. **put you out:** interrupted your recital. **377–78. Commend . . . perdition:** commend them to her service, or, if denied that, condemn them to destruction.

SHEPHERD   Come, your hand;   390
   And, daughter, yours.
POLIXENES   Soft, swain, awhile, beseech you.
   Have you a father?
FLORIZEL   I have; but what of him?
POLIXENES   Knows he of this?
FLORIZEL   He neither does, nor shall.
POLIXENES   Methinks a father
   Is at the nuptial of his son a guest   395
    That best becomes the table. Pray you once more,
    Is not your father grown incapable
    Of reasonable affairs? is he not stupid
    With age and alt'ring rheums? Can he speak? hear?
    Know man from man? dispute his own estate?   400
    Lies he not bed-rid? and again does nothing
    But what he did being childish?
FLORIZEL   No, good sir;
   He has his health, and ampler strength indeed
    Than most have of his age.
POLIXENES   By my white beard,
   You offer him, if this be so, a wrong   405
    Something unfilial. Reason my son
    Should choose himself a wife, but as good reason
    The father (all whose joy is nothing else
    But fair posterity) should hold some counsel
    In such a business.
FLORIZEL   I yield all this;   410
   But for some other reasons, my grave sir,
    Which 'tis not fit you know, I not acquaint
    My father of this business.
POLIXENES   Let him know't.
FLORIZEL   He shall not.
POLIXENES   Prithee let him.
FLORIZEL   No, he must not.
SHEPHERD   Let him, my son. He shall not need to grieve   415
   At knowing of thy choice.
FLORIZEL   Come, come, he must not.
   Mark our contract.
POLIXENES   Mark your divorce, young sir,
                       [*Discovering himself.*]

---

391. Soft: not so fast.   **398. reasonable:** requiring the exercise of reason.   **399. alt'ring rheums:** debilitating diseases.   **400. dispute:** discuss. **estate:** state, condition.   **406. Reason:** it is reasonable that.   **410. yield:** concede.

Whom son I dare not call. Thou art too base
To be [acknowledg'd]. Thou, a sceptre's heir,
That thus affects a sheep-hook! Thou, old traitor,   420
I am sorry that by hanging thee I can
But shorten thy life one week. And thou, fresh piece
Of excellent witchcraft, whom of force must know
The royal fool thou cop'st with—

SHEPHERD   O, my heart!

POLIXENES I'll have thy beauty scratch'd with briers and made   425
More homely than thy state. For thee, fond boy,
If I may ever know thou dost but sigh
That thou no more shalt see this knack (as never
I mean thou shalt), we'll bar thee from succession,
Not hold thee of our blood, no, not our kin,   430
Farre than Deucalion off. Mark thou my words.
Follow us to the court. Thou, churl, for this time,
Though full of our displeasure, yet we free thee
From the dead blow of it. And you, enchantment—
Worthy enough a herdsman, yea, him too,   435
That makes himself (but for our honor therein)
Unworthy thee—if ever, henceforth, thou
These rural latches to his entrance open,
Or [hoop] his body more with thy embraces,
I will devise a death as cruel for thee   440
As thou art tender to't.   *Exit.*

PERDITA   Even here undone!
I was not much afeard; for once or twice
I was about to speak, and tell him plainly
The self-same sun that shines upon his court
Hides not his visage from our cottage, but   445
Looks on alike. Will't please you, sir, be gone?
I told you what would come of this. Beseech you
Of your own state take care. This dream of mine

---

418. dare: will. **420. affects:** affectest, desirest. **422–23. fresh . . . witchcraft:** fair young creature skilled in witchcraft. She is at once bewitchingly beautiful and a wicked witch. In line 434 *enchantment* has precisely the same duality of meaning. **423. whom of force:** who necessarily. **424. cop'st:** dealest. **426. homely:** (1) ugly (with reference to *beauty*); (2) humble (with reference to *state* = station). **fond:** foolish. **428. knack:** crafty contriver. **431. Farre . . . off:** more remote in kinship than Deucalion (the Noah of classical myth and hence the ancestor of all mankind). **432. churl.** He addresses the Shepherd. **434. dead:** death-dealing. **435. Worthy:** worthy of. **436. but . . . therein:** except that my royal honor comes into it, i.e. except that he is the king's son. **448. Of . . . care:** have a proper care for your high station.

Being now awake, I'll queen it no inch farther,
But milk my ewes, and weep.
CAMILLO   Why, how now, father?   450
Speak ere thou diest.
SHEPHERD   I cannot speak, nor think,
Nor dare to know that which I know. [*To Florizel.*] O sir,
You have undone a man of fourscore three,
That thought to fill his grave in quiet; yea,
To die upon the bed my father died,   455
To lie close by his honest bones; but now
Some hangman must put on my shroud and lay me
Where no priest shovels in dust. [*To Perdita.*] O cursed wretch,
That knew'st this was the Prince, and wouldst adventure
To mingle faith with him!—Undone, undone!   460
If I might die within this hour, I have liv'd
To die when I desire.   *Exit.*
FLORIZEL   Why look you so upon me?
I am but sorry, not afeard; delay'd,
But nothing alt'red. What I was, I am:
More straining on for plucking back, not following
My leash unwillingly.   465
CAMILLO   Gracious my lord,
You know [your] father's temper. At this time
He will allow no speech (which I do guess
You do not purpose to him) and as hardly
Will he endure your sight as yet, I fear.   470
Then till the fury of his Highness settle
Come not before him.
FLORIZEL   I not purpose it.
I think Camillo?
CAMILLO   Even he, my lord.
PERDITA How often have I told you 'twould be thus!
How often said my dignity would last   475
But till 'twere known!
FLORIZEL   It cannot fail, but by
The violation of my faith, and then
Let nature crush the sides o' th' earth together,
And mar the seeds within! Lift up thy looks.
From my succession wipe me, father, I   480
Am heir to my affection.
CAMILLO   Be advis'd.

---

459. adventure: dare.   **465. for plucking back:** for having been dragged back.
477. then: i.e. when that happens.   **481. Be advis'd:** take thought.

FLORIZEL I am—and by my fancy. If my reason
    Will thereto be obedient, I have reason;
    If not, my senses, better pleas'd with madness,
    Do bid it welcome.
CAMILLO   This is desperate, sir.   485
FLORIZEL So call it; but it does fulfill my vow;
    I needs must think it honesty. Camillo,
    Not for Bohemia, nor the pomp that may
    Be thereat gleaned, for all the sun sees, or
    The close earth wombs, or the profound seas hides   490
    In unknown fadoms, will I break my oath
    To this my fair belov'd. Therefore, I pray you,
    As you have ever been my father's honor'd friend,
    When he shall miss me (as, in faith, I mean not
    To see him any more), cast your good counsels   495
    Upon his passion. Let myself and Fortune
    Tug for the time to come. This you may know,
    And so deliver: I am put to sea
    With her who here I cannot hold on shore;
    And most opportune to her need I have   500
    A vessel rides fast by, but not prepar'd
    For this design. What course I mean to hold
    Shall nothing benefit your knowledge, nor
    Concern me the reporting.
CAMILLO   O my lord,
    I would your spirit were easier for advice,   505
    Or stronger for your need.
FLORIZEL   Hark, Perdita!   [Drawing her aside.]
    [To Camillo.] I'll hear you by and by.
CAMILLO   He's irremovable,
    Resolv'd for flight. Now were I happy if
    His going I could frame to serve my turn,
    Save him from danger, do him love and honor,   510
    Purchase the sight again of dear Sicilia
    And that unhappy king, my master, whom
    I so much thirst to see.
FLORIZEL   Now, good Camillo,
    I am so fraught with curious business that
    I leave out ceremony.

482. fancy: love. 497. Tug . . . come: contend for the future. 498. deliver:
report. 500. her. Some editors emend to *our*, arguing that the compositor picked
up *her* from the preceding line. 505. easier for: more open to. 507. irremovable: immovable. 514. curious: demanding care.

CAMILLO   Sir, I think   515
  You have heard of my poor services, i' th' love
  That I have borne your father?
FLORIZEL   Very nobly
  Have you deserv'd. It is my father's music
  To speak your deeds; not little of his care
  To have them recompens'd as thought on.
CAMILLO   Well, my lord,   520
  If you may please to think I love the King,
  And through him what's nearest to him, which is
  Your gracious self, embrace but my direction,
  If your more ponderous and settled project
  May suffer alteration. On mine honor,   525
  I'll point you where you shall have such receiving
  As shall become your Highness, where you may
  Enjoy your mistress—from the whom, I see,
  There's no disjunction to be made, but by
  (As heavens forefend!) your ruin—marry her,   530
  And with my best endeavors in your absence,
  Your discontenting father strive to qualify,
  And bring him up to liking.
FLORIZEL   How, Camillo,
  May this (almost a miracle) be done?
  That I may call thee something more than man,   535
  And after that trust to thee.
CAMILLO   Have you thought on
  A place whereto you'll go?
FLORIZEL   Not any yet:
  But as th' unthought-on accident is guilty
  To what we wildly do, so we profess
  Ourselves to be the slaves of chance, and flies   540
  Of every wind that blows.
CAMILLO   Then list to me.
  This follows, if you will not change your purpose
  But undergo this flight: make for Sicilia,
  And there present yourself and your fair princess
  (For so I see she must be) 'fore Leontes.   545
  She shall be habited as it becomes

---

520. as thought on: in accordance with his high estimation of them.
524. ponderous: weighty. **525. suffer:** admit of. **530. forefend:** forfend,
forbid. **532. discontenting:** discontented, angry. **qualify:** appease. **533. liking:**
approval. **538–39. as . . . do:** i.e. as the unexpected discovery is responsible for
whatever course we must rashly undertake.

The partner of your bed. Methinks I see
Leontes opening his free arms, and weeping
His welcomes forth; asks thee there, son, forgiveness,
As 'twere i' th' father's person; kisses the hands   550
Of your fresh princess; o'er and o'er divides him
'Twixt his unkindness and his kindness: th' one
He chides to hell, and bids the other grow
Faster than thought or time.

FLORIZEL   Worthy Camillo,
What color for my visitation shall I   555
Hold up before him?

CAMILLO   Sent by the King your father
To greet him and to give him comforts. Sir,
The manner of your bearing towards him, with
What you (as from your father) shall deliver,
Things known betwixt us three, I'll write you down,   560
The which shall point you forth at every sitting
What you must say; that he shall not perceive
But that you have your father's bosom there,
And speak his very heart.

FLORIZEL   I am bound to you.
There is some sap in this.   565

CAMILLO   A course more promising
Than a wild dedication of yourselves
To unpath'd waters, undream'd shores, most certain
To miseries enough; no hope to help you,
But as you shake off one, to take another;
Nothing so certain as your anchors, who   570
Do their best office, if they can but stay you
Where you'll be loath to be. Besides you know,
Prosperity's the very bond of love,
Whose fresh complexion and whose heart together
Affliction alters.

PERDITA   One of these is true: 575
I think affliction may subdue the cheek,
But not take in the mind.

CAMILLO   Yea? say you so?
There shall not at your father's house these seven years
Be born another such.

---

548. free: generous, welcoming.   **555. color:** pretext, explanation.   **561. point you forth:** direct you.   **sitting:** conference.   **563. bosom:** inmost thoughts.   **565. sap:** vitality, i.e. promise of success.   **573. bond:** uniting tie or force.   **577. take in:** subdue.

FLORIZEL   My good Camillo,
  She's as forward of her breeding as   580
  She is i' th' rear 'our birth.
CAMILLO   I cannot say 'tis pity
  She lacks instructions, for she seems a mistress
  To most that teach.
PERDITA   Your pardon, sir; for this
  I'll blush you thanks.
FLORIZEL   My prettiest Perdita!
  But O, the thorns we stand upon! Camillo,   585
  Preserver of my father, now of me,
  The medicine of our house, how shall we do?
  We are not furnish'd like Bohemia's son,
  Nor shall appear in Sicilia.
CAMILLO   My lord,
  Fear none of this. I think you know my fortunes   590
  Do all lie there. It shall be so my care
  To have you royally appointed, as if
  The scene you play were mine. For instance, sir,
  That you may know you shall not want—one word.
                                          [They talk aside.]

             Enter AUTOLYCUS *[laughing]*.

AUTOLYCUS Ha, ha, what a fool Honesty is! and Trust,   595
  his sworn brother, a very simple gentleman! I have
  sold all my trompery; not a counterfeit stone, not a
  ribbon, glass, pomander, brooch, table-book, ballad,
  knife, tape, glove, shoe-tie, bracelet, horn-ring, to
  keep my pack from fasting. They throng who   600
  should buy first, as if my trinkets had been hallow'd
  and brought a benediction to the buyer; by which
  means I saw whose purse was best in picture, and what
  I saw, to my good use I rememb'red. My clown (who
  wants but something to be a reasonable man)   605
  grew so in love with the wenches' song, that he would
  not stir his pettitoes till he had both tune and words,
  which so drew the rest of the herd to me that all their

578–79. There . . . such. Probably spoken to Florizel: "Even in the royal palace
people of Perdita's quality are not often born." *These seven years* = for a long time to
come (not a definite period).   **580. forward . . . breeding:** far in advance of her up-
bringing.   **581. 'our:** of our, i.e. of my.   **587. medicine:** restorative.   **589. appear:**
appear so.   **597. trompery:** trumpery, cheap wares.   **598. pomander:** scent-ball.
table-book: notebook.   **601. hallow'd:** sacred, like holy relics.   **603. picture:** looks.
605. wants but something: lacks only one thing.   **607. pettitoes:** toes (of a pig).

other senses stuck in ears. You might have pinch'd a
placket, it was senseless; 'twas nothing to geld a   610
codpiece of a purse; I would have fil'd keys off that
hung in chains. No hearing, no feeling, but my sir's
song, and admiring the nothing of it. So that in this
time of lethargy I pick'd and cut most of their festival
purses; and had not the old man come in with a   615
whoobub against his daughter and the King's son, and
scar'd my choughs from the chaff, I had not left a
purse alive in the whole army.

                         [*Camillo, Florizel, and Perdita come forward.*]

CAMILLO Nay, but my letters, by this means being there
    So soon as you arrive, shall clear that doubt.   620
FLORIZEL And those that you'll procure from King Leontes?
CAMILLO Shall satisfy your father.
PERDITA   Happy be you!
    All that you speak shows fair.
CAMILLO   Who have we here? [*Seeing Autolycus.*]
    We'll make an instrument of this; omit
    Nothing may give us aid.   625
AUTOLYCUS [*Aside.*] If they have overheard me now—
    why, hanging.
CAMILLO How now, good fellow? why shak'st thou so?
    Fear not, man, here's no harm intended to thee.
AUTOLYCUS I am a poor fellow, sir.   630
CAMILLO Why, be so still; here's nobody will steal that
    from thee. Yet for the outside of thy poverty we must
    make an exchange; therefore discase thee instantly
    (thou must think there's a necessity in't) and change
    garments with this gentleman. Though the penny-   635
    worth on his side be the worst, yet hold thee, there's
    some boot.   [*Giving money.*]
AUTOLYCUS I am a poor fellow, sir. [*Aside.*] I know ye
    well enough.
CAMILLO Nay, prithee dispatch. The gentleman is   640
    half [flea'd] already.

---

609. stuck in ears: were devoted to listening. **610. senseless:** insensible.
611. codpiece: baglike flap on the front of Elizabethan breeches. **613. nothing:**
nonsense (with pun on *noting,* i.e. tune, pronounced similarly). **614. lethargy:** coma.
616. whoobub: hubbub. **617. choughs:** crows or jackdaws. **632. outside .
. . poverty:** i.e. your ragged clothes. **633. discase:** undress. **635–36. penny-
worth:** bargain. **637. some boot:** something in addition. **640. dispatch:** make
haste. **641. flea'd:** flayed, skinned, i.e. undressed.

AUTOLYCUS Are you in earnest, sir? [*Aside.*] I smell the
  trick on't.

FLORIZEL Dispatch, I prithee.

AUTOLYCUS Indeed I have had earnest, but I cannot with   645
  conscience take it.

CAMILLO Unbuckle, unbuckle.

                      [*Florizel and Autolycus exchange garments.*]
  Fortunate mistress (let my prophecy
  Come home to ye!), you must retire yourself
  Into some covert. Take your sweetheart's hat   650
  And pluck it o'er your brows, muffle your face,
  Dismantle you, and (as you can) disliken
  The truth of your own seeming, that you may
  (For I do fear eyes over) to shipboard
  Get undescried.

PERDITA   I see the play so lies   655
  That I must bear a part.

CAMILLO   No remedy.
  Have you done there?

FLORIZEL   Should I now meet my father,
  He would not call me son.

CAMILLO   Nay, you shall have no hat.
                        [*Giving it to Perdita.*]
  Come, lady, come. Farewell, my friend.

AUTOLYCUS   Adieu, sir.

FLORIZEL O Perdita! what have we twain forgot?   660
  Pray you a word.

CAMILLO [*Aside.*] What I do next shall be to tell the King
  Of this escape, and whither they are bound;
  Wherein my hope is I shall so prevail
  To force him after; in whose company   665
  I shall re-view Sicilia, for whose sight
  I have a woman's longing.

FLORIZEL   Fortune speed us!
  Thus we set on, Camillo, to th' sea-side.

CAMILLO The swifter speed the better.

                  Exit [*with Florizel and Perdita*].

AUTOLYCUS I understand the business, I hear it. To have   670
  an open ear, a quick eye, and a nimble hand, is

---

645. earnest: first payment. **648–49. let . . . ye:** i.e. may I prove a true prophet
in calling you fortunate. **652. disliken:** alter, falsify. **654. eyes over:** spying
eyes.

necessary for a cutpurse; a good nose is requisite also,
to smell out work for th' other senses. I see this is the
time that the unjust man doth thrive. What an ex-
change had this been, without boot! What a boot is   675
here, with this exchange! Sure the gods do this
year connive at us, and we may do any thing extempore.
The Prince himself is about a piece of iniquity: stealing
away from his father with his clog at his heels. If I
thought it were a piece of honesty to acquaint the King   680
withal, I would not do't. I hold it the more
knavery to conceal it; and therein am I constant to
my profession.

Enter CLOWN *and* SHEPHERD.

Aside, aside, here is more matter for a hot brain.
Every lane's end, every shop, church, session, hanging,   685
yields a careful man work.
CLOWN See, see; what a man you are now! There is
no other way but to tell the King she's a changeling,
and none of your flesh and blood.
SHEPHERD Nay, but hear me.   690
CLOWN Nay—but hear me.
SHEPHERD Go to then.
CLOWN She being none of your flesh and blood, your
flesh and blood has not offended the King, and so your
flesh and blood is not to be punish'd by him. Show   695
those things you found about her, those secret
things, all but what she has with her. This being done,
let the law go whistle; I warrant you.
SHEPHERD I will tell the King all, every word, yea, and
his son's pranks too; who, I may say, is no honest man,   700
neither to his father nor to me, to go about to make me
the King's brother-in-law.
CLOWN Indeed brother-in-law was the farthest off
you could have been to him, and then your blood had
been the dearer by I know how much an ounce.   705
AUTOLYCUS [*Aside.*] Very wisely, puppies!
SHEPHERD Well; let us to the King. There is that in
this farthel will make him scratch his beard.
AUTOLYCUS [*Aside.*] I know not what impediment this
complaint may be to the flight of my master.   710

---

675. without: even without.   **679. clog:** impediment (slang for a wife).
681. withal: with it.   **692. to:** ahead.   **708. farthel:** bundle.

CLOWN Pray heartily he be at' palace.

AUTOLYCUS [*Aside.*] Though I am not naturally honest, I
am so sometimes by chance. Let me pocket up my
pedlar's excrement. [*Takes off his false beard.*] How
now, rustics, whither are you bound?   715

SHEPHERD To th' palace, and it like your worship.

AUTOLYCUS Your affairs there? what? with whom? the
condition of that farthel? the place of your dwelling?
your names? your ages? of what having? breeding? and
any thing that is fitting to be known—discover.   720

CLOWN We are but plain fellows, sir.

AUTOLYCUS A lie; you are rough and hairy. Let me have
no lying. It becomes none but tradesmen, and they
often give us soldiers the lie, but we pay them for it
with stamped coin, not stabbing steel, therefore they   725
do not give us the lie.

CLOWN Your worship had like to have given us one,
if you had not taken yourself with the manner.

SHEPHERD Are you a courtier, and't like you, sir?

AUTOLYCUS Whether it like me or no, I am a courtier.   730
Seest thou not the air of the court in these enfoldings? Hath not my gait in it the measure of the court?
Receives not thy nose court-odor from me? Reflect I
not on thy baseness court-contempt? Think'st thou, for
that I insinuate, [that] toze from thee thy business, I am   735
therefore no courtier? I am courtier cap-a-pe, and
one that will either push on or pluck back thy business
there; whereupon I command thee to open thy affair.

SHEPHERD My business, sir, is to the King.

AUTOLYCUS What advocate hast thou to him?   740

SHEPHERD I know not, and't like you.

CLOWN Advocate's the court-word for a pheasant.
Say you have none.

---

711. at': at the. **714. excrement:** outgrowth (of hair). **716. and it like:** if it
please. **719. having:** property. **721. plain.** With following pun on the sense
"smooth." **724. give . . . lie:** (1) practice a deception on us; (2) call us liar
(hence Autolycus' reference to "stabbing steel," the soldier's revenge for an insult).
725. therefore: i.e. because we pay for it (and so they cannot be said to give it).
727–28. Your . . . manner: i.e. you almost told us an untruth (i.e. that the
tradesmen had *given* you the lie) but you caught yourself in time. *With the manner* = in the act. **731–32. enfoldings:** garments. **732. measure:** stately stride.
735. insinuate: pry. **toze:** tease out. **736. cap-a-pe:** from head to foot.
742. pheasant. The Clown confuses the two kinds of court. A pheasant or other
bird was often given as a bribe to a judge.

SHEPHERD None, sir; I have no pheasant cock, nor hen.

AUTOLYCUS How blessed are we that are not simple men! 745
Yet nature might have made me as these are,
Therefore I will not disdain.

CLOWN This cannot be but a great courtier.

SHEPHERD His garments are rich, but he wears them
not handsomely. 750

CLOWN He seems to be the more noble in being
fantastical. A great man, I'll warrant; I know by the
picking on 's teeth.

AUTOLYCUS The farthel there? What's i' th' farthel?
Wherefore that box? 755

SHEPHERD Sir, there lies such secrets in this farthel and
box, which none must know but the King, and which
he shall know within this hour, if I may come to th'
speech of him.

AUTOLYCUS Age, thou hast lost thy labor. 760

SHEPHERD Why, sir?

AUTOLYCUS The King is not at the palace. He is gone
aboard a new ship to purge melancholy and air himself; for if thou be'st capable of things serious, thou
must know the King is full of grief. 765

SHEPHERD So 'tis said, sir—about his son, that should
have married a shepherd's daughter.

AUTOLYCUS If that shepherd be not in hand-fast, let him
fly. The curses he shall have, the tortures he shall feel,
will break the back of man, the heart of monster. 770

CLOWN Think you so, sir?

AUTOLYCUS Not he alone shall suffer what wit can make
heavy and vengeance bitter; but those that are germane
to him (though remov'd fifty times) shall all come
under the hangman; which though it be great pity, 775
yet it is necessary. An old sheep-whistling
rogue, a ram-tender, to offer to have his daughter come
into grace! Some say he shall be ston'd; but that death
is too soft for him, say I. Draw our throne into a sheep-
cote!—all deaths are too few, the sharpest too easy. 780

CLOWN Has the old man e'er a son, sir, do you hear,
and't like you, sir?

---

764. If . . . capable of: if you know anything about. **768. hand-fast:** custody.
772. wit: ingenuity. **773. germane:** related. **776. sheep-whistling:** whistling
after (i.e. tending) sheep. **778. grace:** favor.

AUTOLYCUS He has a son, who shall be flay'd alive; then
'nointed over with honey, set on the head of a wasp's
nest; then stand till he be three quarters and a dram   785
dead; then recover'd again with aqua-vitae or
some other hot infusion; then, raw as he is (and in the
hottest day prognostication proclaims), shall he be set
against a brick-wall, the sun looking with a southward
eye upon him, where he is to behold him with flies   790
blown to death. But what talk we of these traitorly
rascals, whose miseries are to be smil'd at, their
offenses being so capital? Tell me (for you seem to be
honest plain men) what you have to the King. Being
something gently consider'd, I'll bring you where he is   795
aboard, tender your persons to his presence,
whisper him in your behalfs; and if it be in man
besides the King to effect your suits, here is man
shall do it.

CLOWN He seems to be of great authority. Close with   800
him, give him gold; and though authority be a
stubborn bear, yet he is oft led by the nose with gold.
Show the inside of your purse to the outside of his
hand, and no more ado. Remember "ston'd," and
"flay'd alive."   805

SHEPHERD And't please you, sir, to undertake the business for us, here is that gold I have. I'll make it as
much more, and leave this young man in pawn till I
bring it you.

AUTOLYCUS After I have done what I promis'd?   810

SHEPHERD Ay, sir.

AUTOLYCUS Well, give me the moi'ty. Are you a party
in this business?

CLOWN In some sort, sir; but though my case be a
pitiful one, I hope I shall not be flay'd out of it.   815

AUTOLYCUS O, that's the case of the shepherd's son.
Hang him, he'll be made an example.

CLOWN Comfort, good comfort! We must to the
King, and show our strange sights. He must know 'tis

---

785. a dram: i.e. a little more.   **786. aqua-vitae:** brandy.   **788. prognostication:**
prediction in the almanac.   **790–91. with . . . death.** A kind of punishment the
Spaniards used on Negroes and Indians.   **794–95. Being . . . consider'd:** for a
gentlemanly consideration, i.e. a generous bribe.   **800. Close:** come to an agreement.   **812. moi'ty:** half.   **814. case:** (1) plight; (2) skin.

none of your daughter, nor my sister; we are gone else. 820
Sir, I will give you as much as this old man does when
the business is perform'd, and remain (as he says) your
pawn till it be brought you.
AUTOLYCUS I will trust you. Walk before toward the
sea-side, go on the right hand, I will but look upon the 825
hedge, and follow you.
CLOWN We are bless'd in this man, as I may say, even
bless'd.
SHEPHERD Let's before, as he bids us. He was provided
to do us good.   [*Exeunt Shepherd and Clown.*] 830
AUTOLYCUS If I had a mind to be honest, I see Fortune
would not suffer me: she drops booties in my mouth.
I am courted now with a double occasion: gold and a
means to do the Prince my master good; which who
knows how that may turn back to my advancement? 835
I will bring these two moles, these blind ones,
aboard him. If he think it fit to shore them again, and
that the complaint they have to the King concerns him
nothing, let him call me rogue for being so far officious,
for I am proof against that title, and what shame else 840
belongs to't. To him will I present them, there may
be matter in it.   *Exit.*

---

820. gone else: done for otherwise.   **833. occasion:** opportunity.   **837. aboard him:** to him aboard his ship. **shore:** put ashore.   **840. proof against:** invulnerable to.

Act 5

SCENE I

Enter LEONTES, CLEOMINES, DION, PAULINA, SERVANTS.

CLEOMINES Sir, you have done enough, and have perform'd
  A saint-like sorrow. No fault could you make
  Which you have not redeem'd; indeed paid down
  More penitence than done trespass. At the last
  Do as the heavens have done, forget your evil,   5
  With them, forgive yourself.
LEONTES   Whilest I remember
  Her and her virtues, I cannot forget
  My blemishes in them, and so still think of
  The wrong I did myself; which was so much
  That heirless it hath made my kingdom, and   10
  Destroy'd the sweet'st companion that e'er man
  Bred his hopes out of.
PAULINA   True, too true, my lord.
  If, one by one, you wedded all the world,
  Or, from the all that are, took something good
  To make a perfect woman, she you kill'd   15
  Would be unparallel'd.
LEONTES   I think so. Kill'd?
  She I kill'd? I did so; but thou strik'st me
  Sorely, to say I did. It is as bitter
  Upon thy tongue as in my thought. Now, good now,
  Say so but seldom.
CLEOMINES   Not at all, good lady.   20
  You might have spoken a thousand things that would
  Have done the time more benefit, and grac'd
  Your kindness better.
PAULINA   You are one of those
  Would have him wed again.

5.1. Location: Sicilia. The palace of Leontes.   **19. good now:** i.e. please.
22. grac'd: befitted.

DION   If you would not so,
    You pity not the state, nor the remembrance   25
    Of his most sovereign name; consider little
    What dangers, by his Highness' fail of issue,
    May drop upon his kingdom, and devour
    Incertain lookers-on. What were more holy
    Than to rejoice the former queen is well?   30
    What holier than, for royalty's repair,
    For present comfort, and for future good,
    To bless the bed of majesty again
    With a sweet fellow to't?
PAULINA   There is none worthy,
    Respecting her that's gone. Besides, the gods   35
    Will have fulfill'd their secret purposes;
    For has not the divine Apollo said,
    Is't not the tenor of his oracle,
    That King Leontes shall not have an heir
    Till his lost child be found? Which that it shall,   40
    Is all as monstrous to our human reason
    As my Antigonus to break his grave,
    And come again to me; who, on my life,
    Did perish with the infant. 'Tis your counsel
    My lord should to the heavens be contrary,   45
    Oppose against their wills. [*To Leontes.*] Care not for issue,
    The crown will find an heir. Great Alexander
    Left his to th' worthiest; so his successor
    Was like to be the best.
LEONTES   Good Paulina,
    Who hast the memory of Hermione,   50
    I know, in honor, O, that ever I
    Had squar'd me to thy counsel! then, even now,
    I might have look'd upon my queen's full eyes,
    Have taken treasure from her lips—
PAULINA   And left them
    More rich for what they yielded.
LEONTES   Thou speak'st truth: 55
    No more such wives, therefore no wife. One worse,
    And better us'd, would make her sainted spirit

<hr>

25. remembrance: perpetuation (through an heir).   **29. Incertain lookers-on:**
i.e. citizens who cannot decide between rival claimants of the crown.   **30. well:**
i.e. in heaven.   **35. Respecting:** compared to.   **36. have ... purposes:** have their
secret purposes fulfilled.   **41. monstrous:** unnatural, i.e. incredible.   **46. Care not**
for: do not be anxious about.   **52. squar'd me to:** ruled myself by.

Again possess her corpse, and on this stage
(Where we offenders now) appear soul-vex'd,
And begin, "Why to me—?"

PAULINA   Had she such power,   60
She had just cause.

LEONTES   She had, and would incense me
To murther her I married.

PAULINA   I should so:
Were I the ghost that walk'd, I'ld bid you mark
Her eye, and tell me for what dull part in't
You chose her; then I'ld shriek, that even your ears   65
Should rift to hear me, and the words that follow'd
Should be "Remember mine."

LEONTES   Stars, stars,
And all eyes else dead coals! Fear thou no wife;
I'll have no wife, Paulina.

PAULINA   Will you swear
Never to marry but by my free leave?   70

LEONTES Never, Paulina, so be bless'd my spirit!

PAULINA Then, good my lords, bear witness to his oath.

CLEOMINES You tempt him overmuch.

PAULINA   Unless another,
As like Hermione as is her picture,
Affront his eye.

CLEOMINES   Good madam—

PAULINA   I have done.   75
Yet if my lord will marry—if you will, sir,
No remedy but you will—give me the office
To choose you a queen. She shall not be so young
As was your former, but she shall be such
As (walk'd your first queen's ghost) it should take joy   80
To see her in your arms.

LEONTES   My true Paulina,
We shall not marry till thou bid'st us.

PAULINA   That
Shall be when your first queen's again in breath;
Never till then.

Enter a SERVANT.

SERVANT One that gives out himself Prince Florizel,   85
Son of Polixenes, with his princess (she

---

59. now: i.e. now are.   **66. rift:** split.   **73. tempt:** press.   **75. Affront:** confront.

The fairest I have yet beheld), desires access
To your high presence.
LEONTES   What with him? He comes not
  Like to his father's greatness. His approach,
  So out of circumstance and sudden, tells us   90
  'Tis not a visitation fram'd, but forc'd
  By need and accident. What train?
SERVANT   But few,
  And those but mean.
LEONTES   His princess, say you, with him?
SERVANT Ay; the most peerless piece of earth, I think,
  That e'er the sun shone bright on.
PAULINA   O Hermione,   95
  As every present time doth boast itself
  Above a better gone, so must thy grave
  Give way to what's seen now! Sir, you yourself
  Have said and writ so, but your writing now
  Is colder than that theme, "She had not been,   100
  Nor was not to be equall'd"—thus your verse
  Flow'd with her beauty once. 'Tis shrewdly ebb'd,
  To say you have seen a better.
SERVANT   Pardon, madam:
  The one I have almost forgot—your pardon—
  The other, when she has obtain'd your eye,   105
  Will have your tongue too. This is a creature,
  Would she begin a sect, might quench the zeal
  Of all professors else, make proselytes
  Of who she but bid follow.
PAULINA   How? not women?
SERVANT Women will love her, that she is a woman   110
  More worth than any man; men, that she is
  The rarest of all women.
LEONTES   Go, Cleomines;
  Yourself, assisted with your honor'd friends,
  Bring them to our embracement.
                       Exeunt [Cleomines and others].
                       Still, 'tis strange
He thus should steal upon us.

---

88. What: who, what company. **90. out of circumstance:** without ceremony. **91. fram'd:** planned. **93. mean:** of low rank. **94. piece of earth:** mortal.
102. shrewdly: grievously. **108. all professors else:** all who professed other faiths,
i.e. worshippers of all other deities.

PAULINA   Had our prince,   115
  Jewel of children, seen this hour, he had pair'd
  Well with this lord; there was not full a month
  Between their births.
LEONTES Prithee no more; cease. Thou know'st
  He dies to me again when talk'd of. Sure   120
  When I shall see this gentleman, thy speeches
  Will bring me to consider that which may
  Unfurnish me of reason. They are come.

Enter FLORIZEL, PERDITA, CLEOMINES, *and others.*

  Your mother was most true to wedlock, Prince,
  For she did print your royal father off,   125
  Conceiving you. Were I but twenty-one,
  Your father's image is so hit in you
  (His very air) that I should call you brother,
  As I did him, and speak of something wildly
  By us perform'd before. Most dearly welcome!   130
  And your fair princess—goddess! O! alas,
  I lost a couple, that 'twixt heaven and earth
  Might thus have stood, begetting wonder, as
  You, gracious couple, do; and then I lost
  (All mine own folly) the society,   135
  Amity too, of your brave father, whom
  (Though bearing misery) I desire my life
  Once more to look on him.
FLORIZEL   By his command
  Have I here touch'd Sicilia, and from him
  Give you all greetings that a king (at friend)   140
  Can send his brother; and but infirmity
  (Which waits upon worn times) hath something seiz'd
  His wish'd ability, he had himself
  The lands and waters 'twixt your throne and his
  Measur'd to look upon you; whom he loves   145
  (He bade me say so) more than all the sceptres,
  And those that bear them, living.
LEONTES   O my brother,
  Good gentleman! the wrongs I have done thee stir

---

123. Unfurnish: divest. **127. hit:** precisely achieved. **129. wildly:** madly, exuberantly. **137. my life:** i.e. to go on living long enough. **138. him.** Redundant in modern syntax. **140. at friend:** in friendship. **141. but:** except for the fact that. **142. waits . . . times:** attends old age. **142–43. seiz'd . . . ability:** i.e. reduced his strength to less than he would wish it. **145. Measur'd:** journeyed over.

Afresh within me, and these thy offices,
So rarely kind, are as interpreters   150
Of my behind-hand slackness.—Welcome hither,
As is the spring to th' earth. And hath he too
Expos'd this paragon to th' fearful usage
(At least ungentle) of the dreadful Neptune,
To greet a man not worth her pains, much less   155
Th' adventure of her person?

FLORIZEL   Good my lord,
She came from Libya.

LEONTES   Where the warlike Smalus,
That noble honor'd lord, is fear'd and lov'd?

FLORIZEL Most royal sir, from thence; from him, whose daughter
His tears proclaim'd his, parting with her; thence   160
(A prosperous south-wind friendly) we have cross'd,
To execute the charge my father gave me
For visiting your Highness. My best train
I have from your Sicilian shores dismiss'd;
Who for Bohemia bend, to signify   165
Not only my success in Libya, sir,
But my arrival, and my wife's, in safety
Here, where we are.

LEONTES   The blessed gods
Purge all infection from our air whilest you
Do climate here! You have a holy father,   170
A graceful gentleman, against whose person
(So sacred as it is) I have done sin,
For which the heavens, taking angry note,
Have left me issueless; and your father's bless'd
(As he from heaven merits it) with you,   175
Worthy his goodness. What might I have been,
Might I a son and daughter now have look'd on,
Such goodly things as you?

Enter a LORD.

LORD   Most noble sir,
That which I shall report will bear no credit,
Were not the proof so nigh. Please you, great sir,   180
Bohemia greets you from himself by me;

---

149. offices: attentions. **150. rarely:** extraordinarily. **150–51. interpreters Of:** commentators on. **156. adventure:** hazard. **170. climate:** reside. **171. graceful:** full of noble qualities.

Desires you to attach his son, who has
(His dignity and duty both cast off)
Fled from his father, from his hopes, and with
A shepherd's daughter.
LEONTES   Where's Bohemia? speak.   185
LORD Here, in your city; I now came from him.
I speak amazedly, and it becomes
My marvel and my message. To your court
Whiles he was hast'ning (in the chase, it seems,
Of this fair couple), meets he on the way   190
The father of this seeming lady, and
Her brother, having both their country quitted
With this young prince.
FLORIZEL   Camillo has betray'd me;
Whose honor and whose honesty till now
Endur'd all weathers.
LORD   Lay't so to his charge: 195
He's with the King your father.
LEONTES   Who? Camillo?
LORD Camillo, sir; I spake with him; who now
Has these poor men in question. Never saw I
Wretches so quake: they kneel, they kiss the earth;
Forswear themselves as often as they speak.   200
Bohemia stops his ears, and threatens them
With divers deaths in death.
PERDITA   O my poor father!
The heaven sets spies upon us, will not have
Our contract celebrated.
LEONTES   You are married?
FLORIZEL We are not, sir, nor are we like to be.   205
The stars, I see, will kiss the valleys first;
The odds for high and low's alike.
LEONTES   My lord,
Is this the daughter of a king?
FLORIZEL   She is,
When once she is my wife.

---

182. attach: arrest. **183. dignity and duty:** i.e. obligations as a prince and as a son. **187. amazedly:** confusedly. **187–88. it . . . message:** my confused speech befits my bewilderment and the news I have to tell. **198. in question:** under examination. **199. kiss the earth:** i.e. abase themselves on the ground. **202. deaths in death:** tortures. **207. The odds . . . alike:** i.e. prince and shepherdess are equally the playthings of fortune (?). If *high and low* includes also the meaning "false dice," the implication is that fortune is a cheater against whom it is impossible to win.

LEONTES That "once," I see, by your good father's speed,   210
   Will come on very slowly. I am sorry,
   Most sorry, you have broken from his liking,
   Where you were tied in duty; and as sorry
   Your choice is not so rich in worth as beauty,
   That you might well enjoy her.

FLORIZEL   Dear, look up.   215
   Though Fortune, visible an enemy,
   Should chase us with my father, pow'r no jot
   Hath she to change our loves. Beseech you, sir,
   Remember since you ow'd no more to time
   Than I do now. With thought of such affections,   220
   Step forth mine advocate. At your request
   My father will grant precious things as trifles.

LEONTES Would he do so, I'ld beg your precious mistress,
   Which he counts but a trifle.

PAULINA   Sir, my liege,
   Your eye hath too much youth in't. Not a month   225
   'Fore your queen died, she was more worth such gazes
   Than what you look on now.

LEONTES   I thought of her,
   Even in these looks I made. [*To Florizel.*] But your petition
   Is yet unanswer'd. I will to your father.
   Your honor not o'erthrown by your desires,   230
   I am friend to them and you. Upon which errand
   I now go toward him; therefore follow me,
   And mark what way I make. Come, good my lord.

                             Exeunt.

SCENE 2

Enter AUTOLYCUS *and a* GENTLEMAN.

AUTOLYCUS Beseech you, sir, were you present at this
   relation?

I. GENTLEMAN I was by at the opening of the farthel,
   heard the old shepherd deliver the manner how he
   found it; whereupon, after a little amazedness, we   5

---

214. worth: rank. **219–20. since . . . now:** when you were my age. **220. With
. . . affections:** recalling how it felt to be in love. **230. Your . . . desires:** if your
desires are not incompatible with your honor (?) or if your passion has not prema-
turely overcome your chastity (?). **233. way:** progress. **5.2. Location:** Sicilia.
Before the palace of Leontes. **4. deliver:** report.

were all commanded out of the chamber; only this, methought, I heard the shepherd say, he found the child.
AUTOLYCUS I would most gladly know the issue of it.
1. GENTLEMAN I make a broken delivery of the business;
  but the changes I perceiv'd in the King and Camillo   10
  were very notes of admiration. They seem'd almost,
  with staring on one another, to tear the cases of their
  eyes. There was speech in their dumbness, language in
  their very gesture; they look'd as they had heard of a
  world ransom'd, or one destroy'd. A notable   15
  passion of wonder appear'd in them; but the wisest
  beholder, that knew no more but seeing, could not say
  if th' importance were joy or sorrow; but in the
  extremity of the one, it must needs be.

Enter another GENTLEMAN.

Here comes a gentleman that happily knows more.   20
The news, Rogero?
2. GENTLEMAN Nothing but bonfires. The oracle is
  fulfill'd; the King's daughter is found. Such a deal of
  wonder is broken out within this hour that ballad-
  makers cannot be able to express it.   25

Enter another GENTLEMAN.

Here comes the Lady Paulina's steward, he can deliver
you more. How goes it now, sir? This news, which is
call'd true, is so like an old tale, that the verity of it is
in strong suspicion. Has the King found his heir?   30
3. GENTLEMAN Most true, if ever truth were pregnant by
  circumstance. That which you hear you'll swear you
  see, there is such unity in the proofs. The mantle of
  Queen Hermione's; her jewel about the neck of it; the
  letters of Antigonus found with it, which they know to
  be his character; the majesty of the creature in   35
  resemblance of the mother; the affection of nobleness
  which nature shows above her breeding; and many
  other evidences proclaim her, with all certainty, to be

---

9. broken: fragmentary. **11. notes of admiration:** exclamation marks (*admiration* = wonder). **12. cases:** lids. **17. seeing:** what he saw. **18. importance:**
import. **18–19. in . . . be:** it was certainly the extreme degree of one or the
other. **20. happily:** haply, perhaps. **30–31. pregnant by circumstance:** made
convincing by detailed evidence. **35. character:** handwriting. **36. affection of:**
natural inclination toward. **37. breeding:** rearing.

the King's daughter. Did you see the meeting of the
two kings? 40

2. GENTLEMAN No.

3. GENTLEMAN Then have you lost a sight which was to
be seen, cannot be spoken of. There might you have
beheld one joy crown another, so and in such manner
that it seem'd sorrow wept to take leave of them, 45
for their joy waded in tears. There was casting up of
eyes, holding up of hands, with countenance of such
distraction that they were to be known by garment,
not by favor. Our king, being ready to leap out of himself for joy of his found daughter, as if that joy 50
were now become a loss, cries, "O, thy mother, thy
mother!"; then asks Bohemia forgiveness; then embraces his son-in-law; then again worries he his
daughter with clipping her. Now he thanks the old
shepherd, which stands by like a weather-bitten 55
conduit of many kings' reigns. I never heard of such
another encounter, which lames report to follow it, and
undoes description to do it.

2. GENTLEMAN What, pray you, became of Antigonus,
that carried hence the child? 60

3. GENTLEMAN Like an old tale still, which will have
matter to rehearse, though credit be asleep and not an
ear open: he was torn to pieces with a bear. This
avouches the shepherd's son, who has not only his
innocence (which seems much) to justify him, but a 65
handkerchief and rings of his that Paulina knows.

1. GENTLEMAN What became of his bark and his followers?

3. GENTLEMAN Wrack'd the same instant of their master's
death, and in the view of the shepherd; so that all 70
the instruments which aided to expose the child were
even then lost when it was found. But O, the noble
combat that 'twixt joy and sorrow was fought in
Paulina! She had one eye declin'd for the loss of her
husband, another elevated that the oracle was ful- 75
fill'd. She lifted the Princess from the earth, and so

---

47. **countenance:** demeanor (?) or countenances (?). **47–48. of such distraction:** so altered by emotion. **49. favor:** face, features. **54. clipping:** embracing.
56. conduit: i.e. because he is weeping too. **58. do:** i.e. describe; *undoes . . . it* =
utterly defies description. **62. credit:** belief. **63. with:** by. **65. innocence:**
simple-mindedness.

locks her in embracing, as if she would pin her to her
heart, that she might no more be in danger of losing.

1. GENTLEMAN The dignity of this act was worth the
audience of kings and princes, for by such was it
acted.   80

3. GENTLEMAN One of the prettiest touches of all, and that
which angled for mine eyes (caught the water though
not the fish), was when, at the relation of the Queen's
death (with the manner how she came to't bravely   85
confess'd and lamented by the King), how attentiveness
wounded his daughter, till (from one sign of dolor to
another) she did (with an "Alas!"), I would fain say,
bleed tears; for I am sure my heart wept blood. Who
was most marble there chang'd color; some   90
swounded, all sorrow'd. If all the world could have
seen't, the woe had been universal.

1. GENTLEMAN Are they return'd to the court?

3. GENTLEMAN No. The Princess hearing of her mother's
statue, which is in the keeping of Paulina—a   95
piece many years in doing and now newly perform'd by
that rare Italian master, Julio Romano, who, had he
himself eternity and could put breath into his work,
would beguile Nature of her custom, so perfectly he is
her ape. He so near to Hermione hath done   100
Hermione that they say one would speak to her and
stand in hope of answer. Thither with all greediness of
affection are they gone, and there they intend to sup.

2. GENTLEMAN I thought she had some great matter there
in hand, for she hath privately twice or thrice a   105
day, ever since the death of Hermione, visited that
remov'd house. Shall we thither, and with our company piece the rejoicing?

1. GENTLEMAN Who would be thence that has the benefit
of access? Every wink of an eye some new grace   110
will be born. Our absence makes us unthrifty to our
knowledge. Let's along.   *Exeunt [Gentlemen].*

---

78. she: i.e. Perdita. **losing:** being lost. **86. attentiveness:** listening to it.
96. perform'd: completed. **97. Julio Romano:** the name of an actual Italian
artist (died 1546). **99. beguile . . . custom:** drive Nature out of business.
100. ape: imitator. **102–3. greediness of affection:** i.e. eagerness arising out of
love. **103. sup.** Perhaps concluding the figure in *greediness*—satisfy their hunger
to see it. **108. piece:** augment. **111–12. unthrifty . . . knowledge:** wasteful of a
chance to increase our store of knowledge.

AUTOLYCUS Now, had I not the dash of my former life in
   me, would preferment drop on my head. I brought the
   old man and his son aboard the Prince; told him I   115
   heard them talk of a farthel, and I know not what; but
   he at that time, overfond of the shepherd's daughter
   (so he then took her to be), who began to be much
   sea-sick, and himself little better, extremity of weather
   continuing, this mystery remain'd undiscover'd.   120
   But 'tis all one to me; for had I been the finder-out
   of this secret, it would not have relish'd among my
   other discredits.

Enter SHEPHERD *and* CLOWN.

Here come those I have done good to against my will,
   and already appearing in the blossoms of their fortune.   125
SHEPHERD Come, boy, I am past moe children, but thy
   sons and daughters will be all gentlemen born.
CLOWN You are well met, sir. You denied to fight
   with me this other day, because I was no gentleman
   born. See you these clothes? Say you see them   130
   not and think me still no gentleman born. You were
   best say these robes are not gentlemen born. Give me
   the lie, do; and try whether I am not now a gentleman
   born.
AUTOLYCUS I know you are now, sir, a gentleman born.   135
CLOWN Ay, and have been so any time these four
   hours.
SHEPHERD And so have I, boy.
CLOWN So you have. But I was a gentleman born
   before my father; for the King's son took me by   140
   the hand, and call'd me brother; and then the two kings
   call'd my father brother; and then the Prince, my
   brother, and the Princess, my sister, call'd my father
   father; and so we wept; and there was the first gentle-
   man-like tears that ever we shed.   145
SHEPHERD We may live, son, to shed many more.
CLOWN Ay; or else 'twere hard luck, being in so
   preposterous estate as we are.
AUTOLYCUS I humbly beseech you, sir, to pardon me all
   the faults I have committed to your worship, and   150
   to give me your good report to the Prince my master.

113. dash: black mark, stain.   **122. relish'd:** had a pleasing taste.   **148. preposterous:** blunder for *prosperous* (but closer to the truth than the Clown knows).

SHEPHERD Prithee, son, do; for we must be gentle, now
   we are gentlemen.
CLOWN Thou wilt amend thy life?
AUTOLYCUS Ay, and it like your good worship.   155
CLOWN Give me thy hand: I will swear to the Prince
   thou art as honest a true fellow as any is in Bohemia.
SHEPHERD You may say it, but not swear it.
CLOWN Not swear it, now I am a gentleman? Let
   boors and franklins say it, I'll swear it.   160
SHEPHERD How if it be false, son?
CLOWN If it be ne'er so false, a true gentleman may
   swear it in the behalf of his friend; and I'll swear to the
   Prince thou art a tall fellow of thy hands, and that thou
   wilt not be drunk; but I know thou art no tall   165
   fellow of thy hands, and that thou wilt be drunk; but
   I'll swear it, and I would thou wouldst be a tall fellow
   of thy hands.
AUTOLYCUS I will prove so, sir, to my power.   170
CLOWN Ay, by any means prove a tall fellow. If I do
   not wonder how thou dar'st venture to be drunk, not
   being a tall fellow, trust me not. Hark, the kings and
   the princes, our kindred, are going to see the Queen's
   picture. Come, follow us; we'll be thy good masters.

                                             Exeunt.

SCENE 3

Enter LEONTES, POLIXENES, FLORIZEL, PERDITA,
CAMILLO, PAULINA, LORDS, *etc.*

LEONTES O grave and good Paulina, the great comfort
   That I have had of thee!
PAULINA   What, sovereign sir,
   I did not well, I meant well. All my services
   You have paid home; but that you have vouchsaf'd,
   With your crown'd brother and these your contracted   5
   Heirs of your kingdoms, my poor house to visit,
   It is a surplus of your grace, which never
   My life may last to answer.

---

157. honest . . . true: worthy . . . honest. **160. boors and franklins:** peasants and
small landowners. **164. tall . . . hands:** valiant fellow. **169. to my power:** to the
best of my ability. **5.3. Location:** Sicilia. Paulina's house. **4. paid home:** rewarded
fully. **8. last to answer:** last long enough for me to make an adequate return.

LEONTES   O Paulina,
  We honor you with trouble; but we came
  To see the statue of our queen. Your gallery   10
  Have we pass'd through, not without much content
  In many singularities; but we saw not
  That which my daughter came to look upon,
  The statue of her mother.
PAULINA   As she liv'd peerless,
  So her dead likeness, I do well believe,   15
  Excels what ever yet you look'd upon,
  Or hand of man hath done; therefore I keep it
  [Lonely], apart. But here it is; prepare
  To see the life as lively mock'd as ever
  Still sleep mock'd death. Behold, and say 'tis well.   20
           [*Paulina draws a curtain, and discovers*] Hermione
                  [*standing*] *like a statue.*
  I like your silence, it the more shows off
  Your wonder; but yet speak. First, you, my liege;
  Comes it not something near?
LEONTES   Her natural posture!
  Chide me, dear stone, that I may say indeed
  Thou art Hermione; or rather, thou art she   25
  In thy not chiding; for she was as tender
  As infancy and grace. But yet, Paulina,
  Hermione was not so much wrinkled, nothing
  So aged as this seems.
POLIXENES   O, not by much.   30
PAULINA So much the more our carver's excellence,
  Which lets go by some sixteen years, and makes her
  As she liv'd now.
LEONTES   As now she might have done,
  So much to my good comfort as it is
  Now piercing to my soul. O, thus she stood,
  Even with such life of majesty (warm life,   35
  As now it coldly stands), when first I woo'd her!
  I am asham'd; does not the stone rebuke me
  For being more stone than it? O royal piece,
  There's magic in thy majesty, which has
  My evils conjur'd to remembrance, and   40

---

12. singularities: rarities.   **19. lively mock'd:** realistically imitated.   **38. piece:** work of art.   **40. conjur'd:** summoned up (as a magician summons evil spirits).

From thy admiring daughter took the spirits,
Standing like stone with thee.
PERDITA   And give me leave,
And do not say 'tis superstition, that
I kneel, and then implore her blessing. Lady,
Dear queen, that ended when I but began,   45
Give me that hand of yours to kiss.
PAULINA   O, patience!
The statue is but newly fix'd; the color's
Not dry.
CAMILLO My lord, your sorrow was too sore laid on,
Which sixteen winters cannot blow away,   50
So many summers dry. Scarce any joy
Did ever so long live; no sorrow
But kill'd itself much sooner.
POLIXENES   Dear my brother,
Let him that was the cause of this have pow'r
To take off so much grief from you as he   55
Will piece up in himself.
PAULINA   Indeed, my lord,
If I had thought the sight of my poor image
Would thus have wrought you (for the stone is mine),
I'ld not have show'd it.
LEONTES   Do not draw the curtain.
PAULINA No longer shall you gaze on't, lest your fancy   60
May think anon it moves.
LEONTES   Let be, let be.
Would I were dead but that methinks already—
What was he that did make it? See, my lord,
Would you not deem it breath'd? and that those veins
Did verily bear blood?
POLIXENES   Masterly done!   65
The very life seems warm upon her lip.
LEONTES The fixure of her eye has motion in't,
As we are mock'd with art.
PAULINA   I'll draw the curtain.
My lord's almost so far transported that
He'll think anon it lives.

---

41. admiring: wonderstruck. **spirits:** vital forces. **47. fix'd:** i.e. painted.
56. piece . . . himself: make part of himself. **58. wrought:** moved. **62. but . . .
already:** if it doesn't seem to me already (that it moves). **67. The fixure . . . in't:**
i.e. her eye, though stationary, seems to move. **68. As . . . with:** in such a way
that we are deluded by.

LEONTES   O sweet Paulina,   70
  Make me to think so twenty years together!
  No settled senses of the world can match
  The pleasure of that madness. Let't alone.
PAULINA I am sorry, sir, I have thus far stirr'd you; but
  I could afflict you farther.
LEONTES   Do, Paulina;   75
  For this affliction has a taste as sweet
  As any cordial comfort. Still methinks
  There is an air comes from her. What fine chisel
  Could ever yet cut breath? Let no man mock me,
  For I will kiss her.
PAULINA   Good my lord, forbear.   80
  The ruddiness upon her lip is wet;
  You'll mar it if you kiss it; stain your own
  With oily painting. Shall I draw the curtain?
LEONTES No! not these twenty years.
PERDITA   So long could I
  Stand by, a looker-on.
PAULINA   Either forbear,   85
  Quit presently the chapel, or resolve you
  For more amazement. If you can behold it,
  I'll make the statue move indeed, descend,
  And take you by the hand; but then you'll think
  (Which I protest against) I am assisted   90
  By wicked powers.
LEONTES   What you can make her do,
  I am content to look on; what to speak,
  I am content to hear; for 'tis as easy
  To make her speak as move.
PAULINA   It is requir'd
  You do awake your faith. Then, all stand still.   95
  On; those that think it is unlawful business
  I am about, let them depart.
LEONTES   Proceed;
  No foot shall stir.
PAULINA   Music! awake her! strike!   [Music.]
  'Tis time; descend; be stone no more; approach;
  Strike all that look upon with marvel. Come;   100

---

72. settled: stable, sane.   **77. cordial:** heartwarming.   **85. forbear:** withdraw.
86. presently: at once.   **96. On; those.** Many editors emend to *Or those.*
98. strike: strike up.   **100. upon:** on.

I'll fill your grave up. Stir; nay, come away;
Bequeath to death your numbness; for from him
Dear life redeems you. You perceive she stirs.

[*Hermione comes down.*]

Start not; her actions shall be holy, as
You hear my spell is lawful. Do not shun her   105
Until you see her die again, for then
You kill her double. Nay, present your hand.
When she was young, you woo'd her; now, in age,
Is she become the suitor?
LEONTES   O, she's warm!
If this be magic, let it be an art   110
Lawful as eating.
POLIXENES   She embraces him.
CAMILLO She hangs about his neck.
If she pertain to life let her speak too.
POLIXENES Ay, and make it manifest where she has liv'd,
Or how stol'n from the dead.
PAULINA   That she is living,   115
Were it but told you, should be hooted at
Like an old tale; but it appears she lives,
Though yet she speak not. Mark a little while.
Please you to interpose, fair madam, kneel,
And pray your mother's blessing. Turn, good lady,   120
Our Perdita is found.
HERMIONE   You gods, look down
And from your sacred vials pour your graces
Upon my daughter's head! Tell me, mine own,
Where hast thou been preserv'd? where liv'd? how found
Thy father's court? for thou shalt hear that I,   125
Knowing by Paulina that the oracle
Gave hope thou wast in being, have preserv'd
Myself to see the issue.
PAULINA   There's time enough for that;
Least they desire (upon this push) to trouble
Your joys with like relation. Go together,   130
You precious winners all; your exultation
Partake to every one. I, an old turtle,

---

106. then: i.e. if you do. **107. double:** a second time. **129–30. Least . . . relation:** the last thing they want, at this critical moment, is to trouble your happiness
with such an account. **132. Partake to:** share with. **turtle:** turtledove (symbol
of faithful love).

Will wing me to some wither'd bough, and there
My mate (that's never to be found again)
Lament till I am lost.

LEONTES   O, peace, Paulina!   135
Thou shouldst a husband take by my consent,
As I by thine a wife: this is a match,
And made between 's by vows. Thou hast found mine,
But how, is to be question'd; for I saw her
(As I thought) dead; and have (in vain) said many   140
A prayer upon her grave. I'll not seek far
(For him, I partly know his mind) to find thee
An honorable husband. Come, Camillo,
And take her by the hand, whose worth and honesty
Is richly noted; and here justified   145
By us, a pair of kings. Let's from this place.
What? look upon my brother. Both your pardons,
That e'er I put between your holy looks
My ill suspicion. This' your son-in-law,
And son unto the King, whom heavens directing   150
Is troth-plight to your daughter. Good Paulina,
Lead us from hence, where we may leisurely
Each one demand, and answer to his part
Perform'd in this wide gap of time, since first
We were dissever'd. Hastily lead away.   155
                                     Exeunt.

---

145. justified: confirmed.   **148. holy:** chaste.   **149. This':** this is.

NOTE ON THE TEXT

The First Folio (1623) is the only authority for *The Winter's Tale*; all later editions are derived from that source. The F1 text, it is widely agreed, was printed from a transcript made by Ralph Crane, scrivener to the King's Men, and probably specially prepared for the printer. Most of Crane's scribal characteristics are clearly apparent in the printed text (see, e.g., Textual Notes, 1.1.3, 10, 1.2.1, 254, 2.1.61, 179, 2.3.16, 3.2.11, 4.3.32, 41, 4.4.83, 88, 195, 273, 577, 737, 5.1.120, 5.3.21, 49); moreover the list of "The Names of the Actors," the careful act-scene division, and the use of "massed entries," though not entirely consistent, link this play with *The Merry Wives of Windsor* and *The Two Gentlemen of Verona*, both generally agreed to have been printed from Crane transcripts.

It is not clear what sort of manuscript lies behind Crane's transcript: Greg suggests "foul papers" and Wells/Taylor suggest authorial "fair copy," probably a prompt-book. But nothing in the text suggests any use of the official prompt-book; indeed, an entry in the *Office Book* of Sir Henry Herbert, Master of the Revels, strongly suggests that the company's prompt-book was lost at the time copy was needed for F1. The entry reads: "For the king's players. An olde play called *Winter's Tale*, formerly allowed of by Sir George Bucke, and likewyse by mee on Mr. Hemmings his worde that there was nothing prophane added or reformed, thogh the allowed booke was missinge; and therefore I returned itt without a fee, this 19 of August, 1623." (Quoted from Malone's *Shakspeare* (1790), Vol. I, Pt. 2, p. 226, the original *Office Book* being since lost.)

Since the F1 text of *The Winter's Tale* had most probably been printed off by December 1622 (Hinman), E. E. Willoughby's suggestion (in Wilson) that the "booke" submitted to Herbert in 1623 may well have consisted of F1 sheets marked up by the book-keeper for use as the prompt-book is perhaps more credible than Greg allows. See, for example, the so-called Padua First Folio prompt-books of *Macbeth* and *Measure for Measure* (pre-Restoration) and the copy of the Third Folio (1663/4), in which some ten plays were annotated as prompt-books (c. 1674–85) for use in the Smock Alley Theatre in Dublin (G. B. Evans, ed., *Shakespearean Prompt-Books of the Seventeenth Century*, 8 vols., 1960–96).

It has been claimed, with some likelihood, that the "dance of twelve Satyrs" in 4.4 and its introductory lines (324–42) are an addition, which was inserted, perhaps, at a Court performance of *The Winter's Tale* (5 November 1611) as part of the festivities arranged for the coming marriage of Princess Elizabeth with the Elector Palatine, an addition imitating a similar dance of ten (or twelve) satyrs in Ben Jonson's masque, *Oberon, The Fairy Prince*, performed 1 January 1611. Certainly this short episode is completely detachable without affecting the surrounding text and Polixenes' first line after the dance (343) shows no consciousness of the dance action but is addressed to the old Shepherd, whose son (the Clown) has shortly before remarked (310) that the Shepherd is "in sad talk" with the "gentlemen" (i.e., Polixenes and Camillo).

Some suggestive, but inconclusive, evidence has been interpreted to suggest (see J. E. Ballard and W. M. Fox as cited in Greg) that Hermione's intensely moving and dramatic "resurrection" scene, with which the play concludes (5.3), represents a change in Shakespeare's original intention—that is, he had intended to make the reunion between Leontes and Perdita the final climactic episode, thus leaving Hermione dead as in Robert Greene's *Pandosto* (1588), Shakespeare's principal source, and, seemingly, as in Antigonus's reaction to her ghostlike appearance in 3.3.15–46. In *Pandosto*, Bellaria (=Hermione), having been declared guiltless of adultery with Egistus (=Polixenes) by the Oracle of Delphos, dies from grief when news is brought of the sudden death of her son, little Garinter (=Mamillius). Since, then, (1) Shakespeare must have known how Greene had dealt with Bellaria and because Simon Forman, who witnessed a performance of *The Winter's Tale* at the Globe on 15 May 1611, fails to mention Hermione's surprise survival, it may be argued that the performance of the play concluded with a scene showing the reunion of Leontes and Perdita. (2) Antigonus interprets the apparition of Hermione, in pure white robes "like very sanctity," that appeared to him in a kind of waking dream to mean that she has died (3.3.15–46). (3) The reunion of Leontes and Perdita, a naturally climactic scene toward which Acts 4 and 5 would seem, inevitably, to be leading, is, instead of being shown, merely reported by several gentlemen, who describe the event in considerable detail. The arguments advanced above, however, are not perhaps so persuasive as they may at first appear (compare Pafford's discussion). (1) Forman, although he fails to mention Hermione's "resurrection," also fails to report her death. Moreover, he makes no reference to Paulina, an important character not found in *Pandosto*, and it would be absurd to suggest she was also an afterthought and played no part in the play as seen by Forman. (2) Antigonus's belief that it must have been Hermione's ghost that had appeared to him may also be explained as a clever piece of Shakespearean legerdemain intended to make the audience temporarily forget Hermione and hence eventually to heighten the dramatic tension generated by the surprise ending. (3) The use of what is called "reported action" to describe, instead of show, the reunion of Leontes and Perdita is, perhaps, the strongest of the three points discussed above, but, like the first two points, it remains essentially speculative. In other words, an opposite supposition is similarly probable and unprovable: namely, Shakespeare, always intending to end the play with Hermione's "rebirth," realized that the plot-line, as he was developing it, required the prior reunion of Leontes and Perdita and that to show two reunion scenes almost back to back would surely result in reducing the second to an anticlimax, and he thus wisely chose to play down the first by using the distancing "reported action" technique.

The F1 text is unusually clean and good and presents few problems to the editor.

For further information, see: J. D. Wilson, ed., New Shakespeare *The Winter's Tale* (Cambridge, 1931) [Wilson's theory that the F1 text is based on a transcript made up from players' parts is no longer accepted]; W. W. Greg, *The Shakespeare First Folio* (Oxford, 1955); Charlton Hinman, *The Printing and Proof-Reading of the First Folio*, 2 vols. (Oxford, 1963); J. H. P. Pafford, ed., New Arden *The Winter's Tale* (London, 1953; rev. 1965); E. A. J. Honigmann, "On the Indifferent and One-Way Variants in Shakespeare," *The Library*, 5th. ser., XXII (1967), 189–204; Stanley Wells, Gary Taylor, et al., *William Shakespeare: A Textual Companion* (Oxford, 1987).

TEXTUAL NOTES

Dramatis personae: *as given in F1, following the play, with a few additions by Rowe and later eds.*
Mamillius] *F3* (Mamilius); Mamillus *F1*
Act-scene division: *from F1*

I.1

Location: *Theobald (after Rowe)*
3 **on foot]** *F4*; on-foot *F1*
10 **Beseech]** *Capell*; 'Beseech *F1*
   (*sporadically throughout*)
19 **Believe]** *F3*; 'Beleeue *F1*

I.2

Location: *Capell (subs.)*
o.s.d. **and Attendants]** *Theobald*
1 **wat'ry star]** *F4*; Watry-Starre *F1*
32 **by-gone day]** *Rowe*; by-gone-day *F1*
32 **proclaim'd.]** *Rowe (subs.)*;
   proclaym'd, *F1*
42 **good deed]** *Capell*; good-deed *F1*;
   good-heed *F2*
50 **"verily" is]** *F3 (subs.)*; Verely' is *F1*
67 **twinn'd]** *Rowe*; twyn'd *F1*
104 **And]** *F2*; A *F1*
106 **lo you]** *Rowe*; lo-you *F1*
108 s.d. **Gives . . . Polixenes.]** *Capell*
108 s.d. **Aside.]** *Rowe*
121 **hast]** *Capell*; has't *F1*
124 **heckfer]** *ed.*; Heycfer *F1*
129 **full]** *Pope*; full, *F1*
137 **be?—]** *Rowe (question mark, Hanmer)*;
   be *F1*
138 **Affection!]** *Steevens*; Affection? *F1*
141 **unreal]** *Theobald conj.*; vnreall: *F1*
154 **recoil]** *F3*; requoyle *F1*
158 **ornament]** *Capell*; Ornaments *F1*
180 s.d. **Aside.]** *Rowe (subs.; after l. 182);
   placed as in Dyce*
185 s.d. **Exeunt . . . Attendants.]** *Rowe
   (after l. 184); placed as in Cambridge*
203 **south.]** *Johnson*; South, *F1*
208 **they]** *F2*
211 s.d. **Exit Mamillius.]** *Rowe*
217 s.d. **Aside.]** *Hanmer*
254 **forth . . . lord,]** *Theobald*; forth in
   your affaires (my Lord.) *F1*
276 **hobby-horse]** *Rowe*; Holy-Horse *F1*
285 **meeting]** *F4*; meating *F1*
305 **Infected . . . life,]** *Capell (after Rowe)*;
   Infected (as her life) *F1*
307 **medal]** *Rowe*; Medull *F1*
312 **ay]** *Capell*; I *F1*
371 **compliment]** *Rowe*; complement *F1*
403 **guess]** *F3*; ghesse *F1*

421 **nostril]** *F3*; Nosthrill *F1*
462 **off. Hence!]** *Wilson (subs.)*; off,
   hence: *F1*

2.1

Location: *Theobald (subs.)*
o.s.d. **Enter . . . Ladies.]** *Rowe*
   (Mamillus); Enter Hermione,
   Mamillius, Ladies: Leontes, Antigonus,
   Lords. *F1 (the first of the "massed
   entries"; Leontes, Antigonus, and the
   Lords actually enter later in the scene)*
2, 4, etc. s.pp. **1. Lady.]** *Rowe*; Lady. *F1*
27 **Come on . . . come on]** *Rowe*;
   Come-on . . . come-on *F1*
32 s.d. **Enter . . . others.]** *Capell
   (after Rowe)*; Enter L. *F2*
33 **Was . . . him?]** *as verse, Warburton
   (after Rowe); as prose, F1*
34, 53, etc. s.pp. **1. Lord.]** *Capell*;
   Lord. *F1*
35 **ey'd]** *Rowe*; eyed *F1*
38 **knowledge!]** *Capell (subs.)*;
   knowledge, *F1*
61 **big with]** *F3*; big-with *F1*
69 **without-door form]** *Rowe*;
   without-dore-Forme *F1*
71 **petty brands]** *Hanmer*;
   Petty-brands *F1*
104 **afar off]** *F4*; a farre-off *F1*
125 s.d. **Exit . . . Ladies.]** *Theobald*
136 **Than]** *Pope*; Then *F1*
141 **putter-on]** *hyphen, Rowe*
145 **nine,]** *Theobald conj.*; nine: *F1*
147 **geld]** *Rowe*; gell'd *F1*
152 **dead man's]** *Rowe*; dead-mans *F1*
153 s.d. **grasps his arm]** *Hanmer (subs.)*
157 **dungy earth]** *Rowe*; dungy-earth *F1*
160 **true than]** *Dyce (than F4)*; true,
   then *F1*
160 **suspicion,]** *Collier*; suspition *F1*
179 **push on]** *F2*; push-on *F1*
182 **have]** *F2*; hane *F1*
185 **stuff'd sufficiency]** *F3*; stuff'd-
   sufficiency *F1*
191 s.d. **Points at Antigous.]** *Furness conj.*
198 s.d. **Aside.]** *Hanmer*

2.2

Location: *Pope*
o.s.d. **Enter . . . Attendants.]** *Hanmer
   (after Rowe)*; Enter Paulina, a
   Gentleman, Gaoler, Emilia. *F1*
2 s.d. **Exit Gentleman.]** *Rowe (after l. 1);
   placed as in Dyce*

4 s.d. **Enter . . . Jailer.**] *Rowe (after not? l. 5); placed as in Johnson*
15 s.d. **Exeunt . . . Attendants.**] *Theobald (subs.)*
16 s.d. **Exit Jailer.**] *Capell (subs.)*
18 s.d. **Enter . . . Emilia.**] *Capell (subs.);* Enter Emilia. *F2 (opposite ll. 16–17)*
19 **gracious**] *F2;* gtacious *F1*
34 **Queen.**] *Capell (subs.);* Queene, *F1*
45 **presently**] *F2;* presenrly *F1*
51 **let't**] *F3;* le't *F1*

2.3

Location: *Pope (subs.)*
o.s.d. **Enter . . . door.**] *ed.,* Enter Leontes, Seruants, Paulina, Antigonus, and Lords. *F1 (F1 enters Paulina again at l. 26)*
2 **weakness.**] *Collier;* weaknesse, *F1*
4 **harlot king**] *Capell;* harlot-King *F1*
9, 10 s.pp. **1. Serv.**] *Cambridge (after Capell);* Ser. *F1*
9 **Advancing.**] *Capell*
13 **mother!**] *ed.;* Mother. *F1*
16 **Threw off**] *F3;* Threw-off *F1*
18 s.d. **Exit First Servant.**] *Theobald (subs.; after l. 17); placed as in Capell*
26 s.d. **with a Child**] *Rowe*
26 s.d. **endeavoring . . . back**] *ed. (after Wilson)*
26 s.p. **1. Lord.**] *Malone;* Lord. *F1*
31 s.p. **2. Serv.**] *Cambridge (after Capell);* Ser. *F1*
39 **What**] *F2;* Who *F1*
50 **La you**] *Capell (subs.);* La-you *F1*
52 s.d. **Aside.**] *Wilson*
52–7 **come— . . . yours.—**] *Capell (after Rowe);* come: . . . yours. *F1*
61 **good, so**] *Theobald;* good so, *F1*
67 s.d. **Laying . . . child.**] *Rowe*
74 s.d. **To Antigonus.**] *Rowe*
112 **more,**] *Theobald;* more *F1*
140 **bastard brains**] *Theobald;* Bastard-braynes *F1*
147, **197** s.pp. **1. Lord.**] *Capell;* Lord. *F1*
162 **grey—what**] *Pope;* gray. What *F1*
192 s.d. **with the child**] *Rowe*

3.1

Location: *Kittredge (after Capell)*
12 **successful**] *F2;* snccessefull *F1*
18 **business.**] *Theobald (subs.);* Businesse, *F1*
20 **discover,**] *Johnson;* discouer: *F1*

3.2

Location: *Theobald*
o.s.d. **Enter . . . Officers.**] *Theobald (subs.);* Enter Leontes, Lords, Officers:

Hermione (as to her Triall) Ladies: Cleomines, Dion. *F1*
10 s.d. **Enter . . . attending.**] *Theobald (subs.; after Silence! l. 10); placed as in Wilson*
10 **Silence!**] *Rowe; in italics as s.d., F1*
12 s.d. **Reads.**] *Capell*
29 **human**] *Rowe;* humane *F1*
33 **Who**] *Rowe;* Whom *F1*
41 **'fore**] *Pope;* fore *F1*
97 **first-fruits**] *hyphen, Rowe*
105 **Here**] *Pope;* Here, *F1*
116, 174, etc. s.pp. **1. Lord.**] *Capell;* Lord. *F1*
118 s.d. **Exeunt certain Officers.**] *Capell*
123 s.d. **Enter . . . Dion.**] *Capell (subs.);* Enter Dion and Cleomines. *F2 (after l. 116)*
132 s.d. **Reads.**] *Capell*
141 s.d. **Enter a Servant.**] *Rowe*
147 s.d. **Hermione swoons.**] *Rowe (subs.)*
153 s.d. **Exeunt . . . Hermione.**] *Rowe (after l. 150); placed subs. as in Malone*
156 **woo**] *F2;* woe *F1*
172 s.d. **Enter Paulina.**] *Rowe*
179–81 **tyranny, Together . . . (Fancies**] *Theobald (subs., after Pope);* Tyranny (Together . . . Fancies *F1*
205 **eye,**] *Rowe;* eye *F1;* eye; *F4*
238 **perpetual).**] *Rowe (subs.);* perpetuall) *F1*

3.3

Location: *Pope, Kittredge (after Rowe)*
o.s.d. **Enter . . . babe.**] *ed. (after Rowe);* Enter Antigonus, A Marriner, Babe, Sheepeheard, and Clowne. *F1*
11 **Too far**] *F3;* Too-farre *F1*
21 **sorrow,**] *Capell;* sorrow *F1*
29 **thrower-out**] *F2;* Thower-out *F1*
46 s.d. **Laying . . . scroll.**] *Kittredge (after Rowe)*
47 s.d. **Placing . . . it.**] *Johnson (subs.)*
49 s.d. **Thunder.**] *Wilson*
49 **begins.**] *Rowe (subs.);* beginnes, *F1*
58 s.d. **Enter a Shepherd.**] *F2*
61 **in the between**] *Pope;* (in the betweene) *F1*
63 **fighting—Hark**] *Rowe;* fighting, hearke *F1*
63 s.d. **Horns.**] *White*
65 **scar'd**] *Rowe;* scarr'd *F1*
68 **Good luck**] *F4;* Good-lucke *F1*
69 **will!**] *Kittredge (after Theobald);* will) *F1*
114 **new-born**] *hyphen, Theobald*
120 **made**] *Theobald;* mad *F1*

4.1

17–9 **leaving— . . . himself—**] *Staunton;* leauing . . . himselfe. *F1*

4.2

Location: *Pope, Capell*
13 **thee.**] *Rowe;* thee, *F1*
54 **Camillo!**] *Theobald;* Camillo, *F1*
55 **Exeunt.**] *Rowe;* Exit *F1*

4.3

Location: *Malone*
1 s.p. **Aut.**] *Capell*
10 **with heigh,**] *F2*
15 **my dear?**] *Pope;* (my deere) *F1*
17 **here and there,**] *F4;* here, and there *F1;* here and there *F3*
22 **avouch it**] *F3;* auouch-it *F1*
32 **'leven wether**] *Malone;* Leauen-weather *F1*
35 s.d. **Aside.**] *Rowe*
37 **sheep-shearing feast**] *Rowe;* Sheepe-shearing-Feast *F1*
38 **currants**] *Rowe;* Currence *F1*
41 **made me**] *F3;* made-me *F1*
50 s.d. **Grovelling . . . ground.**] *Rowe*
51 **me—**] *Rowe;* me. *F1*
62 **detestable**] *F2;* derestable *F1*
75 s.d. **picking his pocket**] *Capell*
77 **Dost**] *F3;* Doest *F1*
115 **good-fac'd**] *hyphen, Theobald*
123 **Jog on, jog on**] *Rowe;* Iog-on, Iog-on *F1*

4.4

Location: *Sisson (after Theobald)*
o.s.d. **Enter . . . Perdita.**] *Rowe;* Enter Florizell, Perdita, Shepherd, Clowne, Polixenes, Camillo, Mopsa, Dorcas, Seruants, Autolicus. *F1*
2 **Does**] *Rowe;* Do's *F1*
5 **Sir,**] *Pope;* Sir: *F1*
12 **Digest't**] *ed. (after* Digest it *F2);* Digest *F1*
29 **fire-rob'd god**] *Rowe;* Fire-roab'd-God *F1*
32 **beauty**] *Rowe;* beauty, *F1*
54 s.d. **Enter . . . Servants.**] *placed as in Capell;* Enter All. *F2 (after* auspicious! *l. 52)*
54 s.d. **disguised**] *Rowe*
55 **liv'd,**] *Rowe;* liu'd: *F1*
70 s.d. **To Polixenes.**] *Malone (after Rowe)*
72 s.d. **To Camillo.**] *Malone*
83 **bastards). Of**] *Rowe (subs.);* bastards) of *F1*
84 **garden's**] *F2;* Gardens *F1*

88 **creating Nature**] *F4;* creating-Nature *F1*
93 **scion**] *Steevens;* Sien *F1*
98 **your**] *F2;* you *F1*
105 **wi' th'**] *Capell (subs.);* with' *F1*
115 **virgin branches**] *Capell;* Virgin-branches *F1*
134 **Whitsun pastorals**] *Johnson;* Whitson-Pastorals *F1*
162–3 **Mopsa . . . with!**] *as verse, Capell; as prose, F1*
165 s.d. **Music.**] *Capell (after l. 155); placed as in Malone*
195 **jump her**] *F4;* Iump-her *F1*
195 **thump her**] *F3;* thump-her *F1*
214 s.d. **Exit Servant.**] *Capell*
218 s.p. **Aut.**] *Capell*
245 **off**] *Hanmer;* of *F1*
249 **promis'd**] *F2;* ptomis'd *F1*
261 **a-life**] *Tyrwhitt conj.;* a life *F1*
273 **Come on**] *F2;* Come-on *F1*
297–8] *In F1 the first line of the song is preceded by* Song *and the second line by* Aut.; *arranged as in Rowe*
310 **gentlemen**] *Rowe;* Gent. *F1*
313 s.d. **Exit . . . Mopsa.**] *Dyce*
316 **cape**] *F2;* Crpe *F1*
323 s.d. **Enter Servant.**] *Rowe (subs.)*
336 **four threes**] *Capell;* foure-threes *F1*
340 **prating.**] *Rowe (subs.);* prating, *F1*
342 s.d. **Exit.**] *Capell*
344 s.d. **To Camillo.**] *Cambridge*
345 s.d. **To Florizel.**] *Craig*
355 **reply, at least**] *Dyce (after Theobald);* reply at least, *F1*
363 **dove's down**] *F2;* Doues-downe *F1*
381 **better.**] *Rowe;* better *F1*
389 **come on**] *Rowe;* come-on *F1*
390 **'fore**] *F2;* fore *F1*
401 **again**] *Capell;* againe, *F1*
417 s.d. **Discovering himself.**] *Rowe*
419 **acknowledg'd**] *F2;* acknowledge *F1*
428 **shalt**] *Rowe;* shalt neuer *F1*
437 **thee—**] *Capell;* thee. *F1*
439 **hoop**] *Pope;* hope *F1*
446 **Will't**] *Hanmer;* Wilt *F1*
452 s.d. **To Florizel.**] *Rowe*
458 **shovels in**] *Rowe;* shouels-in *F1*
458 s.d. **To Perdita.**] *Rowe*
467 **your**] *F2;* my *F1*
468 **guess**] *Rowe;* ghesse *F1*
470 **sight as yet,**] *Hanmer;* sight, as yet *F1*
473 **think, Camillo?**] *Johnson;* think Camillo. *F1*
482–3 **fancy. . . . obedient,**] *Theobald (after Rowe);* fancie, . . . obedient: *F1*
490 **seas hides**] *F2 (*hide*);* seas, hides *F1*

494 **(as, in]** *Rowe (subs.)*; as (in *F1*
506 s.d. **Drawing her aside.]** *Capell*
507 s.d. **To Camillo.]** *Theobald*
549 **there,]** *ed.*; there *F1*
577 **take in]** *F4*; take-in *F1*
583 **sir; for this]** *Hanmer*; Sir, for this, *F1*
594 s.d. **They talk aside.]** *Rowe*
594 s.d. **laughing]** *ed.*
606 **wenches']** *Johnson*; Wenches *F1*
611 **fil'd]** *F3*; fill'd *F1*
611 **off]** *F3*; of *F1*
615 **old man]** *F3*; old-man *F1*
618 s.d. **Camillo . . . forward.]** *Theobald*
623 s.d. **Seeing Autolycus.]** *Theobald*
626 s.d. **Aside.]** *Theobald*
628–9 **How . . . thee.]** *as prose, Malone; as verse, F1*
637 s.d. **Giving money.]** *Dyce (after Capell)*
638, 642 s.dd. **Aside.]** *Johnson; indicated by parentheses, F1*
641 **flea'd]** *Rowe*; fled *F1*
647 s.d. **Florizel . . . garments.]** *Capell*
658 s.d. **Giving . . . Perdita.]** *Capell*
662, 706 s.dd. **Aside.]** *Rowe*
669 s.d. **with . . . Perdita]** *Capell (subs.)*
709, 712 s.dd. **Aside.]** *Capell*
714 s.d. **Takes . . . beard.]** *Steevens (after Capell)*
730 **like]** *F2*; lke *F1*
735 **that toze]** *Alexander (subs.)*; at toaze *F1*
737 **push on]** *Pope*; push-on *F1*
737 **pluck back]** *Theobald (after Rowe)*; pluck-back *F1*
773 **germane]** *Theobald*; Iermaine *F1*
776 **sheep-whistling]** *F2*; Sheepe-whistiing *F1*
786 **aqua-vitae]** *F2*; Aquavite *F1*
791–2 **traitorly rascals]** *Theobald*; Traitorly-Rascals *F1*
830 s.d. **Exeunt . . . Clown.]** *Rowe*; Exeunt. *F2*
842 s.d. **Exit.]** *Rowe*; Exeunt. *F1*

5.1

Location: *Pope, Capell*
o.s.d. **Enter . . . Servants.]** *Rowe*; Enter Leontes, Cleomines, Dion, Paulina, Seruants: Florizel, Perdita. *F1*
5 **done,]** *Theobald*; done; *F1*
12 **of./Paul. True, too]** *Theobald*; of, true./Paul. Too *F1*

29 **lookers-on]** *hyphen, Capell*
31 **holier than,]** *Capell (subs.; than F4)*; holyer, then *F1*
41 **human]** *Pope*; humane *F1*
44, 52 **counsel]** *Pope*; councell *F1*
46 s.d. **To Leontes.]** *Theobald*
59 **now) appear]** *Theobald*; now appeare] *F1*
61 **just]** *F3*; iust such *F1*
75 **madam—/Paul. I have done.]** *Capell*; Madame, I haue done. *F1 (continued to Cleomines)*
114 s.d. **Exeunt . . . others.]** *Dyce (after Capell)*; Exit. *F1 (after us. l. 115)*
120 **talk'd of]** *F4*; talk'd-of *F1*
160 **his,]** *Hanmer*; his *F1*
211 **come on]** *Rowe*; come-on *F1*
228 s.d. **To Florizel.]** *Theobald*

5.2

Location: *Capell*
78 **losing]** *F2*; loosing *F1*
90 **marble]** *F3*; Marble, *F1*
112 s.d. **Exeunt Gentlemen.]** *Capell*; Exit. *F1*

5.3

Location: *Pope*
o.s.d. **Paulina, Lords]** *Rowe*; Paulina: Hermione (like a Statue:) Lords *F1*
18 **Lonely]** *Hanmer*; Louely *F1*
20 s.d. **Paulina . . . statue.]** *Rowe (after F1 o.s.d.)*
21 **shows off]** *F2* (shewes); shewes-off *F1*
22 **speak.]** *Johnson*; speake, *F1*
31 **go by]** *F4*; goe-by *F1*
49 **laid on]** *Rowe*; lay'd-on *F1*
55 **take off]** *F2*; take-off *F1*
62 **already—]** *Rowe*; alreadie. *F1*
85 **Stand by]** *F2*; Stand-by *F1*
98 s.d. **Music.]** *Rowe*
103 s.d. **Hermione comes down.]** *Rowe*
112 **neck.]** *Theobald (subs.)*; necke, *F1*
115 **dead.]** *Capell*; dead? *F1*
122 **vials]** *Pope*; Viols *F1*
126 **the]** *F2*; the *F1*
128 **time]** *F2*; ttme *F1*
128–9 **that; Least]** *F2*; that,/Least *F1*; that;/Lest *F3*
149 **This']** *W. S. Walker conj.*; This *F1*
155 s.d. **Exeunt.]** *Exeunt. [list of actors]* FINIS. *F1*

Sources and Contexts

Account of *The Winter's Tale*

Simon Forman

From Simon Forman's *Booke of Plaies and Notes thereof per formans for Common Pollicie*, Bodleian Ashmole MS 208, fols. 201^{v}–202^{r}. Reprinted in Chambers, *William Shakespeare*, 2. 340–1; the present text has been modernized.

The first account of a performance of The Winter's Tale *appears in a manuscript by Simon Forman, who saw the play at the Globe on May 15, 1611. He makes no mention of the statue scene, which has led to critical debate about whether the play originally contained the remarkable finale that so distinguishes it in the experience of subsequent generations. The play's primary source, Robert Greene's* Pandosto, *includes no such episode, but some of the play's earlier language and imagery about food and eating and about Hermione's alleged corpse resonates with specific passages in 5.3. Still, Forman may simply have had no special interest in such a moment, and alertness to such nuances of composition requires close reading of a text, not just a single viewing of a play in performance. Moreover, his manuscript's title specifies his concern with "Common Pollicie," or matters of public consequence that affect our life as a community, and his remarks include a warning about our susceptibility to con men like Autolycus. Forman may have been sticking to his particular preoccupations regardless of Shakespeare's tour de force that so predominates in later responses to the play.*

IN THE *Winter's Tale* at the Globe 1611 the 15 of May Wednesday, observe there how Leontes the King of Sicilia was overcome with jealousy of his wife with the King of Bohemia, his friend that came to see him, and how he contrived his death and would have had his cupbearer to have poisoned, who gave the King of Bohemia warning thereof and fled with him to Bohemia.

Remember also how he sent to the oracle of Apollo, and the answer of Apollo, that she was guiltless and that the King was jealous, etc., and how except the child was found again that was lost the King should die without issue, for the child was carried into Bohemia and there laid in a forest and brought up by a shepherd. And the King of Bohemia his son married that wench, and how they fled into Sicilia to Leontes, and the shepherd having showed the letter of the nobleman by whom Leontes sent a was [away?] that child, and the jewels found about her, she was known to be Leontes' daughter, and was then sixteen years old.

Remember also the rogue that came in all tattered like colt-pixie,[1] and how he feigned him sick and to have been robbed of all that he had, and how he cozened the poor man of all his money, and after came to the sheep-shear with a pedlar's pack and there cozened them again of all their money, and how he changed apparel with the King of Bohemia his son, and then how he turned courtier, etc. Beware of trusting feigned beggars or fawning fellows.

1. A mischievous sprite or hobgoblin, especially in the shape of a ragged colt luring men to follow it and then disappearing (*OED*).

From ON SOME OF SHAKESPEARE'S FEMALE CHARACTERS

Helena Faucit

Helena Faucit (1817-1898) began her professional career at Covent Garden in January 1836, when she was eighteen years-old, and she immediately became a sensation. William Macready, who joined the Covent Garden company later in 1836, was already twice her age and a renowned performer with a particular gift for expressing spontaneous emotional impulses. In 1881 Faucit began publishing her memoirs in a series of "Letters on some of Shakespeare's Heroines," which were published in book form as On Some of Shakespeare's Female Characters *(1885). In her account of performing opposite Macready, he conveys explosive energy so powerfully that it almost undoes her composure. She also recounts her enactment of Hermione's awakening and sounds, in the process, as though her body has become completely objectified, a statue indeed.*

PAULINA NOW has no longer any reason for withholding from Leontes the secret of his wife's existence. She ingeniously prepares a mode of revealing it by presenting Hermione to him in the semblance of a statue, on which she tells him a rare artist has been for years at work, and which he has slightly coloured to give it a more lifelike look. It was necessary to lay emphasis on this colouring, as the living Hermione, however skilfully arranged, must of necessity be very different from an ordinary statue. My dress in acting this scene was arranged to carry out this effect. It was composed of soft white cashmere, the draperies and edges bordered with the royal purple enriched with a tracery in gold, and thus harmonising with the colouring of the lips, eyes, hair, &c., of the statue.

To see this peerless work of art Leontes comes to what Shakespeare describes as "a chapel in Paulina's house," accompanied by Polixenes, their children, Camillo, and other members of the Court. They have passed through a gallery of works of art, but, says Leontes—

> We saw not
> That which my daughter came to look upon,
> The statue of her mother.

PAULINA   As she liv'd peerless,

So her dead likeness, I do well believe,
Excels whatever yet you look'd upon,
Or hand of man hath done. Therefore, I keep it
Lonely, apart. But here it is. Prepare to see
The life as lively mock'd as ever
Still sleep mock'd death. Behold, and say, 'tis well.

At the back of the stage, when I acted in this play, was a dais which was led up to by a flight of six or eight steps, covered with rich cloth of the same material and crimson colour as the closed curtains. The curtains when gradually opened by Paulina disclosed, at a little distance behind them, the statue of Hermione, with a pedestal of marble by her side.

Here let me say, that I never approached this scene without much inward trepidation. You may imagine how difficult it must be to stand in one position, with a full light thrown upon you, without moving an eyelid for so long a time. I never thought to have the time measured, but I should say that it must be more than ten minutes—it seemed like *ten* times ten. I prepared myself by picturing what Hermione's feelings would be when she heard Leontes' voice, silent to her for so many years, and listened to the remorseful tender words addressed to what he believed to be her sculptured semblance. Her heart hitherto has been full only of her lost children. She has thought every other feeling dead, but she finds herself forgetting all but the tones of the voice, once so loved, now broken with the accents of repentance and woe-stricken desolation. To her own surprise her heart, so long empty, loveless, and cold, begins to throb again, as she listens to the outpourings of a devotion she had believed to be extinct. She would remember her own words to him, when the familiar loving tones were turned to anger and almost imprecation, "I never wished to see you sorry; now I trust I shall."

Of the sorrow she had thus wished for him she is now a witness, and it all but unnerves her. Paulina had, it seemed to me, besought Hermione to play the part of her own statue, in order that she might hear herself apostrophised, and be a silent witness of the remorse and unabated love of Leontes before her existence became known to him, and so be moved to that forgiveness which, without such proof, she might possibly be slow to yield. She is so moved; but for the sake of the loving friend to whom she has owed so much she must restrain herself, and carry through her appointed task.

But, even although I had fully thought out all this, it was impossible for me ever to hear unmoved what passes in this wonderful scene. My first Leontes was Mr Macready, and, as the scene was played by him, the difficulty of wearing an air of statuesque calm became almost insuperable. As I think over the scene now, his appearance, his action, the tones of his voice, the emotions of that time, come back. There was a dead awe-struck silence, when the curtains were gradually drawn aside by Paulina. She has to encourage Leontes to speak.

> I like your silence, it the more shows off
> Your wonder. But yet speak—first you, my liege,
> Comes it not something near?

Then with what wonderful tenderness of tone Mr Macready answered—

> Her natural posture!
> Chide me, dear stone; that I may say, indeed,
> Thou art Hermione; *or, rather, thou art she*
> *In thy not chiding; for she was as tender*
> *As infancy and grace.*

His eyes seemed to devour the figure before him, as the scene proceeded, and he said—

> Oh, thus she stood,
> Even with such life of majesty,—warm life,
> As now it coldly stands, when first I woo'd her!
> I am ashamed. Does not the stone rebuke me,
> For being more stone than it? Oh, royal piece,
> There's magic in thy majesty, which has
> My evils conjured to remembrance, and
> From thy admiring daughter took the spirits,
> Standing like stone with thee.
> PERDITA   And give me leave
> And do not say, 'tis superstition, that
> I kneel, and then implore her blessing. Lady,
> Dear queen, that ended when I but began,
> Give me that hand of yours to kiss.

But the time for this has not arrived, and Paulina prevents her, saying, the colour on the statue is not yet dry. Leontes stands so broken down with the bitter remembrances the statue calls up, that he is urged by Polixenes and Camillo to subdue his grief. Paulina, also deeply moved, exclaims—

> Indeed, my lord,
> If I had thought the sight of my poor image
> Would thus have wrought you,—for the stone is mine,—
> I'd not have show'd it—

and is about to close the curtain. Never can I forget the manner in
which Mr Macready here cried out, "Do not draw the curtain!" and,
afterwards, when Paulina says—

No longer shall you gaze on't, lest your fancy
May think anon it moves—

"*Let be, let be!*" in tones irritable, commanding, and impossible to resist.
"Would I were dead," he continues, "but that, me thinks already———"
Has he seen something that makes him think the statue lives? Mr
Macready indicated this, and hurriedly went on—

What was he that did make it? See, my lord,
Would you not deem it breathed? And that those veins
Did verily bear blood......
The fixture of her eye has motion in't,
As we are mocked with art.
PAULINA   I'll draw the curtain.
My lord's almost so far transported, that
He'll think anon it lives.
LEONTES   Oh sweet Paulina,
Make me to think so twenty years together;
No settled senses of the world can match
The pleasure of that madness. *Let it alone!*
PAULINA I am sorry, sir, I have thus far stirr'd you: but
I could afflict you further.
LEONTES   Do, Paulina,
For this affliction has a taste as sweet
As any cordial comfort.

His eyes have been so riveted upon the figure, that he sees, what the
others have not seen, that there is something about it beyond the reach
of art. He continues—

        Still, methinks,
There is an air comes from her: What fine chisel
Could ever yet cut breath? Let no man mock me,
For I will kiss her.

Paulina again interposes with the same suggestion as before, that "the
ruddiness on the lip being wet," "he would mar the work," adding,
"Shall I draw the curtain?"

LEONTES No, not these twenty years.
PERDITA   So long could I
Stand by a looker on.

Paulina sees that the strain upon Hermione and all present must not be prolonged; and she tells them—

> If you can behold it,
> I'll make the statue move indeed. . . .
> . . . . It is required
> You do awake your faith. Then, all stand still.
> . . . Music awake her, strike!   (*Music.*)
> 'Tis time, descend, be stone no more: approach!
> Strike all that look upon with marvel; come.

You may conceive the relief I felt, when the first strain of solemn music set me free to breathe! There was a pedestal by my side on which I leant. It was a slight help during the long strain upon the nerves and muscles, besides allowing me to stand in that "natural posture" which first strikes Leontes, and which therefore could not have been rigidly statuesque. By imperceptibly altering the poise of the body, the weight of it being on the forward foot, I could drop into the easiest position from which to move. The hand and arm still resting quietly on the pedestal materially helped me. Towards the close of the strain the head slowly turned, the "full eyes" moved, and at the last note rested on Leontes.

This movement, together with the expression of the face, transfigured as we may imagine it to have been by years of sorrow and devout meditation,—speechless, yet saying things unutterable,—always produced a startling, magnetic effect upon all—the audience upon the stage as well as in front of it. After the burst of amazement had hushed down, at a sign from Paulina the solemn sweet strain recommenced. The arm and hand were gently lifted from the pedestal; then, rhythmically following the music, the figure descended the steps that led up to the dais, and advancing slowly, paused at a short distance from Leontes. Oh, can I ever forget Mr Macready at this point! At first he stood speechless, as if turned to stone; his face with an awe-struck look upon it. Could this, the very counterpart of his queen, be a wondrous piece of mechanism? Could art so mock the life? He had seen her laid out as dead, the funeral obsequies performed over her, with her dear son beside her. Thus absorbed in wonder, he remained until Paulina said, "Nay, present your hand." Tremblingly he advanced, and touched gently the hand held out to him. Then, what a cry came with, "O, she's warm!" It is impossible to describe Mr Macready here. He was Leontes' very self! His passionate joy at finding Hermione really alive seemed beyond control. Now he was prostrate at her feet, then enfolding her in his arms. I had a slight veil or covering over my head and neck, supposed to make the statue look older. This fell off in an instant. The hair, which came unbound, and fell on my shoulders, was reverently kissed and caressed. The whole change was so sudden, so overwhelming, that I suppose I cried out hysterically, for he whispered to me, "Don't be frightened, my child! don't be frightened! Control yourself!" All this went on during a tumult of applause that sounded like a storm of hail. Oh, how glad I was to be released, when, as soon as a lull came, Paulina, advancing with Perdita, said, "Turn, good lady, our Perdita is found." A broken trembling voice, I am very sure, was mine, as I said—

> You gods, look down,
> And from your sacred vials pour your graces
> Upon my daughter's head! Tell me, mine own,
> Where hast thou been preserved? Where lived? How found
> Thy father's court? For thou shalt hear, that I,—
> Knowing by Paulina, that the oracle
> Gave hope thou wast in being,—have preserved
> Myself to see the issue.

It was such a comfort to me, as well as true to natural feeling, that Shakespeare gives Hermione no words to say to Leontes, but leaves her to assure him of her joy and forgiveness by look and manner only, as in his arms she feels the old life, so long suspended, come back to her again.

I was called upon to play Hermione very soon after my *début*. I was still very young, and by my years and looks most unfit even to appear as the mother of the young Mamillius. Why Mr Macready selected me for the task I could not imagine, and most gladly would I have declined it. But his will was law. Any remonstrance or objection was met by reasons and arguments so broad and strong,—you were so earnestly reminded of your duty to sacrifice yourself to the general good, and the furtherance of the effort he was making to regenerate the drama,—that there was nothing left but to give way. All you could urge seemed so small, so merely personal. Therefore play Hermione I must, even as I had not long after to play Constance of Bretagne, a still severer trial and much greater strain upon my young shoulders. Hermione was a character that had not then come within the circle of my favourite Shakespearian heroines. It was, therefore, quite new to me. Mrs Warner had been for years the recognised Hermione of the London stage. On this occasion she was cast for Paulina, a character for which nature had eminently fitted her by a stately figure, fine voice, and firm, earnest manner. How admirably she acted Emilia in *Othello* I must ever remember, especially the way she turned on Othello in the last scene, in which Mr Macready was also very grand.

On the audience, who could see their looks and gestures, the impression they made must have been very great indeed. I, as the smothered Desdemona, could hear only.

My first appearance as Hermione is indelibly imprinted on my memory by the acting of Mr Macready as I have described it in the statue scene. Mrs Warner had rather jokingly told me, at one of the rehearsals, to be *prepared* for something extraordinary in his manner, when Hermione returned to life. But prepared I was not, and could not be, for such a display of uncontrollable rapture. I have tried to give some idea of it; but no words of mine could do it justice. It was the finest burst of passionate speechless emotion I ever saw, or could have conceived. My feelings being already severely strained, I naturally lost something of my self-command, and as Perdita and Florizel knelt at my feet I looked, as the gifted Sarah Adams[1] afterwards told me, "like Niobe, all tears." Of course, I behaved better on the repetition of the play, as I knew what I had to expect and was somewhat prepared for it; but the intensity of Mr Macready's passion was so real, that I never could help being moved by it, and feeling much exhausted afterwards.

The Winter's Tale makes heavy demands upon the resources of a theatre both in actors and *mise en scène.* It was therefore only in such cities as Dublin, Glasgow, and Edinburgh that I was able to have it acted. But in all these cities, even with such inadequate resources as they supplied, the play used to produce a profound impression. The sympathies of my audience for the suffering Hermione were reflected back upon me so warmly as to make me feel that they entered into my conception of her beautiful nature, such as I have here endeavoured to present it. There, as in London, the statue scene always produced a remarkable effect. This I could feel in the intense hush, as though every one present "held his breath for the time." In Edinburgh, upon one occasion, I have been told by a friend who was present that, as I descended from the pedestal and advanced towards Leontes, the audience simultaneously rose from their seats, as if drawn out of them by surprise and reverential awe at the presence of one who bore more of heaven than of earth about her. I can only account for this by supposing that the soul of Hermione had for the time entered into mine, and "so divinely wrought, that one might almost say," with the old poet, my "body thought." Of course I did not observe this movement of the audience, for my imagination was too full of what I felt was then in Hermione's heart, to leave me eyes for any but Leontes. You

1. This sweet accomplished lady wrote many poems and hymns. Her drama in blank verse, founded on the story of "Vivia Perpetua," one of the first Christian martyrs, was greatly admired in a wide literary circle. Her beautiful hymn "Nearer, my God, to Thee," we all know, and are moved by, when sung in our churches as it often is.

may judge of the pleasure it was to play to audiences of this kind. As "there is a pleasure in poetic pains, which only poets know," so there is a pleasure in the actor's pains, which only actors know, who have to deal with the "high actions and high passions" of which Milton speaks. Unless they know these pains, and feel a joy in knowing them, their vocation can never rise to the level of an art.

I fear, my dear Lord Tennyson, I have tried your patience with this long letter. But in this fine play I have had to write of three exquisite types of womanhood—the mother, the maiden, and the friend. In what other play or story do we find three such women? In lingering over their excellences I may have lost account of time and thus wearied you. If I have, pray forgive me this once, and believe me to be ever, with deep admiration and gratitude, very sincerely yours,

HELENA FAUCIT MARTIN.

1st November 1890,
BRYNTYSILIO, LLANGOLLEN.

From *On Some of Shakespeare's Female Characters.* 7th Edition. Edinburgh and London: William Blackwood and Sons, 1904.

"AUTOLYCUS"

Louis MacNeice

In "Autolycus" by Louis MacNeice (1907–1963) two figures especially claim our attention: the Master, who is Shakespeare, and that rogue, who is Autolycus. Or so it seems, although these identities are hardly stable. They merge and overlap in a variety of ways that yield a portrait of the artist as an older man, the author of Shakespeare's late romances. He is a composite of low cunning and romantic fancy. He does not merely rest upon the laurels of achieved mastery. While he enjoys the reassurance that such mastery offers, he confidently writes as he pleases. Is this a satisfying idea of our author and our sense of his accomplishment by the end of his career? Does it illuminate our experience of The Winter's Tale *in ways that might be overlooked without the resources of MacNeice's lyric art?*

In his last phase when hardly bothering
 To be a dramatist, the Master turned away
 From his taut plots and complex characters
To tapestried romances, conjuring
With rainbow names and handfuls of sea-spray
And from them turned out happy Ever-afters.

Eclectic always, now extravagant,
Sighting his matter through a timeless prism
He ranged his classical bric-à-brac in grottos
Where knights of Ancient Greece had Latin mottoes
And fishermen their flapjacks—none should want
Colour for lack of an anachronism.

A gay world certainly though pocked and scored
With childish horrors and a fresh world though
Its mainsprings were old gags—babies exposed,
Identities confused and queens to be restored;
But when the cracker bursts it proves as you supposed—
Trinket and moral tumble out just so.

Such innocence—In his own words it was
Like an old tale, only that where time leaps
Between acts three and four there was something born

Which made the stock-type virgin dance like corn
In a wind that having known foul marshes, barren steeps,
Felt therefore kindly towards Marinas, Perditas . . .

Thus crystal learned to talk. But Shakespeare balanced it
With what we knew already, gabbing earth
Hot from Eastcheap—Watch your pockets when
That rogue comes round the corner, he can slit
Purse-strings as quickly as his maker's pen
Will try your heartstrings in the name of mirth.

O master pedlar with your confidence tricks,
Brooches, pomanders, broadsheets and what-have-you,
Who hawk such entertainment but rook your client
And leave him brooding, why should we forgive you
Did we not know that, though more self-reliant
Than we, you too were born and grew up in a fix?

From *The Collected Poems of Louis MacNeice*. Ed. E. R. Dodds. London: Faber and Faber Ltd., 1966. Used by permission of David Higham Associated Limited.

"INSTRUCTIONS TO AN ACTOR"

Edwin Morgam

"Instructions to an Actor," a dramatic monologue by Edwin Morgan (1920-2010), puts us in the place of a boy actor in 1611. He is listening to directions about how to perform that exceptional part in the final scene of The Winter's Tale: *Hermione's catatonic pose in complete silence for eighty lines. It reminds us not only of the laws that made it illegal for girls and women to perform on the public stage in England during Shakespeare's lifetime but also of the extraordinary demands that this particular scene places upon any performer of this role. Compare this poem's fictional account of a Jacobean actor facing that challenging assignment with Helena Faucit's autobiographical account of her own performance of this part in* On Some of Shakespeare's Female Characters.

Now, boy, remember this is the great scene.
You'll stand on a pedestal behind a curtain,
the curtain will be drawn, and you don't move
for eighty lines; don't move, don't speak, don't breathe.
I'll stun them all out there, I'll scare them,
make them weep, but it depends on you.
I warn you eighty lines is a long time,
but you don't breathe, you're dead,
you're a dead queen, a statue,
you're dead as stone, new-carved,
new-painted and the paint not dry
—we'll get some red to keep your lip shining —
and you're a mature woman, you've got dignity,
some beauty still in middle-age, and
you're kind and true, but you're dead,
your husband thinks you're dead,
the audience thinks you're dead,
and you don't breathe, boy, I say
you don't even blink for eighty lines,
if you blink you're out!
Fix your eye on something and keep watching it.
Practise when you get home. It can be done.

And you move at last—music's the cue.
When you hear a mysterious solemn jangle
of instruments, make yourself ready.
Five lines more, you can lift a hand.
It may tingle a bit, but lift it—
slow, slow—
O this is where I hit them
right between the eyes, I've got them now—
I'm making the dead walk—
you move a foot, slow, steady, down,
you guard your balance in case you're stiff,
you move, you step down, down from the pedestal,
control your skirt with one hand, the other hand
you now hold out—
O this will melt their hearts if nothing does—
to your husband who wronged you long ago
and hesitates in amazement
to believe you are alive.
Finally he embraces you, and there's nothing
I can give you to say, boy,
but you must show that you have forgiven him.
Forgiveness, that's the thing. It's like a second life.
I know you can do it.—Right, then. Shall we try?

From *Collected Poems*. Manchester, UK: Carcanet Press. 1996. Used by permission.

"Letter to Genetically Engineered Superhumans"

Fred Dings

In "Letter to Genetically Engineered Superhumans" Fred Dings (1957-) explores the pathology of perfectionism, when the worthy desire to improve our selves and circumstances becomes excessive and disables our capacity for acceptance and appreciation. We begin not only to "pay a great deal too dear for what's given freely" (1.1.17-8) but also to overlook the ways that everydayness and transcendence, like Bohemia and Sicilia, can nourish and sustain one another. In this regard study the debate between Polixenes and Perdita about grafting (4.4.79–103). With its consideration of our insatiable urge to be better than well and more than we can (humanely) be, does this contemporary poem illuminate such antinomies as art and nature, court and country, gentlemen born and country bumpkins central to The Winter's Tale?

You are the children of our fantasies of form,
    our wish to carve a larger cave of light,
    our dream to perfect the ladder of genes and climb

its rungs to the height of human possibility,
to a stellar efflorescence beyond all injury
and disease, with minds as bright as newborn suns

and bodies which leave our breathless mirrors stunned.
Forgive us if we failed to imagine your loneliness
in the midst of all that ordinary excellence,

if we failed to understand how much harder
it would be to build the bridge of love
between such splendid selves, to find the path

of humility among the labyrinth of your abilities,
to be refreshed without forgetfulness,
and weave community without the threads of need.

Forgive us if you must reinvent our flaws
because we failed to guess the simple fact
that the best lives must be less than perfect.

From *Eulogy for a Private Man*. Evanston, IL: Northwestern University Press, 1999.
Used by permission.

"THE CRITICISM OF SHAKESPEARE'S LATE PLAYS"

F. R. Leavis

F. R. Leavis (1895-1978) defends The Winter's Tale *as "a great work of art," which merits that tribute specifically because, unlike* Cymbeline, *it is "an organic whole." It is organized by "a commanding significance, which penetrates the whole, informing and ordering everything…from a deep center." In so doing Leavis conceives of himself as arriving at a correct judgment by applying appropriate criteria, an apt combination that his precursors had failed to achieve in their criticism of the play, which he sees himself as rescuing from disregard due to misunderstanding. Leavis's influence is vast, due in good part to the impact he had on the English National Curriculum. He advocated the positive influence of literary study on students' moral, psychological and emotional growth. Thus, direct citation of lines from this essay in Simon Gray's play about a degenerate professor,* Butley, *resound with irony and the sort of despair that haunted campuses after the student unrest during the tumultuous late 60s.*

A CAVEAT

I have before me two essays on *Cymbeline*. In the later[1] of them Fr. A. A. Stephenson both criticizes the account of the play offered by F. C. Tinkler in the earlier,[2] and offers a positive account of his own. With the criticisms I find myself pretty much in agreement; but I also find myself as unconvinced by the new interpretation as by Tinkler's—or any other that I have read. Fr. Stephenson, judging that Tinkler's attempt to explain the play in terms of 'critical irony' and 'savage farce' doesn't cover the admitted data, himself observes, and argues from, what he takes to be a significant recurrence of 'valuation-imagery'. But while developing his argument he at the same time—and this is the curious fact that seems to me to deserve attention—makes a firm note of another set of characteristics, and draws an explicit conclusion:

1. *Scrutiny*, Vol. X, No. 4.   2. *Ibid.*, Vol. VII, No. 1.

the inequalities, the incongruities, the discontinuity, the sense of different planes, the only spasmodic and flickering life in *Cymbeline*. It must, I think, be recognized that *Cymbeline* is not an 'organic whole', that it is not informed and quickened by an idea-emotion in all its parts.

The stress laid on these characteristics of the play seems to me much more indisputably justified than that laid on the valuation-imagery. So much so, in fact, that the question arises: Why didn't both Fr. Stephenson and Tinkler (whose argument also derives from observation of these characteristics) rest in the judgment that the play 'is not an "organic whole", that it is not informed and quickened by an idea-emotion in all its parts'? Why must they set out to show that it is, nevertheless, to be paradoxically explained in terms of a pressure of 'significance'—significance, according to Fr. Stephenson, of a kind that cannot be conveyed?

That two such intelligent critics, bent on conclusions so different, should countenance one another in this kind of proceeding suggests some reflections on the difficulties and temptations of Shakespeare criticism—and especially of criticism of the late plays—at the present time. We have left Bradley fairly behind. We know that poetic drama is something more than drama in verse, and that consideration of the drama cannot be separated from consideration of the poetry. We are aware of subtle varieties of possibility under the head of convention, and we know we must keep a vigilant eye open for the development of theme by imagery and symbolism, and for the bearing of all these on the way we are to take character, action and plot. Shakespeare's methods are so subtle, flexible and varied that we must be on our guard against approaching any play with inappropriate preconceptions as to what we have in front of us. By assuming that the organization is of a given kind we may incapacitate ourselves for seeing what it actually is, and so miss, or misread, the significance. What a following-through of F. C. Tinkler's and Fr. Stephenson's account will, I think, bring home to most readers is that we may err by insisting on finding a 'significance' that we assume to be necessarily there.

I have put the portentous word in inverted commas in this last use of it, in order not to suggest a severity of judgment that is not intended. The play contains a great variety of life and interest, and if we talk of 'inequalities' and 'incongruities' it should not be to suggest inanity or nullity: out of the interplay of contrasting themes and modes we have an effect as (to fall back on the usefully corrective analogy) of an odd and distinctive music. But the organization is not a matter of a strict and delicate subservience to a commanding significance, which penetrates the whole, informing and ordering everything—imagery, rhythm, symbolism, character, episode, plot—from a deep centre: *Cymbeline* is not a great work of art of the order of *The Winter's Tale*.

The Winter's Tale presents itself as the comparison with which to make the point, in that it belongs with *Cymbeline* to the late group of plays—plays that clearly have important affinities, though my purpose here is to insist on the differences. In academic tradition *The Winter's Tale* is one of the 'romantic' plays; the adjective implying, among other things, a certain fairy-tale licence of spirit, theme and development—an indulgence, in relation to reality, of some of the less responsible promptings of imagination and fancy. Thus we have the sudden, unheralded storm of jealousy in Leontes, the part played by the oracle, the casting-out and preservation of the babe, the sixteen-year gap in the action, the pastoral scene (regarded as a pretty piece of poetical by-play) and, finally, the return to life after sixteen years' latency of Galatea- Hermione, in the reconciliation-tableau. But all this has in the concrete fulness of Shakespeare's poetry an utterly different effect from what is suggested by the enumeration. *The Winter's Tale*, as D. A. Traversi shows so well in his *Approach to Shakespeare*, is a supreme instance of Shakespeare's poetic complexity— of the impossibility, if one is to speak with any relevance to the play, of considering character, episode, theme, and plot in abstraction from the local effects, so inexhaustibly subtle in their inter-play, of the poetry, and from the larger symbolic effects to which these give life.

Properly taken, the play is not romantically licentious, or loose in organization, or indulgent in a fairy-tale way to human fondness. What looked like romantic fairy-tale characteristics turn out to be the conditions of a profundity and generality of theme. If we approach expecting every Shakespearean drama to be of the same kind as *Othello*, we criticize Leontes' frenzy of jealousy as disconcertingly sudden and unprepared. But if our preconceptions don't prevent our being adverted by imagery, rhythm, and the developing hints of symbolism—by the subtle devices of the poetry and the very absence of 'psychology'—we quickly see that what we have in front of us is nothing in the nature of a novel dramatically transcribed. The relations between character, speech and the main themes of the drama are not such as to invite a psychologizing approach; the treatment of life is too generalizing (we may say, if we hasten to add 'and intensifying'); so large a part of the function of the words spoken by the characters is so plainly something other than to 'create' the speakers, or to advance an action that can profitably be considered in terms of the interacting of individuals. The detail of Shakespeare's processes this is not the place for discussing; anyone who wants hints for the analysis will find all that can be asked in D. A. Traversi's book. It is enough here to remind the reader of the way in which the personal drama is made to move upon a complexity of larger rhythms—birth, maturity, death, birth ('Thou mettest with things dying, I with things new-born'); Spring, Summer, Autumn . . .

> Sir, the year growing ancient.
> Not yet on summer's death, nor on the birth
> Of trembling winter . . .

—so that the pastoral scene is something very much other than a charming superfluity. The power and subtlety of the organization— and this is a striking instance of Shakespeare's ability to transmute for serious ends what might have seemed irremediably romantic effects— are equal to absorbing into the profoundly symbolic significance of the whole even the *coup de théâtre* with which Paulina justifies her sixteen years of double-living and funereal exhortation.

As Fr. Stephenson points out, there is no such organization in *Cymbeline*. The romantic theme remains merely romantic. The reunions, resurrections and reconciliations of the close belong to the order of imagination in which 'they all lived happily ever after'. Cloten and the Queen are the wicked characters, stepmother and son, of the fairy-tale: they don't strike us as the expression of an adult intuition of evil. Posthumus's jealousy, on the other hand (if I may supplement Fr. Stephenson's observation: 'the "evil" characters, in particular, do not receive full imaginative realization'), is real enough in its nastiness, but has no significance in relation to any radical theme, or total effect, of the play. And here there is opportunity for a brief aside in illustration of the variety of Shakespeare's dramatic modes. Jealousy is a theme common to *The Winters Tale*, *Othello* and *Cymbeline*. In *The Winter's Tale* there is no psychological interest; we don't ask (so long as we are concerning ourselves with Shakespeare): What elements in Leontes' make-up, working in what way, explain this storm? The question is irrelevant to the mode of the play. *Othello*, on the other hand, it would not be misleading to describe as a character-study. The explosive elements have been generated between the very specifically characterized Othello and his situation, and Iago merely touches them off. Posthumus's case actually answers to the conventional account of Othello's: the noble hero, by nature far from jealous, is worked on and betrayed by devilish Italian cunning—Iachimo is, quite simply, the efficient cause that Iago, in the sentimentalized misreading of *Othello*, is seen as being. Posthumus suffers remorse for his murderous revulsion, but we are not to consider him degraded by his jealousy, or seriously blamable. Simply, he is a victim. He falls in with a villain who, out of pure malice, deceives him about Imogen, and, after strange vicissitudes, fairy-tale fortune brings the lovers together again to enjoy a life of hapiness. Shakespeare, that is, has taken over a romantic convention and has done little to give it anything other than a romantic significance.[1]

Why then should two such intelligent critics as those in question not settle down in the obvious judgment that the play challenges? I have already suggested that the answer should be sought in terms of a reaction against what may be called the Bradley-Archer[2] approach to Shakespeare. In the case of *Cymbeline* the assumption that a profound intended significance must be discovered in explanation of the peculiarities of the play is fostered by the presence of varied and impressive evidence of the Shakespearean genius.

Strength could be adduced in a wealth of illustration. I myself have long carried mental note of a number of passages from *Cymbeline* that seemed to me memorable instances of Shakespeare's imagery and versification. Two in particular I will mention. One is Posthumus's description of the battle [5. 3, lines 14 to 51]. It is a remarkable piece of vigorous dramatic felicity. The precisely right tone, a blend of breathless excitement, the professional soldier's dryness, and contempt (towards the Lord addressed), is perfectly got. There are some fine examples of Shakespearean compression and ellipsis; and here, surely, is strength in imagery:

> and now our cowards,
> Like fragments in hard voyages, became
> The life of the need: having found the back-door open
> Of the unguarded hearts, heavens, how they wound!

In 'like fragments in hard voyages' and the 'back-door' we have, in imagery, the business-like and intense matter-of-factness, at once contemptuous and, in its ironical dryness, expressive both of professional habit and of controlled excitement, that gives the speech its highly specific and dramatically appropriate tone. The other passage is Posthumus's prison speech in the next scene [5, 4, 3-29], so different in tone and movement:

> Most welcome, bondage! for thou art a way,
> I think, to liberty: yet am I better
> Than one that's sick of the gout; since he had rather

---

1. In *Pericles* he took over a romantic play, and the three acts that are clearly his are remarkable for the potency of the transmuting 'significance'. **2.** See *The Old Drama and the New* by William Archer. T. S. Eliot comments interestingly on the book in the essay called 'Four Elizabethan Dramatists' (*Selected Essays*).

Groan so in perpetuity than be cured
By the sure physician, death, who is the key
To unbar these locks.

This doesn't belong to 'romantic comedy', nor does the dialogue with the gaoler at the end of the scene. And here, and in the many vigorously realized passages, we have the excuse for the attempt, in spite of 'the inequalities, the incongruities, the discontinuity, the sense of different planes', to vindicate the play (for that, paradoxically, is Fr. Stephenson's aim as well as Tinkler's) in terms of a profound significance. But surely there should be no difficulty in recognizing that, wrestling with a job undertaken in the course of his exigent profession, Shakespeare might, while failing to find in his material a unifying significance such as might organize it into a profound work of art, still show from place to place, when prompted and incited congenially, his characteristic realizing genius?

Cymbeline, then, is not like *The Winter's Tale* a masterpiece. *The Tempest* is by more general agreement a masterpiece than *The Winter's Tale*, but it is a very different kind of thing (to complete briefly the hint of comparison I threw out above). Lytton Strachey in his essay on 'Shakespeare's Final Period' (see *Books and Characters*), gives us an opening: 'There can be no doubt that the peculiar characteristics which distinguish *Cymbeline* and *The Winter's Tale* from the dramas of Shakespeare's prime are present here in still greater degree. In *The Tempest*, unreality has reached its apotheosis.' Lytton Strachey's 'unreality', strongly derogatory in intention, has to be understood, of course, in relation to the Bradley-Archer assumptions of his approach. Actually, it seems to me that *The Tempest* differs from *The Winter's Tale* in being much closer to the 'reality' we commonly expect of the novelist. The 'unreality', instead of penetrating and transmuting everything as in *The Winter's Tale*, is in *The Tempest* confined to Prospero's imagery and its agents. Prospero himself, the Neapolitan and Milanese nobility and gentry, Stephano and Trinculo, the ship's crew—all these belong as much to the 'reality' of the realistic novelist as the play of *Othello* does. Prospero manages the wreck, lands the parties and directs their footsteps about the island to the final convergence, but they strike us, in their behaviour and conversation, as people of the ordinary everyday world. The courtiers are Elizabethan quality, and Gonzalo's attempt to distract the king and raise the tone of the conversation with a piece of advanced thought from Montaigne is all in keeping. Even Caliban (though sired by the devil on a witch) leads the modern commentator, quite appropriately, to discuss Shakespeare's interest in the world of new discovery and in the impact of civilization on the native.

The 'unreality' functions in Ariel and in the power (as it were a daydream actualized) that enables Prospero to stage the scene of repentance and restitution. But the nature of this power as a licence of imagination stands proclaimed in the essential symbolism of the play; and not only does Prospero finally renounce magic, break his staff and drown his book, but the daydream has never been allowed to falsify human and moral realities. That Alonso should, without the assistance of magic, suffer pangs of conscience is not in the least incredible; on the other hand, we note that the sinister pair, Sebastian and Antonio, remain what they were. They may be fairly set over against Ferdinand and Miranda, and they represent a potent element in that world to which the lovers are returning, and in which, unprotected by magic, they are to spend their lives.

O brave new world,
That has such people in't!

—that is both unironical and ironical. Shakespeare's power to present acceptably and movingly the unironical vision (for us given in Miranda and Ferdinand) goes with his power to contemplate the irony at the same time.

Rightly, then, is *The Tempest* accounted a masterpiece; but I am not sure that it deserves the relative valuation it commonly enjoys. The judgment that *The Winter's Tale* is a masterpiece would not, I think, in general be as readily concurred in; and it is true that *The Tempest* has nothing in it to trouble in the same way the reader who finds difficulty in arriving at an unqualified acceptance of the statue business as part of a total unromantic response. But the perfection (or something like it) of *The Tempest* is achieved within limits much narrower than those of *The Winter's Tale*; and the achievement by which, in *The Tempest*, the time-gap of *The Winter's Tale* is eliminated ought not to be allowed to count improperly in the comparative valuation. With the absence of the time-gap goes also an absence of that depth and richness of significance given, in *The Winter's Tale*, by the concrete presence of time in its rhythmic processes, and by the association of human growth, decay and rebirth with the vital rhythms of nature at large. The range, the depth, the effect that I have described as both generalizing and intensifying, for which *The Winter's Tale* is remarkable, are missing in *The Tempest*. Not that while reading *The Tempest* we are at all inclined to judge that this inspired poetry and this consummate art reveal any falling-off in the poet's creative vigour; yet we may perhaps associate the mood expressed in Prospero's farewell to *his* art and in the 'insubstantial pageant' speech (the mood in which Shakespeare can in the symbolic working of the drama itself so consciously separate his art from the life it arranges and presents—life that is 'such stuff as dreams are made on')—perhaps we may associate this mood with an absence of that effect as of the sap rising from the root which *The Winter's Tale* gives us. No doubt it might as truly be said of Florizel and Perdita as it has been of Ferdinand and Miranda, that they are lovers seen by one who is himself beyond the age of love, but Florizel and Perdita are not merely two individual lovers; they are organic elements in the poetry and symbolism of the pastoral scene, and the pastoral scene is an organic part of the whole play.

From *The Common Pursuit*. New York: George W. Stewart, 1952. Used by permission of the author.

The Triumph of Time in *The Winter's Tale*

Inga-Stina Ewbank

Inga-Stina Ewbank (1932–2004) writes of "the triumph of time" in The Winter's Tale. *She takes this phrase as her essay's title from the subtitle of Shakespeare's main source,* Pandosto, *a prose romance that also bears, as its epigraph, this Latin adage:* Temporis filia veritas, *or* Truth is the daughter of Time. *It is a commonplace that Erasmus glosses in his* Adages *under the variant form:* Tempus omnia revelat, *or* Time reveals all things. *Amid the host of classical authors in whom he discovers complementary sentiments, Erasmus also cites Matt. 10:26, a sign that he reads Christian culture in harmony with classical precedents, both of which form a continuous tradition, as they do in* The Winter's Tale. *Ewbank perceives time in the play not only as a voracious exterminator but also as a beneficent revealer of meaning, though Leontes is so out of sync that such understanding cannot penetrate his perverse defiance. The figure of Time was familiar to Shakespeare's first audiences, and Ewbank helpfully relates such elements in* The Winter's Tale *to elaborate entertainments like the masque and the Lord Mayor's show and the royal entry that were a part of London culture and Stuart pageantry during the rule of James I.*

IT IS OFTEN assumed that, while Shakespeare's middle plays and many of his sonnets show a keen awareness of, and even obsession with, the power of time over man, his final plays are not concerned with the theme of time and change. In these plays we are, according to one critic, in 'a fairyland of unrealities' in which 'injurious time plays no controlling part';[1] and another critic sees Shakespeare as abandoning time-thinking in order to devote himself to 'myths of immortality'.[2] Yet *The Tempest*, for all that it celebrates values which are not subject to time, also balances these against time in its 'injurious' capacity, time which triumphs over

> The cloud-capped towers, the gorgeous palaces,
> The solemn temples, the great globe itself,
> Yea, all which it inherit.[3]

Prospero's island may be a 'fairyland of unrealities', but it is also the land of Petrarch's *Trionfi*:

Our Tryumphs shal passe our pompes shal decay
Our lordshyppes our kyngdomes shall all awaye
And al thynge also that we accompt mortall
Tyme at the length shal clene deface it al.[4]

And when Shakespeare was looking around for material for the play which was to become *The Winter's Tale*, he chose a story with the sub-title 'The Triumph of Time' and developed it in a fashion which suggests a deepening and enrichment, rather than abandonment, of time-thinking.

The Time which triumphs on the title-page of Greene's *Pandosto* is not the dreaded *tempus edax* but the beneficent Revealer who shows that 'although by the means of sinister fortune Truth may be concealed, yet by Time in spight of fortune it is most manifestly revealed'.[5] The *Pandosto* story itself fails to work out its motto—*Temporis filia veritas*—for it puts all the emphasis on Fortune, with her wheel, as the ruling agent of human affairs. Shakespeare, on the other hand, makes the Triumph of Time into a controlling theme of his tale; and in doing so he transforms what the conventional motto suggests—a simple victory of Time, the Father of Truth—into a dramatic exploration of the manifold meanings of Time.

The chief evidence of Shakespeare's time-thinking in his middle period lies in the time allusions and time imagery of the plays and sonnets. The chief evidence for assuming a lack of concern with time in the last plays has been, it would seem, their almost total lack of time imagery. But, as I hope to show, while in *The Winter's Tale* time has largely disappeared from the verbal imagery, it is all the more intensely present as a controlling and shaping figure behind the dramatic structure and technique. It is true that certain features of the dramatic technique in *The Winter's Tale* are aimed at achieving an effect of timelessness: S. L. Bethell has shown how Shakespeare uses deliberate anachronisms to create the never-never world of a winter's tale.[6] It would be wrong, however, to conclude that the absence of the objective, social time of history which characterizes the setting of the tale, means that in the human issues of the play Shakespeare is unaware of, or uninterested in, man's subjection to time in its various aspects, injurious as well as benevolent.

The most obvious indication of Shakespeare's concern with time is the overall structure of the play. Not only does the action span a long period, so as—and this never happens in the tragedies—to give working-space to time, both as Revealer and as Destroyer; but, through the arrangement of the play into two halves separated by the 'wide gap' of sixteen years, past and present can be emphatically juxtaposed.[7] The structure thus becomes a vehicle for the exploration of the meanings of time—in the sense of what time does to man. The intricacy and complexity of this exploration is revealed, in parts of the play, by subordinated structural features, and it is to these we must first turn if we are to see the full relevance of the larger structure.

The scene of exposition (1.1) is a dialogue between Camillo and Archidamus, which proceeds via a series of references to time seen as natural growth; it places the play in a perspective of naturally ripening time, opening backwards as well as forwards. Camillo describes the span of the relations between the Kings of Sicilia and of Bohemia: from an indicative past—'They were trained together in their childhoods'—to a present consequent upon that past—'there rooted betwixt them then such an affection, which cannot choose but branch now'—and on to a desired (but soon to be threatened) future—'The heavens continue their loves'! Similarly he introduces the whole span of human life by way of talking about the little Prince Mamillius: 'they that went on crutches ere he was born desire yet their life to see him a man'; and this subject is expanded to provide, as the scene closes, an ironically foreboding note: 'If the king had no son, they would desire to live on crutches till he had one'. Linking up with this introduction, the beginning of 1.2 is a conversation which modulates from one subject to another, with time as the shared note. It opens with the most immediate time-concern, conditioned by the plot: how long Polixenes has stayed already and how much longer, if at all, he may be prevailed upon to stay. Even this persuasion (for which there is no source in *Pandosto*) has about it a peculiar urgency, as if love could be measured in time-units:

> When at Bohemia
> You take my lord, I'll give him my commission
> To let him there a month behind the gest
> Prefix'd for's parting: yet, good deed, Leontes
> I love thee not a jar o 'the clock behind
> What lady-she her lord.

Hermione's fatal victory leads naturally on to remembrances of things past, first of the two Kings' blissful childhood as 'twinn'd lambs'. Here Shakespeare deliberately juxtaposes time's destruction with things as they were: 'We were', says Polixenes,

> Two lads that thought there was no more behind
> But such a day to-morrow as to-day,
> And to be boy eternal.

Polixenes' speeches create a strong sense of time as destructive, as equalling the passing of innocence, making nonsense of the ideals of youth. The transition from this stage of the scene to the next is delicately made via the courtly banter of Polixenes and Hermione. The next remembrance is of the long-seeming courtship of Leontes and Hermione, when finally, so he tells her, after 'three crabbed months', 'then didst thou utter "I am yours forever"'. It is, I think, noteworthy that this recollection of Hermione's forward-looking statement is what triggers off Leontes' first outburst of jealousy. The 'forever' (which the rest of the play is going to prove true[8]), spoken in innocent remembrance, suddenly becomes tormentingly ironical to Leontes. From his next words, 'Too hot, too hot', all is feverish haste, in word and deed.

For the action centering on Leontes, from this moment until the end of Act 3, is not only a vivid realization of Polixenes' words about the loss of innocence, but it is also a dramatization of the failure to trust Time the Revealer. If Leontes had given himself time to observe the behaviour of Hermione and Polixenes and to listen to his advisers, he would have discovered that his suspicions were rootless. Instead he goes, as it were, against time and is therefore blind to truth; for time, when not allowed to ripen, can only *make*, not *unfold*, error. From now on, speech-patterns, as well as the structure of individual scenes and their combination, are so devised as to bring out the unnatural haste of Leontes' thoughts and acts; and this frenzied hurry is all the more marked for being set against the references to naturally progressing time with which the play opened. The telescoped syntax and half-finished sentences of Leontes' speeches image the frenzy within. His heated imagination fabricates evidence the very nature of which adds to the sense of rush:

> Is whispering nothing?
> Is leaning cheek to cheek? is meeting noses?
> Kissing with inside lip? stopping the career
> Of laughter with a sigh?—a note infallible
> Of breaking honesty—horsing foot on foot?
> Skulking in corners? *wishing clocks more swift?*
> *Hours, minutes? noon, midnight?*

and it repeatedly draws time itself into its scope:

> Were my wife's liver
> Infected as her life, she would not live
> The running of one glass.

The arrangement of events is partly responsible for the hectic effect of these scenes. Shakespeare here greatly condenses the sequence in the source story. For example, in *Pandosto*, Egistus (Polixenes), having been told of Pandosto's (Leontes') intention to poison him, waits six days for favourable winds before he sets sail; whereas in *The Winter's Tale* the events up to the end of Act 1, when Camillo urges Polixenes 'please your highness To take the urgent hour', would seem to happen in as little time as it takes to act them. Camillo's function, in relation to Leontes, is to try to brake the speed:

> Good my lord, be cured
> Of this diseased opinion, and *betimes*;
> For tis most dangerous;

and indeed, when brought to insight at the end of Act 3, Leontes looks back and sees Camillo as the voice of time whose 'good mind . . . *tardied* My *swift* command'. But he is not listened to in time; and in a sense he is himself guilty of untimeliness in urging Polixenes to leave at once. Polixenes' hasty departure cannot but tie the knot of error more firmly by confirming Leontes' 'true opinion' (2.1.37).

In *Pandosto* Bellaria finds herself quick with child only after Egistus is gone, and she is kept in prison, awaiting trial, till after the child is born. In *The Winter's Tale* Hermione's lying-in is imminent at the outset of the play (Polixenes has been in Sicilia for 'nine changes of the watery star'), and it is in keeping with the onrush of time in these Acts that she is '*something before her time* deliver'd'. Although at least twenty-three days must have passed during the course of Acts 2 and 3, the structure of events is shaped so as to give the impression that Leontes has not once stopped to think—'nor night nor day no rest'. The child is no sooner born than it is doomed to suffer (probable) death. Hermione is rushed into court,

> hurried
> Here to this place, i'the open air, before
> I have got strength of limit.

The verdict of the Oracle is no sooner announced than flouted: 'There is no truth at all i'the oracle: The sessions shall proceed: this is mere falsehood'. Shortly before, Leontes had hailed the early return of the messengers:

> Twenty three days
> They have been absent; tis good speed; foretells
> The great Apollo suddenly will have
> The truth of this appear.

Indeed Apollo has been 'sudden' in revealing the truth, but Leontes is even more sudden in rejecting it, thereby demonstrating to the full his perversion of truth and justice.

In terms of Elizabethan thought the injustice done to Hermione is linked up with the time theme more closely than a modern reader or audience may realize. Her arraignment can be seen as the epitome of Leontes' rejection of Time, the Father of Truth, for Justice, like her sister virtue Truth, was conceived of as closely associated with Time.[9] Rosalind points to the connection in her parting words to Orlando after the mock-wooing: 'Time is the old Justice that examines all . . . offenders, and let Time try' (*As You Like It*, 4.2.203). Leontes does not let Time try, despite Antigonus's warning: 'Be certain what you do, sir, lest your justice Prove violence' (2.2.127). And throughout the court scene (3.2) the word 'justice' rings ironically, coming from Leontes:

> Let us be clear'd
> Of being tyrannous, since we so openly
> Proceed in justice, which shall have due course,
> Even to the guilt or the purgation.

Significantly, no one else in this scene uses the word. Hermione never appeals to Leontes 'justice', for all along is stressed her awareness that she and Leontes—now that time is out of joint—do not use words in the same sense: 'You speak a language that I understand not: My life stands in the level of your dreams'.

It is, I think, important to notice that it is the first actual death to happen in the play which stops the mad onrush. Previously death has been spoken of, envisaged theoretically, even planned and arranged for; but now Leontes is brought face to face with its actuality. The fact that his son is 'gone', his own issue cut off, his future in terms of the Sonnets' 'lines of life that life repair' interrupted, is what shocks Leontes into seeing in a true perspective the present and the immediate past: 'I have too much believed mine own suspicion'. Too late, this conversion and repentance. The queen is reported dead, too, and suddenly, in a deliberate contrast with what has gone before, time cannot be long enough:

> A thousand knees
> Ten thousand years together, naked, fasting,
> Upon a barren mountain, and still winter
> In storm perpetual,

could not atone for the deeds of a few hectic days of error.

This is the lowest point in the play. The sands have, as it were, rushed through the dramatic hour-glass to measure the decline in Leontes' fortune, his self-inflicted loss of wife and issue. But in the final scene of Act 3 the finding of the babe replaces things dying with things new-born; and so we are prepared for the visible turning of the hour-glass by 'Time, the Chorus': 'I turn my glass and give my scene such growing As you had slept between'.

If we have been aware of the insistence on, and the importance of, the time theme in the first half of the play, we are, I think, prepared to see the introduction of Father Time here as more than a mere stop-gap, a desperate attempt to tidy over the Romance breach of the unities.[10] He has come, at a crucial moment in the play, not merely to substitute for a programme note of something like 'Act 4: Sixteen years later',[11] but to provide a pivotal image, part verbal part visual, of the Triumph of Time. The last fifteen lines of his speech are indeed a *résumé* of events during the sixteen-year lapse, but they are set in the context of the first fifteen lines, where Time is presented as a principal and power: 'I, that please some, try all, both joy and terror Of good and bad, that makes and unfolds error . . .' Far from having abandoned time-thinking, Shakespeare presses home the fact that the 'wide gap' of dramatically 'untried growth' is part of the universal process of time who 'makes and unfolds error' in his immutable onward flight. Rather than being timeless, *The Winter's Tale* is thus set in a context of *all* time.

We have seen error being made; now, it is suggested, it is to be unfolded by Time the Revealer. Of course, in a mere plot sense, error had been unfolded at the end of Act 3. But truth is more than just getting the facts straight: it is not enough for Leontes to find out that he has been mistaken in his jealousy. He has to become aware of truth in a wider sense, and that can only be achieved through subjection to Time the Revealer—and through grappling with Time the Destroyer. For Time, the Chorus reminds us of his destructive qualities, too: of his power 'To o' erthrow law and in one self-born hour To plant and o' erwhelm custom'. Above all—anticipating Prospero in his use of the very form of the work of art of which he himself is a part, as an image of transience—he reminds us that 'brightness falls from the air':

> I witness to
> The times that brought them in; so shall I do
> To the freshest things now reigning and make stale
> The glistering of this present, as my tale
> Now seems to it.

These lines are less haunting than Prospero's, because they are written in a kind of pageant doggerel, and because the speaker here is the triumphant agent, not the object; so that the element of human nostalgia is lacking. Their effect is to establish the play's connection with Time's triumph; and the total effect of the choric speech is to invite a dual response to such triumph.

Needless to say, Shakespeare's audience in 1610–11 would have been familiar with the figure of Father Time, from innumerable verbal and pictorial representations and from pageants and masques.[12] Time as the Father of Truth had appeared in the last three royal entries, and Middleton was soon going to use him in the 1613 Lord Mayor's show, *The Triumphs of Truth*. He had become a popular figure in the allegorical masque, because as Revealer he could be used as an effective *deus ex machina* to solve the central conflict and turn anti-masque into masque. Thus he appears, for example, in the fourth of Beaumont and Fletcher's *Four Plays in One*, the masque called *The Triumph of Time*: 'helping triumphantly, Helping his Master Man'. Yet, to the Elizabethan or Jacobean imagination, Time is never for long allowed to remain a purely beneficent figure. Beaumont and Fletcher's triumphant Time first appears 'mowing mankind down'. When represented iconographically as the Father of Truth, he also has his scythe and his hour-glass—an example of this is the emblem of *Veritas temporis filia* in Whitney's *Choice of Emblemes*[13]—and thus remains connected with transience and death. One of the fullest catalogues of the characteristics of Time is Lucrece's diatribe, and there we hear within one stanza that 'Time's glory' is both 'to calm contending kings, To unmask falsehood and bring truth to light', and 'To ruinate proud buildings with [his] hours, And smear with dust their glittering golden towers' (*The Rape of Lucrece*, 939-44).

Those who tried to put Father Time on the stage in his dual significance often found themselves ending up with an unresolved contradiction, as in Middleton's *Triumphs of Truth*, where Time, the agent of good, suddenly and incongruously turns destructive:

TIME, standing up in TRUTH'S Chariot, seeming to make an offer with his sithe to cut off the glories of the day, growing neere now to the season of rest and sleepe, his daughter TRUTH thus meekely stayes his hand.[14]

It was easier for non-dramatic poets to combine destructive and truth-revealing Time, and perhaps the most complete fusion of the two attributes takes place when truth is seen not just as the opposite of falsehood but as, in itself, the realization of the immutable flux of time:

When *Trewth (Tymes daughter)* doth owr triall touch,
Then take the Glasse and wee shal hardly knowe,
Owreselves therein we shalbe changed so.[15]

This is the truth connected with time in many of Shakespeare's sonnets on mutability, and indeed in the wrinkled Hermione at the end of *The Winter's Tale*. Shakespeare's choric Time is in a firm Elizabethan tradition when he insists on the multiplicity of his powers—and rather more successful than most pageant Father Times in reconciling his opposed attributes. He needs no disintegrationists or apologists for Shakespeare's 'bad poetry' to justify his appearance in the play, for he is more than a self-contained emblem: he is a concrete image[16] of the multiplicity which the play as a whole dramatizes and which is a leading theme of the second half of the play.

When Act 4 opens, sixteen years of time have acted as a healer through the process of growth—natural in the case of Perdita and moral in the case of Leontes. But Leontes himself is withheld from our view till Act 5, and two whole scenes precede the appearance on stage of Perdita, thus preparing our acceptance of growth and change before they are actually demonstrated. It is Camillo (just as in 1.1) who at the beginning of Act 4 brings in the sense of time and puts the immediate action into a time perspective: 'It is fifteen years since I saw my country: . . . I desire to lay my bones there'. We are not, it should be noted, introduced at once to the positive result of the 'wide gap'—the growth into womanhood of the child Perdita—but are first asked to realize what the sixteen years have meant in terms of deprivation for Camillo and, more importantly, of suffering for Leontes: 'that penitent . . . and reconciled king . . . whose loss of his most precious queen and children are even now to be afresh lamented'. This scene, then, as well as preparing for the rest of Act 4, also forms the foundation of the whole of Act 5.

The importance of the pastoral scene as an image of regeneration has often been commented on, and even seen as mythical. In the context of the present discussion it is important that Perdita, who is herself almost an image of time seen as natural growth, should first appear in a world where time equals the life of nature and the cycle of the seasons. Perdita's flower-speeches and flower-giving become the epitome of this world. She starts in a vein which may recall Ophelia:

> For you there's rosemary and rue; these keep
> Seeming and savour all the winter long:
> Grace and remembrance be to you both;

but while Ophelia's flowers are altogether emblematic and distributed according to the emotional significance of the situation and the recipient, Perdita's turn out to be mainly a measure of time and age. Polixenes at once takes her meaning thus: 'well you fit our ages With flowers of winter'; but Perdita, whether out of courtesy or of chronological accuracy, would assess the ages of Polixenes and Camillo as

> the year growing ancient,
> Not yet on summer's death, nor on the birth
> Of trembling winter.

The famous discussion on Art versus Nature arises from the 'streak'd gillyvors' allegedly representing Polixenes' time of life; and, having agreed to differ, Perdita returns to her identification of time in nature's year with age in man, giving 'flowers Of middle summer' to 'men of middle age' and lamenting the lack of early spring flowers which would have typified youth, particularly Florizel. Despite their sheer lyrical beauty, these speeches are not just decorative or just meant to create atmosphere: they not only establish a contrast between this world and the world of most of the first three Acts, but also define the contrast as being between a world where time is taken for granted as a natural progression and one where time is altogether defied.

Timeless the pastoralism in *The Winter's Tale* is not. Pastoral poets soon discovered that death and transience were in Arcadia, too;[17] and the love of Florizel and Perdita in a central passage pits itself against time and change. Florizel's adoration is formulated as a desire to arrest time, to achieve permanence outside the flux of time:

> When you speak, sweet,
> I'ld have you do it ever . . .
> when you do dance, I wish you
> A wave o' the sea, that you might ever do
> Nothing but that; move still, still so.

We are reminded of Polixenes' reference, in 1.2, to how he and Leontes assumed that 'there was no more behind' than to be 'boy eternal' (and indeed the joint childhood of the two kings is referred to in pastoral terms); but in Florizel's case the thinking is not naive, it is wishful, and consciously so. Both Florizel and Perdita are aware of the precariousness of their love in relation to the extra-pastoral world, and throughout the scene the audience sees the threat to it literally present, in the shape of the disguised Polixenes. Before the scene is over, Polixenes has broken up this world of natural time, as Leontes did with the one remembered at the beginning of Act 1.

Up till Polixenes' intervention, this scene had presented a structural contrast with the first three acts: long speeches—lyrical, meditative or descriptive—had set a leisurely pace, relaxed further by singing and dancing. With the King's outburst, the pursuit is on, but instead of our following the hectic activity, as we do in Acts 2 and 3, it takes place off-stage; and we are, as Act 5 opens, finally brought face to face with Leontes.

In 5.1 the emphasis is again on the past sixteen years. Time, which we know has to Perdita meant growing up in step with nature, has to Leontes meant unceasing grief over a self-inflicted loss. His sense of time is entirely retrospective; he looks into the future only to lament that it does not exist to him because of

The wrong I did myself; which was so much,
That heirless it hath made my kingdom and
Destroy'd the sweet'st companion that e'er man
Bred his hopes out of.

'Heirless' and 'issueless' are thematic words in this scene, made even more poignant (though also ironical in terms of what the audience knows) when Florizel and Perdita arrive to emphasize the difference between what is and what was. It is significant that Hermione is mourned not only for her own sweetness' sake but also as 'the sweet'st companion that e'er man Bred his hopes out of'. Leontes has robbed himself not only of love and friendship but also of that other means of defeating time: issue.

After the first acute reminder of loss, the arrival of the young couple (allegedly bearing with them also the loving greetings of Polixenes) strikes a new note in Leontes. The form of his greeting to them—'Welcome hither, As is the spring to the earth'—echoes the many references to 'natural' time in the pastoral scene, and hints at an acceptance of the possibility of time as healing and restoring. Critics of the myth-making school read these lines as a confirmation of the essentially mythical nature of the play: here, they argue, is the first direct sign of the regeneration of the King. But if we see the coming of Perdita and Florizel into Leontes' court as altogether an archetypal situation, then we miss some very human aspects of it which are clearly recognized by Shakespeare. True, the pair are first of all representatives of a second generation, of youth and innocence and regenerative forces—and in being so, they represent to us the beneficial effects of time. But indirectly—through other characters' reaction to her—Perdita also indicates something about time's destructiveness. Paulina is used by Shakespeare in this scene as a choric commentator, turning people's admiration of Perdita into a reminder, though in a muted fashion, that time hath a wallet at his back. Before Perdita appears, the Gentleman's praise of her beauty provokes Paulina to a lamentation much reminiscent of some of the words of Time the Chorus earlier in the play:

> O Hermione,
As every present time doth boast itself
Above a better gone, so must thy grave
Give way to what's seen now! . . .
>   'She had not been
Nor was not to be equall'd'—thus your verse
Flow'd with her beauty once: 'tis shrewdly ebb'd,
To say you have seen a better . . . [18]

The Gentleman's defence, as concerns Hermione, is a simple 'I have almost forgot'; and at this point it contrasts markedly with Leontes' insistence, a few lines earlier, that *he* cannot forget. But by the end of the scene, in the one possible approach to what in *Pandosto* is a fully developed and elaborated incestuous passion, Leontes himself seems to find the past dimming before the beauty of the present; and again Paulina is there to comment on the treachery:

> not a month
> Fore your queen died, she was more worth such gazes
> Than what you look on now.

Perdita's return, then, becomes the occasion for several and varied insights into what time does to man. What it really means to Leontes, when her identity is known, is dramatized in the final scene; for by letting this reunion be merely reported, Shakespeare reserves its impact to combine it with that of the ultimate reunion.

In the last scene the time themes are drawn together and acted out in a unique way. The whole scene has about it a sense of the fulness of time—pointed at the climactic moment by Paulina's 'Tis time; descend'—of stillness and solemnity. Speeches are short, the diction plain, the language almost bare of imagery: as if Shakespeare is anxious not to distract attention from the significance of action and movement. Characters' reactions to the statue are patterned in a fashion which approaches ritual An unusual number of speeches are devoted just to underlining the emotions and postures of people on-stage, as in Paulina's words to Leontes: 'I like your silence, it the more shows off Your wonder'; or in Leontes' to the statue:

> O royal piece,
> There's magic in thy majesty, which has
> My evils conjured to remembrance and
> From thy admiring daughter took the spirits,
> Standing like stone with thee.

Verbal repetitions in the first three Acts imaged Leontes' obsession and frenzied hurry, as in the 'nothing' speech; here they give the effect of ritual:

> What can you make her do
> I am content to look on, what to speak,
> I am content to hear.

When the statue comes alive, it is as though we were witnessing the central movement of a masque, with music as accompaniment, Paulina as the presenter and Hermione as the main 'device'. Paulina's commands—

> Music, awake her; strike!
> 'Tis time; descend; be stone no more; approach;
> Strike all that look upon with marvel—

are in tone and phrasing very like a presenter's call for the chief figure of the masque to appear.[19]

Into this ritual and revelation Shakespeare has woven the various time-concerns of the play so closely that the scene can be said, in the widest sense, to represent a Triumph of Time. In the widest sense only, for at this stage in the play the simple identification of time as either Revealer or Destroyer has been obliterated. At first the statue seems to bring back the past so vividly that time itself is obliterated:

> O, thus she stood,
> Even with such life of majesty, warm life,
> As now it coldly stands, when first I woo'd her!

As on another, fatal, occasion Leontes harks back to his courtship. But the past is present with a difference, for Leontes' reaction also is: 'Hermione was not so much wrinkled, nothing So aged as this seems'; to which Paulina replies:

> So much the more our carver's excellence;
> Which lets go by some sixteen years and makes her
> As she lived now.

The intervening time has meant physical decay, symbolized as in the Sonnets, by 'necessary wrinkles'. As the sense of the distance between now and sixteen years ago sharpens in Leontes, it again becomes identified with guilt and penance: he speaks of how the statue conjures his evils to remembrance, and Camillo recalls the sorrow 'Which sixteen winters cannot blow away, So many summers dry'.

But the statue comes alive. Paulina's words suggest that Hermione's return is a kind of resurrection:

> Come
> I'll fill your grave up: stir, nay, come away,
> Bequeath to death your numbness, for from him
> Dear life redeems you;

and so it is, of course, to Leontes. As he stands there with Hermione and Perdita, many of the sonnets' resolutions are fused into one dramatic situation. Leontes has defeated time in that his lines of life are stretching into the future. Not only is Perdita restored, but she is in love and about to be married and is herself the potential mother of future generations. Hermione's return represents another form of victory over time; she is a living proof that 'Love's not Time's fool, though rosy lips and cheeks Within his bending sickle's compass come' (Sonnet 116). These sonnet lines could perhaps also paraphrase the truth that time has finally revealed to Leontes: paradoxically, time has at last in its triumph brought about its own defeat. This does not efface the human suffering that has gone before, however, and that weighs so heavily on the play right till the very end. Rather than a myth of immortality, then, this play is a probing into the human condition, and—as a whole as well as in details—it looks at what time means and does to man.

It would, needless to say, be wrong to think of *The Winter's Tale* as a treatise on time. The play does not state or prove anything. But through its action, its structure and its poetry, it communicates a constant awareness of the powers of time. Shakespeare, had his small Latin allowed, might well have substituted for the motto of *Pandosto* the words of St Augustine, *Quid est ... tempus? si nemo ex me quaerat, scio; si quaerenti explicare velim, nescio.*[20]

NOTES

1. J. M. Nosworthy, New Arden ed. of *Cymbeline* (1955), Introduction, p. lxiii.
2. G. Wilson Knight, *The Crown of Life* (1947), p. 30.
3. All quotations are taken from *The Works of Shakespeare*, ed. W. G. Clark, J. Glover, and W. A. Wright (1866). [The Globe edn.]
4. *The Tryumphes of Fraunces Petrarcke, translated out of Italian into English by Henrye Parker knyght, Lorde Morley (1565?),* fol. M2r.
5. Greene's *Pandosto*, ed. P. G. Thomas (1907), p. xxiii.
6. *The Winter's Tale* (1947), pp. 47 ff.
7. Cf. Ernest Schanzer's discussion of how the juxtaposition of the two parts is pointed by structural parallels and contrasts (above, pp. 72–82).
8. Leontes is, in a sense, an inverted Troilus. Troilus believes that Cressida's love will last forever, and is disillusioned by Time. Leontes does not believe in Hermione's 'forever', and is converted by Time. In each case there is a failure to know the love offered for what it is worth.
9. For a discussion of this association, see S. C. Chew, *The Virtues Reconciled*, Toronto (1947), pp. 90 ff. An example of the close connection of Time and Justice can be seen in the last of Beaumont and Fletcher's *Four Plays in One*, the masque-play called *The Triumph of Time*. The central Everyman character here abandons false friends, to turn to Time and Justice. The function of Time in this piece is to set things right by unmasking falsehood.
10. See the Introduction to the New Cambridge edn. of the play (1931), p. xix '... having to skip sixteen years after Act 3, he desperately drags

in Father Time with an hour-glass.... Which means on interpretation that Shakespeare ... simply did not know how to do it, save by
invoking some such device'.

11. I cannot agree with Panofsky's criticism of Father Time in this play:
'Sometimes the figure of Father Time is used as a mere device to
indicate the lapse of months, years, or centuries, as in Shakespeare's
Winter's Tale, where Time appears as Chorus before the fifth (*sic*) act'.
(*Studies in Iconology*, New York, 1939, p. 81.)

12. For example of these, see, e.g., S. C. Chew, 'Time and Fortune', *ELH*,
VI (1939): pp. 83-113; F. Saxl, 'Veritas Filia Temporis', in *Philosophy and
History: Essays presented to Ernst Cassirer*, ed. R. Klibansky and H. J.
Paton, Oxford (1936), pp. 203 ff.; Rudolf Wittkower, 'Chance, Time
and Virtue', *Journal of the Warburg Institute*, I (1937-8), pp. 313-21 and
D.J. Gordon, 'Veritas Filia Temporis: Hadrianus Junius and Geoffrey
Whitney', *Journal of the Warburg and Courtauld Institutes*, III (1939-40),
pp. 228-40.

13. Plate 34b.

14. Nichols, *Progresses of James I* (1828), II, p. 695.

15. Gascoigne, *The Grief of Joye*, ed. Cunliffe, Cambridge (1910), St. 52,
II. 5-7.

16. Unfortunately in productions of *The Winter's Tale* Father Time often
looks like some kind of wizard. The most successful Time I have seen
was in a Munich performance in 1959, when he was acted by an
octogenarian with little make-up and no paraphernalia other than an
hourglass.

17. See E. Panofsky, 'Et in Arcadia Ego', in *Philosophy and History*.

18. Cf. the Chorus lines, 'so shall I do To the freshest things now
reigning and make stale The glistering of this present'.

19. Cf., to take just one example, the call for Neptune in the masque
in *The Maid's Tragedy*, I.1 (ed. Waller and Glover, p. 10). Various critics (e.g. Alice Venezky, *Pageantry on the Shakespearean Stage*, p. 128 and
T. M. Parrott, *Shakespearean Comedy*, p. 386) have suggested that the
statue which comes alive is an adaptation of a masque-device; but
I have never seen it pointed out that in fact no masque-writer had
used this device before *The Winter's Tale* was first performed. Soon
after *The Winter's Tale*, however, both Campion and Beaumont in
their respective masques for the Princess Elizabeth's wedding, made
use of statues coming alive. Campion's main masque consists of eight
women statues, which come to life, four at a time; but in Beaumont's
masque the 'statuas' are relegated to the first anti-masque: a variation
on the theme is needed by now, and so, 'having but half life put into
them, and retaining still somewhat of their old nature', they give 'fit
occasion to new and strange varieties both in the music and paces'.
It was obviously statues used in this fashion that Bacon had in mind
when in his essay 'Of Masques and Triumphs' he placed 'statuas'

among the baboons, fools and other grotesques of the anti-masque.
(*A Harmony of the Essays*, ed. E. Arber, 1871, pp. 539-40. The essay first
appeared in the 1625 edition.) It might be noted that the Beaumont
masque referred to was in fact 'ordered and furnished' by Bacon.
20. *Confessions*, II. 14. (What is time? If no one asks me, I know. If I
wish to explain it to someone who asks me, I do not know.)

From *Review of English Literature* 5 (1964). Reprinted with the permission of
Roger Ewbank.

SHAKESPEARE'S ROMANCES:
THE WINTER'S TALE
Northrop Frye

*Northrop Frye (1912–1991) gathered his lectures on Shakespeare into a collec-
tion at the urging of another scholar, and they derive from the notes he prepared
for his undergraduate survey of Shakespeare's plays. As such they contain traces
of his voice as it was heard in the classroom, where clarity was at a premium
and the presence of students sometimes inspired a conversational tone. Frye's
criticism always reflects his wide-ranging acquaintance with apt analogues and
traditions that illuminate basic structures of literary form and meaning. In his
teaching voice, however, we can hear essential points made in terms accessible
to an audience ready to learn but not so erudite as the academic profession-
als whom Frye usually addressed in his writings and whom he influenced as
profoundly as any other twentieth-century critic. Such lectures open up Frye's
scholarship to students of all ages who wish to learn how a major critic invites
the young to join him on an intellectual journey that can ultimately provide a
lifetime of rewarding adventures.*

THE FIRST Folio says it contains Shakespeare's comedies, histories,
and tragedies, and that suggests a division of the main genres
of Shakespeare's plays that has pretty well held the field ever
since. The main change has been that we now tend to think of four
very late plays, *Pericles, Cymbeline, The Winter's Tale* and *The Tempest*,
as "romances," to distinguish them from the earlier comedies. These
plays reflect a new vogue in playwriting, which Shakespeare probably established, and in which he was followed by younger writers,
notably Fletcher and his collaborator Beaumont. One of these plays,
Fletcher's *The Faithful Shepherdess*, has a preface that speaks of its being
in a new form described as a "tragicomedy." These four romances have
not always been favourites: only *The Tempest* has steadily held the stage,
though it's often done so in some very curious distortions, and *Pericles*
and *Cymbeline*, though superbly actable, are not very often performed
even now.

Nevertheless, the romances are popular plays, not popular in the
sense of giving the public what it wants, which is a pretty silly phrase
anyway, but popular in the sense of coming down to the audience

response at its most fundamental level. We noticed a primitive quality in *Measure for Measure* linking it with folk tales and there's a close affinity between the romances and the most primitive (and therefore most enduring) forms of drama, like the puppet show. To mention some of their characteristics: first, there's a noticeable scaling down of characters; that is, the titanic figures like Hamlet, Cleopatra, Falstaff and Lear have gone. Leontes and Posthumus are jealous, and very articulate about it, but their jealousy doesn't have the *size* that Othello's jealousy has: we're looking at people more on our level, saying and feeling the things we can imagine ourselves saying and feeling. Second, the stories are incredible: we're moving in worlds of magic and fairy tale, where anything can happen. Emotionally, they're as powerfully convincing as ever, but the convincing quality doesn't extend to the incidents. Third, there's a strong tendency to go back to some of the conventions of earlier plays, the kind that were produced in the 1580s: we noticed that *Measure for Measure* used one of these early plays as a source.

Fourth, the scaling down of characters brings these plays closer to the puppet shows I just mentioned. If you watch a good puppet show for very long you almost get to feeling that the puppets are convinced that they're producing all the sounds and movements themselves, even though you can see that they're not. In the romances, where the incidents aren't very believable anyway, the sense of puppet behaviour extends so widely that it seems natural to include a god or goddess as the string puller. Diana has something of this role in *Pericles*, and Jupiter has it in *Cymbeline: The Tempest* has a human puppeteer in Prospero. In *The Winter's Tale* the question "Who's pulling the strings?" is more difficult to answer, but it still seems to be relevant. The preface to that Fletcher play I mentioned says that in a "tragicomedy" introducing a god is "lawful," i.e., it's according to the "rules."

It may seem strange to think of Shakespeare rereading, as he clearly was, old plays that had gone out of fashion and been superseded by the highly sophisticated productions that came along in the early 1600s. But if we think of him as trying to recapture the primitive and popular basis of drama, it makes more sense. *Mucedorus* (anon.), for example, was a play written in the 1590s and revived (something rather unusual for that period) around 1610 or so, about the time of Shakespeare's romances. It tells the story of how a young prince fell in love with a picture of the heroine, a princess in a faraway country, and journeyed in disguise to her land to court her. It's advertised on its title page as "very delectable and full of mirth," as it has a clown who mixes his words.

The hero finds himself in the woods while the heroine and her suitor, a cowardly villain, are taking a walk. A bear appears; the heroine says whatever heroines say when they're confronted with bears; the cowardly villain mutters something like "Well, nice knowing you," and slopes off; there's a scuffle in the bushes and the hero appears carrying the bear's head. He says to the heroine, in effect: "Sorry this beast has been annoying you, but he won't be a problem now; by the way, here's his head, would you like it?" As far as we can make out from the dialogue and stage directions, the heroine says, "Thanks very much," and goes offstage lugging what one might think would be a somewhat messy object. As you see, it's all very delectable and full of mirth: it's a good-natured, harmless, simpleminded story, and the audience of Shakespeare's time ate it up. (So did readers: it went through seventeen Quartos.) But when we look at *The Winter's Tale* and see a stage direction like "Exit, pursued by a bear," we wonder if we're really in so very different a world, for all the contrast in complexity. Shakespeare himself didn't seem to think so: in the winding up of the two main stories in the play, he has a gentleman say of one, "This news which is called true is so like an old tale that the verity of it is in strong suspicion" (5.2.27), and Paulina remarks of the other:

> That she is living,
> Were it but told you, should be hooted at
> Like an old tale.   (5.3.115-17)

I think the "romance" period of Shakespeare's production covers seven plays altogether. We know the approximate dates of Shakespeare's plays, but we can't pinpoint them all exactly in relation to the others: in any case a dramatist of his ability could have worked on more than one play at a time. The rest of this paragraph is guesswork, but not unreasonable guesswork. I think that after finishing *Antony and Cleopatra*, Shakespeare turned over the pages of Plutarch's *Lives* until his eye fell on the life of Coriolanus. Coriolanus makes a perfect contrast to Antony, because his tragedy is the tragedy of a genuine hero who rejects the theatrical, the continuous acting role that made Antony so magnetic a figure. Coriolanus performs amazing feats of valour, but he has to do everything himself: he can't hold an army together. There's an immature and mother-dominated streak in him that won't let him develop beyond the stage of a boy showing off. Plutarch's scheme, you remember, was to write "parallel" lives, taking two at a time, one Greek and the other Roman, who suggested resemblances or contrasts with each other, and then comparing them. The Greek counterpart of Coriolanus was Alcibiades, who was prominent in the Athens-Sparta war, and in the life of Alcibiades there's a digression telling the story of Timon the misanthrope or man hater.

Timon of Athens seems to me to be really Shakespeare's first romance: it differs completely from the great tragedies both in its choice of hero and, more important, in its structure. It breaks in two, like a diptych: we've seen that structure already in *Measure for Measure*. Timon is at the centre of his society, a wealthy man giving parties and being a patron of the arts, for the first half of the play; then he loses his money and his so-called friends drop quickly out of sight, and he's a hermit getting as far as he can from the human race for the second half. Of course we soon realize that he was completely isolated in his sociable phase, just as he's pestered with a great variety of visitors, cursing every one of them, in his hermit stage. The stylizing of the action is typical of the romances, and Timon himself, who dies offstage with a couple of lines of epitaph, is a scaled-down tragic hero.

Pericles is a curiously experimental play that recalls the early plays I mentioned, including an early play of Shakespeare's, *The Comedy of Errors*. *Pericles* is based, as the conclusion of the earlier comedy is, on the traditional story of Apollonius of Tyre. The poets who had retold this story included Gower, a contemporary of Chaucer, and Gower is brought on the stage to help tell the story of *Pericles*. This seems to be partly to suggest the authority of the story being told: you may not believe anything that happens in the story, but if someone gets up out of his grave after two hundred years to tell it to you, you don't start saying "yes, but." *Pericles* also tells its story partly by means of "dumb shows," like the one in the *Hamlet* mousetrap play. In *The Comedy of Errors* there's a priestess of Diana's temple in Ephesus, but no Diana: in *Pericles* Diana appears to the hero in a dream to tell him where to go next. I have no idea why the name Apollonius got changed to Pericles, except that Shakespeare probably made the change himself. The first two acts of *Pericles* don't sound at all like Shakespeare, but no collaborator has been suggested who wasn't considerably younger, and I'd expect the senior collaborator to be in charge of the general design of the play.

Cymbeline, like *Pericles*, is a "tragicomedy" (in fact it's included with the tragedies in the Folio). Cymbeline was king of Britain at the time of the birth of Christ, and, unlike Lear, is a fully historical character: his coins are in the British Museum. Nonetheless the main story told in the play is practically the story of Snow White. No dwarfs, but a very similar story, along with a jealousy story in which the villain, Iachimo, is, as perhaps his name suggests, a small-scale Iago.

The Winter's Tale and *The Tempest* we'll be dealing with next. *Henry VIII*, which seems to be later than *The Tempest*, is a history play assimilated to romance by concentrating on the central theme of the wheel of fortune, which keeps turning all through the play, and coming to an ironic conclusion with Anne Boleyn, Thomas Cromwell and Cranmer (two later beheaded and one burned alive) at the top of the wheel. There follows a very strange play called *The Two Noble Kinsmen*, a bitter, sardonic retelling of the story of Chaucer's *Knight's Tale*. We remember that the names Theseus and Hippolyta in *A Midsummer Night's Dream* were apparently taken from this tale, but nothing of its sombreness got into the earlier play. *The Two Noble Kinsmen* appeared, long after Shakespeare's death, in a Quarto saying it was the joint work of Shakespeare and Fletcher. Most scholars think that the play is mainly Fletcher's (it was included in the Beaumont and Fletcher Second Folio), but that the Quarto is right in assigning part of it to Shakespeare. After that the trail fades out, although there is a rumour of another collaboration with Fletcher which is lost. Many critics also think that *Henry VIII* is partly or largely Fletcher's, but I've never found this convincing, and I suspect that the motivation for believing it is partly that *The Tempest* seems a logical climax for the Shakespeare canon, and *Henry VIII* doesn't.

I spoke earlier of Greek New Comedy, which provided the original plots for Plautus and Terence. A spinoff from New Comedy was prose romance, which featured such themes as having someone of noble birth abandoned on a hillside as an infant, rescued and brought up as a shepherd, and eventually restored to his or her birthright, the essential documentary data having been thoughtfully placed beside the infant, and brought out when it's time for the story to end. Infants did get exposed on hillsides in ancient Greece, though it may not have happened as often, or with such hospitable shepherds, in life as it does in literature. One of these late Greek romances, by a writer named Heliodorus, was available to Shakespeare and his contemporaries in English, and is alluded to in *Twelfth Night*. The imitating of such romance formulas became fashionable in Elizabeth's time, and one such story was written by Robert Greene, Shakespeare's older contemporary, and called *Pandosto*. This story is the main source of *The Winter's Tale*, and its subtitle, *The Triumph of Time*, should also be kept in mind.

The first thing to notice about the play is that, like *Measure for Measure*, it breaks in the middle: there are two parts to the play, the first part all gloom and tragedy, the second part all romantic comedy. But in *Measure for Measure* there's no break in time: the action runs continuously through the same scene in the prison, where the deadlock between Claudio and Isabella is ended by the Duke's taking over the action. In *The Winter's Tale* Time himself is brought on the stage, at the beginning of the fourth act, to tell you that sixteen years have gone by, and that the infant you just saw exposed on the coast of Bohemia in a howling storm has grown up into a lovely young woman. It was still a general critical view that such breaks in the action of a play were absurd, and Shakespeare seems to be not just ignoring such views but deliberately flouting them.

The next thing to notice is that there are two breaks in the middle, and they don't quite coincide. (In speaking of breaks, of course, I don't mean that the play falls in two or lacks unity). We do have the sixteen-year break at the end of the third act, but just before that there's another break, of a type much more like the one in *Measure for Measure*. We see Antigonus caught in a terrific storm and pursued by a bear: the linking of a bear with a tempest is an image in a speech of Lear's, and the storm here has something of the Lear storm about it, not just a storm but a world dissolving into chaos. After Antigonus's speech, the rhythm suddenly shifts from blank verse to prose, just as it does in *Measure for Measure*, and two shepherds come on the scene. So while we have the two parts of the time break, winter in Sicilia and spring in Bohemia sixteen years later, we also have another break suggesting that something is going on that's even bigger than that. We don't have a deputy dramatist like the Duke constructing the action of the second part. But we notice that Shakespeare follows his source in *Pandosto* quite closely up to the point corresponding to the two breaks, and after that he gets much more detached from it. Greene's *Pandosto*, the character corresponding to Leontes, never regenerates: toward the end he's attempting things like incest with his daughter, and his death is clearly a big relief all round.

Near the end of this play we have two scenes of the type critics call "recognition scenes," where some mystery at the beginning of the play is cleared up. One of these is the recognition of Perdita as a princess and daughter of Leontes. This recognition scene takes place offstage: it's not seen by us, but simply described in rather wooden prose by some "gentlemen," so however important to the plot it's clearly less important than the bigger recognition scene at the end, with Hermione and Leontes. Some of the things the gentlemen say, though, seem to be pointing to the real significance of the double break we've been talking about. One of them describes the emotional effect on all concerned of the discovery of the identity of Perdita, and says "they looked as they had heard of a world ransomed, or of one destroyed" (5.2.14-15). Another, in recounting the death of Antigonus, says that the whole ship's crew was drowned: "so that all the instruments which aided to expose the child were even then lost when it was found" [i.e., by the shepherds] (5.2.71-72). Tough on them, considering that they were only carrying out a king's orders, but, as we remember from the last speech of *Richard II*, kings have a lot of ways of keeping their hands clean. We notice that back in the scene where the shepherds find the baby, the shepherd who does find it says to the one who saw the bear eating Antigonus, "thou mettest with things dying, I with things newborn" (3.3.112). The New Arden editor says that this is just a simple statement of fact, whatever a "fact" may be in a play like this. The two halves of the play seem to be not just Sicilian winter and Bohemian spring, but a death-world and a life-world.

Ben Jonson remarked to his friend Drummond, as an example of Shakespeare's carelessness in detail, that in this play he'd given a sea-coast to Bohemia, which was a landlocked country. It's just possible that Shakespeare knew this too: in *The Tempest* he also gives a seacoast to the inland Duchy of Milan. *The Winter's Tale* was one of many plays performed in connection with the festivities attending the marriage of King James's daughter, Elizabeth, to a prince who came from that part of the world. In a few years the Thirty Years' War broke out and he lost his kingdom, and was known thereafter as "the winter king of Bohemia." (However, that story has a long-term happy ending: it was through this marriage that the House of Hanover came to the British throne a century later.) The names Sicilia and Bohemia came from *Pandosto*, but Shakespeare reverses their relation to the characters. I doubt that the name Bohemia means much of anything, and the setting of the play doesn't stay there: it changes back to Sicilia for the end of the play, so that we begin with Sicilia dying and end with Sicilia newborn. And I think the name Sicilia may mean something. It was in Sicily that the literary pastoral—and this play is full of pastoral imagery—originated, and it was in Sicily that the beautiful maiden Proserpine was kidnapped and carried off to the lower world by Pluto, forcing her mother, Ceres, to search all over the upper world for her. In this play Hermione doesn't search, but she doesn't come to life either (or whatever she does) until Perdita, whose name means the lost maiden, is said to be found.

We start off, both in the prose introductory scene and the dialogue of the main scene that follows it, with a heavy, cloying, suetpudding atmosphere that feels like a humid day before a thunderstorm. Leontes, king of Sicilia, is entertaining Polixenes, king of Bohemia, as a guest, and they're crawling over each other with demonstrations of affection. Leontes' queen, Hermione, is just about to give birth, and Polixenes has been visiting for nine months, so it's technically possible for Leontes to do some perverted mental arithmetic. Before long, with no warning, the storm strikes, and Leontes, who's been playing the gracious host role up to now, suddenly turns insanely jealous, setting in motion an extremely grim train of events. In a romance, we just accept Leontes' jealousy as we would a second subject in a piece of music: it's there, and that's all there is to it, except to keep on listening. There are references to a period of innocence in the childhood of the two kings, then some teasing about the role of their two wives in losing their innocence, and finally Hermione says to Polixenes:

Th' offences we have made you do, we'll answer,
If you first sinn'd with us, and that with us
You did continue fault, and that you slipp'd not
With any but with us.   (1.2.83–86)

In its context, all this is harmless badinage, but to a poisoned mind every syllable suggests a horrible leering innuendo, as well as an in-joke that Leontes is excluded from.

Leontes is caught in the strong tricks of imagination that Theseus spoke of in *A Midsummer Night's Dream*, where nothing, under the pressure of what Leontes calls "affection" or emotional stress, consolidates into something, and creates an irrational fantasy. The wife of Greene's *Pandosto* does at least hang around her guest's bedchamber, but Leontes has nothing in the way of "evidence" of that kind, and even the most perverse director couldn't give us a justified Leontes trapped by designing women. We notice how this creation of something out of nothing is associated with the contact senses: he says he smells and feels and tastes his situation, but seeing and hearing, the primary senses of the objective, he takes less account of.

Here again we start rolling down a steep slide, as in *King Lear*, except that in *King Lear* the degenerating is in the king's outer circumstances, whereas here it's in his character. Before long Leontes is trying to get his courtier Camillo to murder Polixenes; foiled by Camillo's flight, he turns coward and (as he says explicitly) is resolved to take it out on Hermione. He hits perhaps his lowest point when he complains that he can't sleep, and wonders if having Hermione burnt alive would give him rest. Later he speaks of burning the infant Perdita, who's just been born in the middle of this hullabaloo, and when Hermione's friend Paulina speaks her mind, he threatens to burn her too. Other images of useless sacrifice run all through this part of the play. Leontes is also obsessed by the notion that people are laughing at him behind his back (which of course they are, though not for the reason he thinks). He can say, however, "How blest am I" in acquiring his totally illusory knowledge of good and evil.

And yet every so often the fog clears a bit, and we realize that the Paulina-Leontes relation is really that of a nanny and a child in a screaming tantrum. Leontes says to Paulina's husband, Antigonus:

I charg'd thee that she should not come about me.
I knew she would.   (2.3.43-44)

There is a quite funny scene where Paulina sweeps in, Leontes orders her out, a swarm of male courtiers make futile efforts at pushing her, and Paulina brushes them off like insects while Leontes blusters. We realize that as soon as he gets rid of his obsession he'll be quite a decent person again, though one doesn't go through such things unmarked. At least he has had the sense to consult the oracle of Apollo, which tells him the exact truth about his situation. But Leontes has fallen into what he calls, in the last lines of the play, a "gap in time," and so the timing goes all wrong.

First comes the news of Mamillius's death from shame at the accusation of his mother. He seems a trifle young for such a reaction, but this is romance. It's this news that shatters Leontes' ugly world: nothing has lessened his affection for this boy, and he has never seriously questioned his legitimacy. Now he's in a very bad situation for a king, without an heir to succeed him. For very soon afterward comes the news of Hermione's death, brought by Paulina. "She's dead, I'll swear't," says Paulina—a remark we might put away for future reference. Then again, the machinery has already been set in motion to make Antigonus go to Bohemia to leave the infant Perdita on Polixenes' territorial doorstep. We notice that Hermione returns to visit Antigonus as a ghost in a dream—by Jacobean dramatic conventions a pretty reliable sign that she's really dead. As Antigonus has not heard the oracle's report, he disappears into a bear, thinking that Polixenes after all must be the infant's father.

The Winter's Tale is set in a pagan and Classical world, where Apollo's oracle is infallibly inspired, and where the man who survived the flood is referred to by his Ovidian name of Deucalion and not his Biblical name of Noah. As always, Shakespeare is not rigorously consistent: there are Biblical allusions, such as Perdita's to the Gospel passage about the sun shining on all alike, which may be considered unconscious, but Polixenes' reference to Judas Iscariot hardly could be. We also seem to be back to "anointed kings," and the awfulness of injuring them: doubtless the more Shakespeare's reputation grew, the more carefully he had to look out for long ears in the audience. But no one can miss the pervading imagery or the number of links with Ovid's *Metamorphoses*: in this play we're not only in the atmosphere of folk tale, as we were in *Measure for Measure*, but in that of Classical mythology as well.

At the centre of the play there's the common folk-tale theme of the calumniated mother. This is a cut-down version of a myth in which a hero or heroine has a divine father and a human mother, so that the man who would normally expect to be the father becomes jealous and wants to kill at least the child, if not the mother too. So the calumniated-mother theme is usually connected with a threatened-birth theme, which is also in the play. We're reminded of two famous Ovidian myths in particular. One is the myth of Ceres and Proserpine, already mentioned, and referred to by Perdita in speaking of her spring flowers. (I give the Ovidian Latin names: the Greek ones, Demeter and Persephone or Kore, may be more familiar now.) The other is the story of Pygmalion and the statue Venus brings to life for him. There is another faint mythical theme in the resemblance between Florizel and Mamillius, a resemblance commented on by Leontes. After Leontes has lost his own son and heir, Florizel becomes his heir in the old-fashioned mythical way, by coming from afar, marrying the king's daughter, and succeeding by what is called mother right.

There are two main stories in the play, contrapuntally linked as usual. One is a straight New Comedy story of Perdita and her lover, Florizel; of how their marriage is blocked by parental opposition, and released by the discovery that Perdita is really a princess after all. The other is the story of the separation and reunion of Leontes and Hermione, which, again as usual in Shakespeare, seems to be the more important story of the two. The cultural environment is more extra-Christian than pre-Christian as in *King Lear*. A tragedy reveals the impotence of the Classical gods; a comedy can give us something of the sunnier side of paganism. The opening dialogue refers to the boyhood of Leontes and Polixenes as a state of innocence that was clear even of original sin.

In *King Lear* we met two levels of nature: an upper level of human nature, which includes many things that in Shakespeare's day would also be called "art," but which are natural to man, and a lower level associated with predatory animals and what we call the law of the jungle. In *The Winter's Tale* there are also two aspects of nature, but they're in more of a parallel than a hierarchical relation. Philosophers have always distinguished two categories of nature. One is nature as a structure or system, the physical aspect of it; the other is the biological aspect, nature as the total power of growth, death and renewed life. They're sometimes called *natura naturata* and *natura naturans*. In *King Lear*, again, the upper, human level is associated with nature as an order; the lower level is associated mainly with ferocity, Tennyson's nature "red in tooth and claw." But in *The Winter's Tale* we have the story of Florizel and Perdita associated with a genial nature of renewing power, the other aspect being more emphasized in the Leontes-Hermione one. There are still different levels, but these exist in both the forms of nature emphasized in the two stories.

There seem to be three main levels in all. In the Leontes-Hermione world, there is a low or demonic level in the chaos released by Leontes' jealousy, a world full of treachery and murder, pointless sacrifice, sterility and utterly needless pain. This is a world of fantasy below reason, the imagination working in its diseased or "imaginary" aspect. Above this is a middle world of rationality, where the court is functioning normally. This middle world is represented particularly by two characters, Camillo and Paulina, who, like Kent in *King Lear*, combine outspoken honest criticism with a fierce loyalty. Above that again is the world we enter in the final scene, a world of imagination in its genuine creative sense, as far above reason as jealousy is below it.

In the Florizel-Perdita world, which is set mainly in Bohemia, there are also three main levels of the action. At the bottom is Autolycus the thief, by no means as sinister a figure as the jealous Leontes, but still something of a nuisance. He would like to be the standard New Comedy tricky servant, but, as I remarked earlier, Shakespeare doesn't care much for this character type, and manoeuvres the main action around him. He lives in a somewhat mindless present: for the life to come, he says, he sleeps out the thought of it. Above him comes the normally functioning level of this world, which is represented primarily by the sheep-shearing festival (4.4). The imagery of this scene is that of the continuous fertilizing power of nature, with Perdita distributing flowers appropriate to all ages, and with a dance of twelve "satyrs" at the end, who perhaps celebrate the entire twelve-month year. Perdita seems, her lover tells her, like the goddess Flora presiding over "a meeting of the petty gods." In her turn Perdita speaks with the most charming frankness of wanting to strew her lover with flowers, not "like a corse," but as "a bank for love to lie and play on." She has Autolycus warned not to use any "scurrilous words" in his tunes, and while of course the primary meaning is that she is a fastidious girl who dislikes obscenity, her motives are magical as well as moral: a festive occasion should not be spoiled by words of ill omen. The top level of this world, the recognition and marriage, we do not see, but merely hear it reported, as mentioned earlier.

In the Florizel-Perdita world the relation of art to nature has a different aspect at each of these levels. When Autolycus first enters (4.3) he is singing the superb "When daffodils begin to peer" song, one of the finest of all spring songs, and we welcome this harbinger of spring as we do the cuckoo, who is also a thief. Later he comes in with a peddler's pack of rubbish, which he calls "trumpery." We should note this word, because it's used again in a similar context by

Prospero in *The Tempest*: it's connected with *tromper*, deceive, and, at the risk of sounding moralizing, we can say that his ribbons and such are "artificial" in the modern derogatory sense of an art that is mainly a corruption of nature. He also produces a number of broadside ballads, which were quite a feature of Elizabethan life: they were the tabloid newspapers of the time, and some of the alleged news they carried was so extravagant that Shakespeare's examples are hardly caricatures. It is on the next level that Polixenes offers his Renaissance idealistic view of the relation of art to nature: in grafting, we use art in implanting a bud on a stock, but the power of nature is what makes it grow. The emphasis on the power of nature is appropriate, even though Perdita will have nothing to do with any interference from art on "great creating nature." And in the reported recognition, the gentlemen tell us that such wonderful things have happened "that ballad-makers cannot be able to express it." So it seems that Autolycus and his preposterous ballads have something to do with the function of art in this world after all.

In the Leontes-Hermione story we have at the bottom the parody art of Leontes' jealousy making something out of nothing, a demonic reversal of the divine creation. On the middle level we have, in the conversation of the gentlemen, a very curious reference to a painted statue of Hermione made by Julio Romano. Romano was an actual painter, widely touted as the successor of Raphael, but the reason for mentioning his name here eludes us: perhaps there was some topical reason we don't know about. He is said to be a fanatically realistic worker in the technique we'd now call *trompe l'oeil*: there's the word *tromper* again. If what we're told is what we're to believe, there's no statue at all, so there was no point in mentioning him, although the conception of art as an illusion of nature perhaps fits this level and aspect of the story. The final scene involves all the arts in the most striking contrast to the Perdita-Florizel recognition: the action takes place in Paulina's chapel; we are presented with what we're told is painting and sculpture; music and oracular language are used at appropriate moments; and another contemporary meaning of the word "art," magic, so important in *The Tempest*, is also referred to.

If we look at the words that get repeated, it seems as though the word "wonder" has a special connection with the Florizel-Perdita story, and the word "grace" with the Leontes-Hermione one. "Grace" has a bewildering variety of meanings in Shakespearean English, many of them obsolete. In the opening dialogue Hermione uses it so frequently and pointedly that we don't just hear it: it seems to stand out from its context. When she becomes the victim of Leontes's fantasy, she says that what's happening to her is for her "better grace," and when she finally speaks at the end of the play, what she says is a prayer for the graces of the gods to descend. We may, perhaps, isolate from all the possible meanings two major ones: first, the power of God (the Classical gods in this play) that makes the redemption of humanity possible, and, second, the quality that distinguishes civilized life, of the kind "natural" to man, from the untutored or boorish.

Let's see what we have now:

A. The Leontes-Hermione story of the order of nature; winter tale of "grace."	B. The Florizel-Perdita story of the power and fertility of nature; spring tale of "wonder."

Upper Level

A. Transformation of Hermione from illusion to reality; union of all the arts.	B. Recognition of Perdita as princess by birth (i.e., nature); ballads of wonder.

Middle Level

A. Court world of Camillo and Paulina; art as Romano's illusion of nature.	B. World of festival; image of art as grafting or attachment to power of nature.

Lower Level

A. Illusory world of Leontes' jealousy: parody of imaginative creation. Mamillius's aborted "winter's tale."	B. Autolycus: pure present; songs of spring; also "trumpery" or arts corrupting nature.

In the final scene, what we are apparently being told is that Paulina has kept Hermione hidden for sixteen years, Hermione consenting to this because the oracle seemed to hint that Perdita would survive. There was never any statue. But other things seem to be going on that don't quite fit that story. In the first place, Paulina's role, partly actor-manager and partly priestess, seems grotesquely ritualistic and full of pretentious rhetoric on that assumption; some of the things she says are really incantations:

> Music, awake her; strike!
> 'Tis time; descend; be stone no more; approach. . .
>
> (5.3.98–99)

Later she remarks that Hermione is not yet speaking, and then pronounces the words "Our Perdita is found," as though they were the charm that enabled her to speak. In several comedies of Shakespeare, including this one and *The Tempest*, the action gets so hard to believe that a central character summons the rest of the cast into—I suppose— the green room afterward, where, it is promised, all the difficulties will be cleared away. The audience can just go home scratching their heads. Here it looks as though the green room session will be quite prolonged; Leontes says:

> But how, is to be question'd; for I saw her,
> As I thought, dead; and have in vain said many
> A prayer upon her grave.   (5.3.139-41)

One might perhaps visualize Leontes saying, "Do you mean to tell me," etc., then erupting into fury at the thought of all those wasted prayers and starting the whole action over again.

We notice the importance of the word "faith" in this play: it's applied by Camillo to Leontes' fantasy, which is below reason, and by Florizel to his fidelity to Perdita despite parental opposition, which, he says explicitly, is a "fancy" above reason. And in this final scene Paulina tells her group that they must awaken their faith, which would hardly make sense unless Hermione were actually coming to life. Such things don't happen in real life, but they happen in myths, and *The Winter's Tale* is a mythical play. We seem to be getting two versions of the scene at once: which is real and which is the illusion? On the stage there's no difference: the illusion and the reality are the same thing. But if even Leontes can say "how, is to be questioned," what price us as we leave the theatre?

I've spoken of the popularity of Ovid's *Metamorphoses* as a kind of poet's bible, and in no play of Shakespeare, except perhaps *A Midsummer Night's Dream*, is its influence more obvious and insistent than it is here. This is partly because poetic language, a language of myth and metaphor, is the language best adapted to a world of process and change, where everything keeps turning into something else. Even in *King Lear* we saw that a new kind of language was getting born out of all that suffering and horror. Here something equally mysterious is going on, but in the context of comedy. To use Theseus's words "apprehend" and "comprehend": in this final scene we "apprehend" that we're looking at a real Hermione, and "comprehend" that she's been hidden by Paulina for sixteen years and there's no statue. That's the "credible" version: we call it credible because there's nothing to believe. Or, perhaps, we "apprehend" that first there was Hermione, then there was a statue of her after she died, and now there's Hermione again. How do we "comprehend" that? Obviously not by trying to "believe" it.

In Ovid most of the "metamorphoses" are changes downward, from some kind of personal or human being into a natural object, a tree, a bird or a star. But there can also be metamorphosis upward. This happens every year when winter turns into spring and new forms of life appear: this kind of metamorphosis we've been associating with the story of Perdita. The story of Hermione seems to imply something more: new possibilities of expanded vision that such people as Shakespeare have come into the world to suggest to us.

As so often in Shakespeare, expanded vision seems to have a good deal to do with time and the ways we experience it. We noted that *The Triumph of Time* was the subtitle of Greene's *Pandosto*, and the early part of the play stresses such words as "push" and "wild" (meaning rash), which suggest a continuous violation of the normal rhythms of time. Then Time appears as chorus: perhaps it is he, not Apollo, who controls the action. We might even give the two parts of the play the Proustian subtitles of *Time Lost* and *Time Regained*. The concluding speech, by Leontes, speaks of the "gap of time" he fell into with his jealousy, and ends "Hastily lead away." There is no time to be lost, once one has found it again.

From *Northrop Frye on Shakespeare*. Ed. Robert Sandler. New Haven: Yale UP, 1986. Used by permission of Fitzhenry & Whiteside Limited, Publishers.

MASCULINE AUTHORITY AND THE MATERNAL BODY IN *THE WINTER'S TALE*

Janet Adelman

Janet Adelman (1941-2010) characterizes the tragic crisis that erupts in the Sicilian court as an outbreak of extreme insecurity about gender identity. Leontes's masculine sense of authority cannot brook any bond of dependence upon maternal fertility and nurturance, even though it is built into the very process of human generation that created us all. Absolute ideals of male autonomy drive Leontes to seek control over Hermione's sexual capacity by any means necessary. Her transformation into a marble statue aptly signifies Leontes's unwavering compulsion to control her, which leads to her imprisonment, trial, and death during the second and third acts of The Winter's Tale. *Adelman views this murderous quality of tragic masculinity as a legacy of themes fully elaborated in* Hamlet *and variously reprised in Shakespeare's Jacobean tragedies. In the final acts of* The Winter's Tale *tragic masculinity undergoes a beneficent reversal in the younger generation and, ultimately, in Leontes himself. The pastoral episode in Bohemia marks a shift in the divine auspices under which the action unfolds. Apollo, with his appetite for order and control, becomes like a mere mortal in his vulnerability to erotic feeling, and Nature, the goddess who wields power over such irresistible emotions as well as the cosmic forces of animal and vegetable growth and decay, assumes precedence.*

WITHIN SHAKESPEARE'S career, *Antony and Cleopatra* functions as a fragile pastoral moment. Its pastoral is shorn of the power to bring even its modest gains back to the dominating culture: as Egypt's female pastoral is in the end contained and colonised by Rome, so *Antony and Cleopatra*'s moment of festive possibility is largely contained by the surrounding texts. The generative maternal power celebrated in Cleopatra's recreation of Antony is severely curtailed in *Coriolanus*, where maternal presence is once again construed as paternal absence, where mothers are once again fatal to their sons. This construction is, I have argued, the legacy of *Hamlet*, where the mother's sexual body is itself poisonous to the father on whom the son would base his identity; its consequences are variously played out in the problem plays and tragedies that follow from *Hamlet*. Taken together, the romances can be understood as Shakespeare's final attempt to repair the damage of this legacy, in effect to reinstate the ideal parental couple lost at the beginning of *Hamlet*: the idealised mother is recovered in *Pericles* and *The Winter's Tale*, the idealised father in *Cymbeline* and *The Tempest*. But the attempt at recovery itself reinscribes the conditions of loss: in the plays of maternal recovery, the father's authority must be severely undermined and the mother herself subjected to a chastening purgation; in the plays of paternal recovery, the mother must be demonised and banished before the father's authority can be restored.

From beginning to end, the romances reiterate the terms of *Hamlet*, working and reworking his problematic confrontation with the sexualised maternal body: if *Pericles* begins where Hamlet does, in the psychic world poisoned by female sexuality, *The Tempest* answers his need for a bodiless father immune to the female, able at last to control her unweeded garden. Except for a moment in *The Winter's Tale*, when the generative female space of Cleopatra's monument recurs in Paulina's own sheltering monument, the mother and father lost in *Hamlet* cannot be fully recovered together. Instead, the romances oscillate between them, broadly structured by a series of gendered either/or's: either maternal or paternal authority; either female deity or male; either nature or art; either trust in processes larger than the self or the attempt to control these processes.[1] Each play is in effect written in defensive response to the one before it; each destabilises the resolution previously achieved, working and reworking the problematic relationship of masculine authority to the female.

[...]

If *Cymbeline* ends with the magical restoration of paternal authority and the fantasy-accomplishment of a parthenogenetic family in which women need not be half-workers, *The Winter's Tale* begins with the pregnant female body. In its opening lines, the play seems initially to replicate aspects of Belarius's male pastoral, giving us the image of the 'natural' male world from which women have been wholly excluded: in the dialogue between Camillo and Archidamus, the 'rooted' affection (1.1.23) between the brother-kings and the healing powers of fathers' sons take centre stage, with no mention of wives or mothers, and certainly no need for daughters. Though there is tension in this world[2]—the hospitality is distinctly competitive and leaves a residue of anxiety about indebtedness, the kings can 'branch' into 'great difference' from their common root—nonetheless there seems 'not in the world either malice or matter to alter' their love (1.1.33-4). Hermione's entrance—perhaps literally between the two kings?— disrupts this male haven. The visual impact of her pregnant body[3] inevitably focuses attention on her, reminding the audience of what has been missing from the gentlemen's conversation; and her body immediately becomes the site of longing and terror, its very presence disruptive of male bonds and male identity.

Even before Leontes' jealousy makes Hermione's pregnant body the sign of betrayal between the brothers, Polixenes has recast the covert tensions of the first scene in its image:

> Nine changes of the watery star hath been
> The shepherd's note since we have left our throne
> Without a burden. Time as long again
> Would be fill'd up, my brother, with our thanks;
> And yet we should, for perpetuity,
> Go hence in debt: and therefore, like a cipher
> (Yet standing in rich place) I multiply
> With one 'We thank you' many thousands moe.
> That go before it.
>
> (1.2.1-9)

'Nine changes', 'watery star', 'burden', 'fill'd up': in Polixenes' opening lines, anxieties about indebtedness and separation are registered through the imagery of pregnancy,[4] as though Hermione's body provided the language for the rupture in their brotherhood. In fact, as Polixenes goes on to tell us in his mythologised version of the kings' childhood, the sexualised female body has already been assigned this role:

> POLIXENES We were as twinn'd lambs that did frisk i' th' sun,
> And bleat the one at th'other: what we chang'd
> Was innocence for innocence: we knew not
> The doctrine of ill-doing, nor dream'd
> That any did. Had we pursu'd that life,
> And our weak spirits ne'er been higher rear'd
> With stronger blood, we should have answer'd heaven
> Boldly 'not guilty', the imposition clear'd
> Hereditary ours.
> HERMIONE   By this we gather
> You have tripp'd since.
> POLIXENES   O my most sacred lady,
> Temptations have since then been born to's: for
> In those unfledg'd days was my wife a girl;
> Your precious self had not yet cross'd the eyes
> Of my young play-fellow.
>
> (1.2.67-80)

Once again, the female body disrupts the idealised male pastoral, becoming the sign of 'great difference' between the kings: 'crossing'[5] the eyes of the young playfellows, Hermione and the unnamed woman who will be Polixenes' wife unmake their symbiotic innocence, plummeting them simultaneously into adult differentiation—now there is 'my' and 'your' where there had been only 'we' and 'our'—and into their newly sexualised bodies, in effect recording the fall in them as their phallic spirits are higher reared with stronger blood.[6] Polixenes may call Hermione 'most sacred lady', but he makes her body the locus and the sign of division and original sin, as Hermione herself is quick to note (1.2.80-2). Moreover, her visible pregnancy stages the submerged logic of his account of original sin: temptations have been born to us, her presence suggests, because we have been born to them, acquiring original sin at the site of origin.

Both in Polixenes' opening speech and in his pastoral myth, the sexualised female body is the sign of male separation and loss. Moreover, in its very fullness, that body becomes the register of male emptiness. The final metaphorics of Polixenes' opening speech bizarrely transform an expression of his indebtedness to Leontes into an expression of chronic male indebtedness to the female in the procreative act: 'like a cipher/(Yet standing in rich place) I multiply/With one "We thank you" many thousands moe/That go before it.' Nothing in himself, he is able to multiply only when he stands in a rich place: his computational joke barely conceals anxiety about the male role in procreation, an anxiety made visible on stage in the rich place that is Hermione's body.[7] But in thus figuring male emptiness and female fullness, Polixenes allows for a transvaluation of sexuality and of the female body. If women are the first temptation, if the phallic rearing of the spirits with higher blood is the sign of the fall in Polixenes' mythologised account of childhood, here it is only by such standing in rich place that man becomes generative: the rich place itself confers value on him. These sharply contrasting attitudes toward sexuality and toward the female body that engenders it mark the trajectory of the play: from an idealised male pastoral to a pastoral richly identified with the generative potential of the female body; from a sterile court in which the maternal body and the progeny who bear its signs must be harried to death to a court in which that body can be restored, its regenerative sanctity recognised and embraced.

If Polixenes' initial speeches give us the image of what must be cured before the play can end happily and hint at the direction from which cure will come, Leontes' psyche is presented as the locus of the disease. Leontes' jealousy erupts out of nowhere and breaks his world apart, as it breaks the syntax and rhythms of his own speeches apart;

in the violence and obscurity of its expression; it draws the audience into its own sphere, causing us to snatch at nothings, to reconstruct the world (as Leontes himself does) in a reassuringly intelligible image. Any attempt to explain its strangeness away or to make it wholly coherent violates the dramatic principles through which it communicates itself to us; Shakespeare has deliberately left its expression fragmentary and incoherent, the better to engage us in its processes, making us—like Leontes—communicate with dreams (1.2.140). But whether or not we think we can pinpoint the onset of the jealousy or the exact progress of its aetiology, it is far from the psychologically un-motivated 'given' of the plot that it is sometimes taken to be.[8] For the jealousy erupts in response to the renewed separation from a mirror-ing childhood twin and the multiple displacements and vulnerabilities signalled by Hermione's pregnant body;[9] it localises and psychologises the myth of loss embedded in Polixenes' version of Eden. And through it, Shakespeare floods the play with the fantasies that have haunted his male protagonists since *Hamlet*, articulating with astonishing economy and force the anguish of a masculinity that conceives of itself as be-trayed at its point of origin, a masculinity that can read in the full maternal body only the signs of its own loss. In Leontes, Shakespeare condenses the destructive logic of tragic masculinity itself; and then, wrenching the play out of the obsessional space of Leontes' mind, he moves beyond tragedy.

In the fantasies given a local habitation in Leontes' jealousy, the fall into original sin is once again registered through the rupture of an ide-alised mirroring relationship with the brother-twin; genital sexuality once again marks the moment of separation and contamination by women. Polixenes' fantasy of twinship functions in effect as Leontes' prehistory, the shaky foundation from which his jealousy erupts: it is his guarantee of a pure male identity, an identity unproblematised by sexual difference, shaped by a mirroring other who reassuringly gives back only himself;[10] its generative equivalent is the fantasy of male parthenogenesis, with its similar denial of otherness and the woman's part. The alternative to the masculine identity conferred through this mirror is the masculine identity originating in the female and everywhere marked by vulnerability to her: the conflicted identity for which Hermione's pregnant body comes to stand. Either the mir-roring twin or the pregnant wife-mother: like Polixenes' fragile pastoral, Leontes' psychic world cannot contain both together. Hence the re-peated insistence—visual and metaphoric—that Hermione's pregnant body comes between the two kings: as the emblem of a male identity always already contaminated at its source, that body is the limiting condi-tion to the fantasy of an identity formed through male parthenogenesis or a pure male twinship. Its presence in effect forces Leontes to acknowledge his own maternal origins, immersing him in the dangerous waters—the contaminated 'pond' (1.2.195)—of a female sexuality he can neither excise nor control.

The fantasy of twinship functions in effect to protect Leontes from immersion in those waters.[11] His jealousy erupts at the first sign of rupture in that protective mirroring relationship, as though its loss returned him to the site of his vulnerability to the female; 'At my request he would not' (1.2.87) is the first sign of danger. As though newly cast out of his equivalent to the all-male Eden, he finds in Hermione's pregnant body the sign of all he stands to lose: remembering their courtship, he remakes her as the unreliable maternal object, capable of souring the entire world to death by withholding herself from him (1.2.102-4). And this withholding is in his imagination tantamount to annihilation: imagining himself excluded from her rich place, he responds as though he has become Polixenes' cipher, flooded with the sense of his own and the world's nothingness; as he later tells Camillo,

> Why then the world, and all that's in't, is nothing,
> The covering sky is nothing, Bohemia nothing,
> My wife is nothing, nor nothing have these nothings,
> If this be nothing.
>
> (1.2.293-6)[12]

But this nothingness is not tolerable: and Leontes retaliates against it, attempting through a monstrous birth of his own—the 'something' born of his affection's copulation with nothing (1.2.138-43)[13]—to recreate himself and the world in the shape of his delusion. If the possibility of Hermione's betrayal first plunges him into the nothingness of maternal abandonment, it becomes his stay against nothingness as it hardens into delusion: the world is nothing, he tells Camillo, *if Hermione is not unfaithful*. Threatened by absolute loss, he seizes on the fantasy of Hermione's adultery as though it in itself could give him something to hold on to: better the 'something' of cuckoldry than the nothingness into which he would otherwise dissolve. Naming himself a cuckold, insisting on his identity as cuckold and his community with other men (1.2.190-200), he finds in the culturally familiar fiction of female betrayal in marriage both an acceptable narrative for his sense of primal loss and a new adult selfhood. Through the self-born delusion of Hermione's betrayal, he thus gives himself a recognisable place to stand; without it, 'the centre is not big enough to bear/A schoolboy's top' (2.1.102-3).

The fantasy of Hermione's adultery initially seems to serve Leontes well, answering several of his psychic needs at once. Through it, Leontes can attempt to undo his subjection to the rich place of Hermione's body, making her—rather than himself—nothing and securing his 'rest' by giving her to the fire (2.3.8). His monstrous birth in effect undoes hers: if she is unfaithful, then he can deny his connection to her body, both as husband and as son. Through his delusion, he can imagine her pregnant body as the sign of her infidelity, rather than the sign of his sexual concourse with her; and the baby she carries thus becomes no part of him. For in his mobile fantasy, her pregnant body threatens to display him in the foetus she bears; he keeps dissolving into that foetus. The delusion of Hermione's adultery affords Leontes secure ground in part because it helps him resist this regressive pull back toward her body; in its own way, it serves the same needs as the initial fantasy of twinship. But it is ultimately no more successful than that fantasy; in the end, it returns him to what refuses to stay repressed. In Leontes' fluid formulations, cuckoldry fuses with sexual intercourse and with birth, implicating him once again in the maternal origin he would deny. If Othello and Posthumus conflate adultery with marital sexuality,[14] Leontes conflates both with cuckoldry: all three 'sully/The purity and whiteness' of his sheets (1.2.326-7). For the sexually mature male body is one with the cuckold's body, both marked by the deforming signs of female betrayal: differentiating himself from Mamillius—'thou want'st a rough pash and the shoots that I have/To be full like me' (1.2.128-9)—Leontes identifies the bull's horns with the cuckold's, as though the sexually mature male body were by definition the cuckold's body. And both sexuality and cuckoldry return him to the original site of betrayal: imagining himself a cuckold—'Inch-thick, knee-deep; o'er head and ears a fork'd one' (1.2.186)—he simultaneously imagines himself sexually entering Hermione's body between her forked legs[15] and immersed in that body, knee-deep, over head and ears, as though returned to the foetal position. Cuckold, adulterer and foetus fuse in their entry into the maternal womb, the belly that 'will let in and out the enemy,/With bag and baggage' (1.2.205-6).[16] And the foetus itself becomes that enemy: in the most bizarre and violent of Leontes' conflations—his brutal 'let her sport herself/With that she's big with' (2.1.60-1)—he imagines the unborn baby he would disown as the mother's illicit sexual partner,[17] graphically literalising the sexualised return to the womb.

Deprived of his protective mirroring relationship, thrust back to his origin in the maternal body, Leontes attempts to escape that body through the fantasy of his own cuckoldry; but the fantasy itself betrays him, returning him to his source. But Leontes has simultaneously been pursuing another strategy against nothingness: virtually as soon as his jealousy erupts, Leontes turns toward Mamillius and attempts to recreate a mirroring twin in him.[18] He begins with the familiar patriarchal worry that his son might not be his son: his thrice-repeated assertions of likeness (1.2.130, 135, 159) serve, first of all, to guarantee his own paternity, as if it were in doubt. But—as in *King Lear* and *Cymbeline*—worries about illegitimacy turn out to be in part a cover for worries about the female role in procreation, legitimate or illegitimate. As Leontes makes clear when he violently separates the boy from his mother—as though she were 'infectious', Hermione says later (3.2.98)—his fear is not that Mamillius resembles Polixenes, but that he resembles his mother:

> Give me the boy: I am glad you did not nurse him:
> Though he does bear some signs of me, yet you
> Have too much blood in him.
>
> (2.1.56–8)

In this construction of likeness, the signs of Mamillius's difference from him are signs not of an illegitimate father but of his mother's contaminating presence in her son: if he is her child, then he is not fully his father's. Hence the drive toward absolute identity in Leontes' early assertions of the likeness between father and son: those assertions —especially the anxiety-filled assertion that they are 'almost as like as eggs' (1.2.130)[19]—move from a (just barely) rational concern with paternity toward a deeply irrational attempt to replace the lost twin-ship by reinstating the fantasy of male parthenogenesis in Mamillius. Leontes' pet names for his son increasingly identify the child as a part —perhaps specifically a sexual part—of his own body, his 'bawcock', a 'collop' of his flesh (1.2.121, 137), as though he could be made without his mother's participation; in effect, those names would make him a split-off portion of his father's masculinity, hence a secure repository for Leontes' threatened identity.[20]

But this defensive fantasy cannot be sustained: like the fantasy of cuckoldry, the attempt at protective identification with Mamillius turns back on itself, ultimately returning Leontes to the corrupt maternal body. Seeing himself in his 'unbreech'd' son may temporarily relieve Leontes of the guilt associated with the use of his own dangerous orna-ment (1.2.155, 158), but it must simultaneously recall the period when he himself was not securely differentiated from his mother.[21] For the inescapable fact of maternal origin is always there in Mamillius—as much a part of him as his name, with its unmistakable allusion to the maternal nursery Leontes so dreads.[22] Approaching the boy sitting by his mother's side, Leontes recoils as though he were seeing himself; and he immediately acts to remove the child from her infectious presence. Conflating his own danger with what he imagines to be Mamillius's, he figures Hermione's betrayal as the source of infection in his drink:

> There may be in the cup
> A spider steep'd, and one may drink, depart,
> And yet partake no venom (for his knowledge
> Is not infected); but if one present
> Th'abhorr'd ingredient to his eye, make known
> How he hath drunk, he cracks his gorge, his sides,
> With violent hefts. I have drunk, and seen the spider.
>
> (2.1.39-45)

'I have drunk, and seen the spider'; 'I am glad you did not nurse him': only eleven lines apart, the phrases echo and explicate one another, identifying Hermione's maternal body with the spider in the cup.[23] In Leontes' infected imagination, maternal nursery is that spider, the infection taken in at the source; his spasmodic attempts to disown Hermione are the psychic equivalents of the violent hefts he images, violent attempts to heave out the internalised mother, the contaminated origin within, like a child spitting up infected—or soured—milk.[24]

Leontes' psychosis illustrates in its purest form the trauma of tragic masculinity, the trauma of contamination at the site of origin. Hermione's pregnant body in effect returns him to this point of origin, and to the sense of contamination culturally registered as original sin; and, despite all his best efforts, the Mamillius in whom he would see himself originally pure gives him back only the reflection of her taint in him. But this taint is ultimately epitomised for Leontes in the baby Hermione now carries; the drama of his expulsion and recovery of the female is thus played out through her. Like everyone else (2.1.17; 2.2.26), Leontes apparently expects this baby to be a boy; that she turns out to be a girl merely confirms her mother's presence in her and hence—according to the familiar logic of illegitimacy[25]— her status as a 'female bastard' (2.3.174): for Leontes at this stage, 'female' and 'bastard' might as well be interchangeable terms. But her supposed illegitimacy nonetheless serves a defensive purpose. When Paulina brings the baby to him and attempts to make him see himself in her, he reacts with panic, summoning up all the cultural tropes for overpowering women—the shrew, the mannish woman, the husband-beating wife, the witch, the bawd, the midwife—with a nearly comic haste:[26] to see himself in his daughter would be the final blow to his threatened masculinity.[27] Paulina's strategy must therefore backfire: the more convincingly she can represent the baby girl as his likeness, the more desperately he will need to dissociate himself from her, hysterically naming her bastard (seven times within roughly forty lines) and casting her out 'like to itself,/No father owning it' (3.2.87-8). He has already managed to isolate Hermione with her women, as though their femaleness were catching; now he phobically drives Paulina off the stage and refuses to go near his infant daughter, violently disowning her as though she too could contaminate him.

In casting her out, Leontes begins counter-phobically to remake himself in the shape of the overwhelming mother he most fears: he would dash his infant's brains out with his own hands (2.3.139-40) or abandon her in a landscape of absolute deprivation (2.3.175).[28] It is diagnostic of this play's radical re-valuation of the maternal that Leontes should thus appropriate the imagery of Lady Macbeth: here the ultimate source of danger is not the overwhelming mother but the tyrannical husband/father. Localising tragic masculinity in Leontes and decisively moving beyond it, Shakespeare thus recasts the gendered aetiology of tragedy as he had defined it in *Hamlet*, *King Lear*, *Macbeth*, and *Coriolanus*: no longer the province of maternal contamination, it is now the province of the male ego that fears such contamination, the ego that would remake the world in the image of its own desired purity. With the casting out of his baby girl, the death of the son too obviously born of woman, and the apparent death of his wife, Leontes has arrived at this point: he has in effect exorcised female generativity and achieved the all-male landscape he thought he wanted. But he discovers in it not the timeless spring of Polixenes' pastoral fantasy but the landscape of tragedy, an endless winter of barrenness and deprivation the psychic equivalent of the 'barren mountain, and still winter/In storm perpetual' (3.2.212-13) that Paulina describes as the fitting setting for his repentance. But the same exorcism that locates Leontes in this psychic landscape allows Shakespeare to undertake a radical recuperation of the maternal body: exorcised and banished from the stage, it can in effect be reconstituted and revalued; and thus released from the confines of Leontes' obsessions, the play itself can begin the turn from tragedy to romance.

The first hints of this release come with the birth of Perdita, 'lusty, and like to live' (2.2.27), herself 'free'd and enfranchis'd' from the womb (2.2.61.). The short scene in which her birth is reported is filled with the promise of release from the tyrannous hold of Leontes' mind. The entrance of Paulina brings not only a new character but a new voice— shrewd, self-assured, funny—strong enough to provide an authoritative countervoice to Leontes'; and from her we hear for the first time of the 'great nature' (2.2.60), the 'good goddess Nature' (2.3.103), who will become the presiding deity of recuperation.[29] Through her, Shakespeare begins the move toward romance, simultaneously underscoring a new alliance between gender and genre: her husband allows himself to become the agent of Leontes' delusions (though he recognises the sanctity of the Hermione who appears to him [3.3.23], he nonetheless believes her guilty); she becomes the advocate for mother and baby, aligning herself firmly with the female forces of recovery.[30] While Paulina sees birth as the promise of freedom and enfranchisement, Antigonus repeats the tragic paradigm linking birth and mortality: in what are virtually his last words—'poor wretch,/That for thy mother's fault art thus expos'd/To loss and what may follow!' (3.3.49-51)—he rewrites the baby's exposure not as the consequence of Leontes' phobic delusion but as a parable for birth itself, the exposure to loss that is always the mother's fault.[31] But Perdita lives, while he himself dies as the sacrificial (and gendered) representative of tragedy.[32] And with his death, the play turns decisively away from the tragic paradigm, increasingly aligning its own artistic processes with the good goddess whom Paulina invokes.

Shakespeare achieves the recuperation of the maternal body and the attendant turn from tragedy to romance by immersion in the fertile space of a decidedly female pastoral. Though the entrance to the pastoral domain is mediated by a series of male figures—Time, Polixenes and Camillo, Autolycus—that domain itself is deeply allied with the fecundity of 'great Creating nature' (4.4.88); filled with the vibrant energies of sexuality and seasonal change, it stands as a rebuke to Polixenes' static and nostalgic male pastoral and to the masculine identity that would find itself there.[33] And it reaches back, behind Polixenes, toward the nightmare version of the female body that could provoke his consolatory dream: the circumstances of Antigonus's death at the entrance to this pastoral allude to Lear's great tragic pastoral, replicating its storm and literalising its bear and sea (*King Lear*, 3.4.9-11), as though signalling that it too must be revised before the play can proceed. And through Florizel, Shakespeare hints at just such revision. Lear sees in his pastoral the emblem of an horrific female sexuality utterly beyond male control; like Leontes lashing out at the Hermione who 'rounds apace' (2.1.16), he would attack the generative female body, 'Strike flat the thick rotundity o' th' world!/Crack Nature's moulds, all germens spill at once' (3.2.7-8). Florizel recalls this body in his vow to Perdita:

> It cannot fail, but by
> The violation of my faith; and then
> Let nature crush the sides o' th' earth together,
> And mar the seeds within!
>
> (4.4.477-80)

But he would recuperate what Lear would destroy,[34] aligning his faith with its generative potential and cherishing the seeds within.

If Leontes founds his masculine identity on separation from the female, Florizel embraces the female. He has already told Perdita 'I cannot be/Mine own, nor anything to any, if/I be not thine' (4.4.43-5); now he disowns the ordinary patriarchal identifiers: 'From my succession wipe me, father; I/Am heir to my affection' (4.4.481-2). Mirrored not in an idealised male twin or in a father but in Perdita—Florizel to her Flora—he founds his identity in his relation to her, in the process recuperating the word—'affection'—that had figured Leontes' monstrous birth. And in return, Perdita promises him not the static eternity of Polixenes' pastoral but an aliveness that springs out of the very conditions of his mortality. She would 'strew him o'er and o'er' with the 'flowers o' th' spring' that Proserpina let 'fall/From Dis's waggon' (4.4.113, 117-18, 129), flowers that allude to the seasonal cycles of birth and death. 'What, like a corpse?' Florizel asks playfully, recapitulating the fears of all those men who find only death in love, only mortality in the sexual body; and Perdita replies,

> No, like a bank, for love to lie and play on:
> Not like a corpse; or if—not to be buried,
> But quick, and in mine arms.
>
> (4.4.130-2)

In these wonderful lines, Perdita encapsulates the whole process of regeneration enacted by the play, herself becoming the presiding deity of recuperation. Immersed in her pastoral, covered with the flowers that are her sign as Flora, Florizel is immersed in the mortal body: hence the pun on *corpse*. But Perdita does not let that body stay dead. She first rewrites it as the literal ground of love—the bank, for love to lie and play on—and then she revives it, making it 'quick' by taking it into her embrace. *Quick* is the decisive word, in which all the anxieties about maternal origin can meet and be resolved: as he quickens in her embrace, she herself imagistically becomes quick with him; restoring him through the pregnant fecundity of her own body.

If Lear's anti-pastoral storm figures the horrific female body that teaches man his mortality, Perdita's pastoral refigures that body in Perdita herself. Imagining Florizel a bank for love to lie and play on, she remakes herself in the image of Love, the Venus genetrix who is one with great creating nature:[35] her words are in fact anticipated by Shakespeare's earlier Venus ('Witness this primrose bank whereon I lie' [*Venus and Adonis*, 1.151]). Polixenes will later equate the pastoral landscape itself with her body, forbidding his son entrance to both and threatening death to Perdita 'if ever henceforth thou/These rural latches to his entrance open' (4.4.438-9).[36] But within her 'rural latches', in the sheltering womb of her pastoral, the mortal body is refigured: death is not denied but embraced and redefined as the condition of the body's aliveness. Perdita's imagistic revival of Florizel turns crucially on her astonishing *or if*, with its acknowledgment that the body is indeed like a corpse: for only what can die can live. Perdita thus reverses the logic of tragedy, restoring aliveness to the mortal body: if Leontes' logic is 'if alive, then dead', the logic of her pastoral is 'if dead, then alive'. As an extension of her body, Perdita's version of pastoral thus repairs the fall implicit in Polixenes' pastoral vision; through it, Shakespeare in effect returns to the source of original sin, rewriting it as the source of wholeness and life.

Florizel stakes his faith on the generative female body, and his extravagant gesture predicts the movement of the play: for with the recovery of the benign maternal body as a source of life comes the recovery of faith, the recovery that enables the play's final restitutions. In its most primitive form, Leontes' crisis has been a crisis of faith.[37] For him as for Othello, doubt is intolerable: the merest possibility of his wife's infidelity spoils her as a source of inner or outer goodness; doubt itself is tantamount to the loss of the sustaining object. Through his doubt, Leontes relives as though for the first time the infant's discovery that the world is separate from him and is not subject to his desires: if his wife can betray him, she is one with the mother who can seduce and betray, souring his inner world as he takes her into himself. All his fantasies of betrayal, of contamination by the female, of spoiling at the maternal site of origin, reflect this fear: in his loss of faith, he can locate only contamination and dread in the female space outside the self. Hence the logic through which he imagines Hermione's betrayal as the spoiling of nurturance: the spider in the cup condenses and epitomises the unreliable outer world that can contaminate the self, the world that is always figured first in the mother's body. Unable to trust in this world, he rejects it, reshaping it in its original form as a promiscuous woman and banishing it, reducing it to nothingness in order to stave off its capacity to hurt him and the contamination he fears from it.

But a world so reduced is a world from which no good can come. As Leontes increasingly manages to do away with the world—casting off wife, friend, children, counsellors, reducing everything external to the level of his dreams (3.2.81)—he not only reflects but sustains and ensures his own inner hopelessness, his doubt that there is anything good out there. In his panic at the possibility of loss, he unmakes the world; and his cure can come only from the world's refusal to stay unmade. Hence, I think, the primary psychic significance of the play's radical break with Leontes' consciousness: though that break seems to court dramatic discontinuity, it is in fact the only possible antidote to his disease. If Leontes seems to have succeeded in reducing the world to the level of his dreams, what he—and we—need to learn is that the world will go on existing, that it will survive despite his best efforts at destroying it.[38] And the pastoral, first of all, signifies this fact: it is the place neither he nor we knew about, the place outside the sphere of his omnipotent control. Such a place is by definition dangerous: for Lear, it is epitomised by his monstrous daughter-mothers and by the overwhelming maternal body of the storm that shows him he is not ague-proof; and in his disease, Leontes too can see only betrayal there, in the region beyond his control. But if this place is dangerous, it is also the only place from which hope can come: blotting out the world, making it nothing, can lead only to the stasis of Leontes' winter's tale, in which there is no possibility of renewal. The pastoral of Act 4 acknowledges the danger—hence its bear and storm—but it insists on the possibility of hope: here, the mother's body is full of promise. Through its association with the female and its structural position in the play—outside Leontes' control, outside his knowledge—the pastoral can figure this body, the unknown place outside the self where good things come from.

If the world's treachery is first figured in the maternal body, then the recovery of faith requires the recuperation of that body. The pastoral in effect initiates this recuperation: *The Winter's Tale* moves from tragedy to romance by demonstrating that this place of 'otherness' can be the source of richness as well as poverty, making the promise that the world is worth having faith in. And in the end, Shakespeare's deep intuition makes Leontes' recovery of trust in the world tantamount to his recovery of the benign maternal body in the literal form of Hermione: if Leontes' attempt to control the world by banishing the female had unmade the world for him, locating him in his own dead inner spaces, Hermione's coming to life figures the return of the world to him and his capacity to tolerate and participate in its aliveness, with all its attendant risks.[39] This return is tellingly mediated by a series of female figures, each beyond the sphere of his control: by Paulina, the archetypically unruly woman; by Perdita, the daughter who outlives his destructive fantasies, growing beyond his knowledge; and by the 'good goddess Nature', the 'great creating nature' they both invoke. For the male effort to make the self safe by controlling the female body is what must be relinquished before Hermione can return:[40] in this play's gendering of doubt and faith, faith means willingness to submit to unknown processes outside the self, processes registered as female. Hence, I think, the shift in status of the play's ruling deity:

though Apollo is at first clearly the god in charge, his authority diminishes as the play gathers toward an ending; named eleven times before the end of Act 3, scene 3, he is mentioned only twice after, and not at all in the recognition scenes that ostensibly manifest his power by fulfilling his oracle. We too as audience must learn to trust in the female: control of the play is increasingly given over to the numinous female presence invoked by Paulina and Perdita, the goddess nature who is named eleven times in Act 4, scene 4 and Act 5, scene 2. The pastoral scene is again the point of transition: there the 'fire-rob'd god' (4.4.29) becomes merely one of those subject to the erotic energies of great creating nature; the ceremonious solemnity and unearthliness (3.1.7) of his sacred habitat give way to the profound earthliness of hers, as sacredness itself is redefined and relocated in the female body of the natural world.

The shift from male to female deity thus epitomises the movement of the play: for Apollo stands for the reassurances of male control, including artistic control, conventionally gendered male and set against a female nature;[41] and this control is what Leontes must be willing to give up. The conventional gendering of the art-nature debate thus suits the purposes of Shakespeare's gendering of the process of faith; and given that the crisis of faith is initiated by Hermione's pregnant body, it is no wonder that the debate turns crucially on the issue of breeding. For Polixenes, the prototypical artist is the gardener who manages nature's generativity, marrying 'a gentler scion to the wildest stock', making her 'bark of baser kind' conceive 'by bud of nobler race' (4.4.92-5). And though he claims that this artist's power derives from and is subservient to nature herself (4.4.89-92), the incipient pun on 'kind' tells a different story: the implicit fusion of class and gender terms—a fusion played out for Polixenes in Perdita's supposedly lower-class body—represents art as the masculine taming of nature's wildness, the ennobling of her base material. But of course Perdita's body turns out not to be base: Polixenes may seem to win this debate; but the structure of the play overturns his temporary victory. In the end, the play decisively rejects the artificial generation of another male artist—Julio Romano, who 'would beguile Nature of her custom' (5.2.98), outdoing nature by making people in her place. In the context of the gendered art-nature debate, Paulina's introduction to the statue takes on a new emphasis: for the statue who can come alive 'excels' specifically 'whatever . . . hand of man hath done' (5.3.16-17). As Apollo gives way to nature, art gives way to her great creating powers: Leontes asks, 'What fine chisel/Could ever yet cut breath?' (5.3.78-9).

In Act 2, scene 1, Leontes' entrance had violently shattered the sheltering female space occupied by Hermione and her ladies; the death of Mamillius was the consequence of that shattering and the attendant loss of maternal presence, without which—his death tells us—we cannot live. Now that space is recreated in Paulina's refuge, which Leontes' long penitential submission entitles him to enter; and here maternal presence can be restored. And the restoration turns on bringing him face to face with exactly what he has done, so that he can undo it step by step, vesting Hermione with life as he has earlier deprived her of it. For the statue grants him what he thought he wanted: the unreliable female body reduced to an icon he could possess forever, static and unchanging; in Othello's words over the Desdemona he has similarly turned to alabaster, 'No more moving' (*Othello*, 5.2.94). Now, in his wife's 'dead likeness' (5.3.15), he sees the consequences of his inability to tolerate her difference, his attempt at absolute control:[42] confronting in its stoniness both the cold barrenness he has made of the world and the deadness of his own inner world—he has been 'more stone than it' (5.3.38)—he is overwhelmed by longing for sheer aliveness—hers, and his own—whatever the risks. And in the end, his longing creates her alive for him, recreating aliveness in them both: for the process of her restoration to him has always been interior; all that is required is that he awaken his faith (5.3.95). Brought through Paulina's ministrations to accept what he knows cannot be true, what is beyond not only his control but his rational understanding, he gives himself over to a magic 'lawful as eating' (5.3.111): as the spider in the cup had registered the loss of faith in the world, the sanctity of this moment is registered through an image of renewed nurturance. For now 'greediness of affection' (5.2.102) can be fed in a world made newly trustworthy: in response to his desire, the statue moves, at once embodying and rewarding his faith.

If in his rage and fear Leontes had obliterated the maternal body of the world, his long submission to the female rewards him in the end by returning the world alive to him in the shape of his wife. And though Leontes has—from his point of view—created her aliveness, she is nonetheless alive beyond his need of her: she exists on her own terms, beyond the sphere of his omnipotence. Shakespeare signals her independent existence by insisting that we see her awakening into life from her point of view as well as his: for Hermione awakens only at Paulina's repeated urging ("'Tis time; descend; . . . approach; . . ./ Come! . . . stir, nay, come away' [5.3.99-101]), as though unwilling to risk coming alive; 'Be stone no more. . . . Bequeath to death your numbness' (5.3.99, 102) makes us feel what her transformation feels like to her. And once alive, she remains outside the sphere of Leontes' omnipotence; though she answers his desire with her embrace, she then turns away from him, turns toward Perdita, insisting on her own agency, her own version of her story: 'Thou shalt hear that I . . . have preserv'd/Myself to see the issue' (5.3.125-8). This turning away seems to me extraordinary and wonderful; we need only try to imagine Cordelia turning thus from Lear to see what is at stake. For through it, Shakespeare marks and validates Hermione's separateness as the source of her value, accepting female separateness for himself as well as for Leontes; and he simultaneously opens up a space for the female narrative—specifically the mother-daughter narrative—his work has thus far suppressed. As the mark of his own renewed capacity to tolerate female separateness, he rewrites his own rewriting of one of the governing myths of his imagination, in the process restoring it to its original form: if in *Lear* he occludes the mother-daughter bond central to the story of Proserpina and Ceres, reshaping it as a mother-son or father-daughter narrative, here he restores that bond, as though acknowledging a female continuity and generativity outside the sphere of male desire.

The Hermione who awakens is thus both the creation of Leontes' renewed desire and independent of that desire; she exists at the boundary between inner and outer, self and other. Situated thus, she epitomises the recovery of fruitful relatedness with the world: the relatedness that Winnicott saw modelled in the infant's relation with its first not-me possession, the relatedness that enables creative and recreative play in the potential space that is neither self nor other.[43] And if Leontes is brought to this place, we are brought there, too:[44] in the last moments of the play, Shakespeare aligns his own theatre with Paulina's female space, where we too can 'sup' (5.2.103), where our desires can be safely fed in recreative play. For the female space of Hermione's recovery is also the space of Shakespeare's theatre: as many have noted, Hermione's aliveness alludes to the risky aliveness of theatre itself, with its moving actors; and like Paulina's, Shakespeare's is a participatory theatre, in which the awakening of our faith is required.[45] Like Leontes, we must first be willing to relinquish control: Shakespeare requires us to give up our position as knowing audience while he transports us to the place we did not know about and gives us the recognition scene we were not looking for, asking that we recreate Leontes' faith in ourselves by our own willingness to believe in what we know cannot be happening. For just this willingness to suspend our own mistrust, to participate in the rich illusionistic play of Hermione's recovery without undue anxiety that we are being played upon, signals the recovery of potential space in us. In the first half of the play we had witnessed the shattering of this space in Leontes, who, in his inability to tolerate the unreliable world outside himself, had retreated to the space of his delusion. From this position of dread, free play across the boundary between inner and outer becomes impossible: any intrusion of the world merely bolsters his conviction that he is being played upon, that his wife's sexual play has forced him to play a role not of his own choosing (1.2.187-9). We witness the restored possibility of play in the rich festivity of pastoral;[46] now, as we choose with Leontes to make Hermione live, submitting ourselves both to our own desires and to Shakespeare's control of us, we participate in the restoration of the zone of trust, where we discover our own aliveness by allowing the world to come alive for us in the play of her return.

NOTES

1. My account of this oscillation, like much else in this chapter, is deeply indebted to Richard Wheeler, specifically to his powerful description of the oscillation between trust/merger and autonomy/ isolation throughout Shakespeare's tragedies and romances (*Shakespeare's Development and the Problem Comedies* [Berkeley, CA, 1981], esp. pp. 156-7, 200-8, and 213-14).

2. The tension is noted by many; see especially Peter Erickson on the corruption of the male entertainment on which patriarchy rests (*Patriarchal Structures in Shakespeare's Drama* [Berkeley, CA, 1985], pp. 149-51) and Ruth Nevo on the reversible images of estrangement in the kings' togetherness (*Shakespeare's Other Language* [New York, 1987], pp. 100-1).

3. Among those who stress the centrality of Hermione's pregnancy, see especially Erickson (*Patriarchal Structures*, pp. 148-9), Carol T. Neely (*Broken Nuptials in Shakespeare's Plays* [New Haven, CT, 1985], pp. 191-2), and Stanley Cavell (*Disowning Knowledge* [Cambridge, 1987], pp. 208-13). I am particularly indebted to Neely's account here.

4. For many, the pregnancy imagery here primes the audience for Leontes' suspicions; see, e.g., Charles Frey (*Shakespeare's Vast Romance: A Study of 'The Winter's Tale'* [Columbia, 1980], p. 120) and Nevo (*Shakespeare's Other Language*, pp. 101-3). Cavell's extraordinary account of telling, counting, indebtedness, and revenge turns complexly on the imagery of pregnancy and indebtedness here (*Disowning Knowledge*, p. 209).

5. For *cross*, see *OED* 12, *to cross the path of*: 'to come in the way of; often implying obstruction or thwarting', and *OED* 14, 'to thwart, oppose, go counter to'. Shakespeare often uses the word in this general sense: of numerous uses, see, e.g., 3 *Henry VI*, 3.2.127; *Much Ado*, 1.3.59; *Antony and Cleopatra*, 1.3.9; and *Pericles*, 5.1.229.

6. For the specifically phallic connotations of *spirit*, see Stephen Booth (*Shakespeare's Sonnets* [New Haven, CT, 1977], pp. 441-3) and *Romeo and Juliet*, 2.1.24. Many have noted that Polixenes' version of Eden

unorthodoxly exempts the boys from original sin, figuring the sexual woman as temptation and making phallic sexuality equivalent to the fall; see, e.g., Murray M. Schwartz ('Leontes' Jealousy in *The Winter's Tale*', *American Imago*, 30 [1973], 257), Mark Taylor (*Shakespeare's Darker Purpose: A Question of Incest* [New York, 1982], pp. 35-8), Peter Lindenbaum ('Time, Sexual Love, and the Uses of Pastoral in *The Winter's Tale*', *Modern Language Quarterly*, 33 [1972], 7-8), and W. Thomas MacCary (*Friends and Lovers: The Phenomenology of Desire in Shakespearean Comedy* [New York, 1985], p. 203).

7. Howard Felperin notes the imagery of copulation implicit in Polixenes' 'standing' and finds in it evidence of the play's contagious suspicion, its self-conscious representation of the fall from verbal innocence into multivocality or linguistic indeterminacy ('"Tongue-tied our queen?": The Deconstruction of Presence in *The Winter's Tale*', in *Shakespeare and the Question of Theory*, ed. Patricia Parker and Geoffrey Hartmann [New York, 1985], p. 9). In Nevo's wonderfully suggestive account, Polixenes' phrase registers Leontes' 'nothing-ness, the emptiness of exclusion from a once experienced plenitude' (*Shakespeare's Other Language*, p. 103).

8. Among the many who find the jealousy unmotivated and see in it evidence of Shakespeare's declining interest in verisimilitude and individualistic character, see, e.g., Rosalie L. Colie (*Shakespeare's Living Art* [Princeton, NJ, 1974], p. 266) and Frey (*Shakespeare's Vast Romance*, pp. 28, 45). Psychoanalytic and feminist critics have of course found motive a-plenty. Many see in the jealousy primarily Leontes' generalised fear of sexuality, displaced onto women (e.g., Lindenbaum, 'Time, Sexual Love', pp. 10-11; Patricia Southard Gourlay, '"O my most sacred lady": Female Metaphor in *The Winter's Tale*', *English Literary Renaissance*, 5 [1975], 376, 380; Carol Thomas Neely, 'Women and Issue in *The Winter's Tale*', *Philological Quarterly*, 57 [1978], 182-3, extended in *Broken Nuptials*, pp. 193-4; Mark Taylor, *Shakespeare's Darker Purpose* [New York, 1982] pp. 38-9; Frey, *Shakespeare's Vast Romance*, p. 130; Diane Elizabeth Dreher, *Domination and Defiance* [Lexington, MA, 1986], pp. 150-5). Many follow Stewart in attributing the jealousy specifically to Leontes' attempt to suppress his homoerotic bond with Polixenes (J. I. M. Stewart, *Character and Motive* [New York, 1949], pp. 31-6; John Ellis, 'Rooted Affection: the Genesis of Jealousy in *The Winter's Tale*', *College English,* 25 [1964], 525-7; Leslie A. Fielder, *The Stranger in Shakespeare* [London, 1972], pp. 151-2); for some, that bond itself is a response to oedipal desires and fears (C. L. Barber, '"Thou That Beget'st Him"', *Shakespeare Survey*, 22 [1969], 65, extended in Barber and Richard P. Wheeler, *The Whole Journey* [Berkeley, CA, 1986], pp. 18, 329-30; Stephen Reid, '*The Winter's Tale*', *American Imago*, 27 [1970], 266-74) or to an underlying narcissistic crisis (Coppélia Kahn, *Man's Estate*, [Berkeley,

CA, 1986], pp. 214-17; MacCary, *Friends and Lovers*, pp. 203, 206).
For René Girard, the jealousy reflects Leontes' realistic appraisal
of the mimetic desire upon which such bonds are based ('Jealousy
in *The Winter's Tale*', in *Alphonse Juilland: D'une passion l'autre,* ed.
Brigitte Cazelles and René Girard [Saratoga, CA, 1987], pp. 47-57).
For others, the motivational centre is less in the male bond than
in the fantasised relationship with the mother per se: see especially
Schwartz's account of Leontes' response to the fear of separation
from an idealised maternal presence and the recovery of that presence through sanctioned communal bonds ('Leontes' Jealousy', pp.
256-73; "'*The Winter's Tale:* Loss and Transformation', *American Imago*,
32 [1975], 145-99); Richard Wheeler's account of the loss and recovery of trust in the 'hallowed presence' on which sustained selfhood
can be based (*Shakespeare's Development and the Problem Comedies*
[Berkeley, CA, 1981], pp. 82-4, 214-21); Erickson's account of the patriarchal transformation and appropriation of an untrustworthy maternal bounty (*Patriarchal Structures*, pp. 148-70); and Nevo's account
of the fears of maternal abandonment and annihilation played out in
Mamillius's death (*Shakespeare's Other Language*, pp. 104-14). (Among
these, Schwartz's seems to me still the fullest and most nuanced
psychoanalytic account of the play; I am deeply indebted to it, and
to the work of Barber, Wheeler, Neely, Kahn, and Erickson, all of
which has influenced my thinking about the play.)

9. In Erickson's elegant formulation, 'The place of Iago is here filled by
   Hermione's pregnancy' (*Patriarchal Structures*, p. 148).
10. See Schwartz, Kahn, and MacCary for similar readings of the narcis-
    sism implicit in the fantasy of twinship.
11. In 'Male Bonding in Shakespeare's Comedies', I argued for this de-
    fensive function: the fantasy of twinship 'allows for a new sense of
    self based on separateness from the mother while maintaining the
    fluidity of boundaries between self and other characteristic of that
    first relationship. In that sense it offers protection against engulfment
    by the mother while allowing for the comforts of union' (in *Shake-
    speare's Rough Magic: Renaissance Essays in Honor of C. L. Barber,* ed.
    Peter Erickson and Coppelia Kahn. [Newark, NJ 1985], p. 92).
12. Leontes is ostensibly proclaiming the world something, not nothing,
    in his speech to Camillo: the world dissolves into nothingness only
    if he is mistaken in his reading of the signs of Hermione's guilt. But
    despite this ostensible logic, any audience subjected to the relentless
    nothing of these lines will probably hear in them the pull toward an-
    nihilation more clearly than the initial if-clause. For me, at any rate,
    they are terrifying. See Nevo (*Shakespeare's Other Language*, p. 114),
    for a similar reading of these lines.
13. The distorted copulative and birth imagery of Leontes' 'affection'
    speech has often been noted; see especially Schwartz ('Leontes'

Jealousy,' pp. 264-5), Carol Neely (*The Winter's Tale*: The Triumph of Speech', *Studies in English Literature, 1500-1900*, 15 [1975], 325-7), and MacCary *(Friends and Lovers*, pp. 204-6).

14. See Janet Adelman, *Suffocating Mothers: Fantasies of Maternal Origin in Shakespeare's Plays* (London, 1992), p. 213.

15. See *King Lear*, 4.4.121

16. Nevo notes the conflation of birth and intercourse here (*Shakespeare's Other Language*, p. 109).

17. See Eric Partridge, *Shakespeare's Bawdy* (New York, 1960), p. 192, for the sexualisation of 'sport'.

18. Neely ('Women and Issue', 183), Kahn *(Man's Estate*, p. 216), and Erickson (*Patriarchal Structures*, pp. 154-5) all note this attempt.

19. Although medical science did not attribute the *ovum* to women until well after Shakespeare's time (see Audrey Eccles, *Obstetrics and Gynaecology in Tudor and Stuart England* [Kent, OH, 1982], pp. 30-2), common observation in the barnyard would suffice to ensure the association of eggs with female generativity.

20. Schwartz notes that Leontes would identify with Mamillius as a 'symbol of phallic integrity' ('Leontes' Jealousy,' p. 268).

21. For the custom of breeching, see Adelman, *Suffocating Mothers*, p. 7. As Maynard Mack notes, the unbreeched Mamillius would have been 'wearing a costume very like [his] mother's' ('Rescuing Shakespeare' [Oxford, 1979], p. 11).

22. As Neely says, 'Mamillius, since not created by some variety of male parthenogenesis, ... is declared infected by his physical connection with Hermione' ('Women and Issue', p. 183). Latin *mamilla* = breast or teat; Schwartz ('Leontes' Jealousy', p. 268) and Kahn *(Man's Estate*, p. 216), among others, note the maternal valence of Mamillus's name.

23. Schwartz's account is the *locus classicus* for the identification of the spider with the catastrophic preoedipal mother, specifically here in the nursing situation ('Leontes' Jealousy', pp. 269-72); Erickson too associates the spider with 'oral contamination' (*Patriarchal Structures*, p. 155). But for MacCary, the spider is the 'sexually insatiable oedipal mother' (*Friends and Lovers*, pp. 209, 215). Whatever their precise interpretations, most psychoanalytically oriented critics find this speech central to Leontes' character.

24. G. Wilson Knight notes this quality in Leontes' linguistic style: 'The spasmodic jerks of his language reflect Leontes' unease: he is, as it were, being sick; ejecting ... something he has failed to digest, assimilate' (*The Crown of Life* [London, 1947], p. 81).

25. See Adelman, *Suffocating Mothers*, pp. 106-7.

26. See Gourlay's fine analysis of their interchange and of the negative stereotypes Leontes invokes ('"O my most sacred lady"', pp. 282-3). D'Orsay W. Pearson argues that Shakespeare invokes and refutes

Paulina's association specifically with the stereotypical urban witch throughout the play ('Witchcraft in *The Winter's Tale*: Paulina as "Alcahueta y un Poquito Hechizera"', *Shakespeare Studies*, 12 [1979], 195-213).

27. Schwartz similarly notes Leontes' difficulty in ' equat[ing] himself with his feminine issue' ('*The Winter's Tale*', p. 150). For Frey, daughters always betoken 'a guilty loss of patrilineal procreative power' (*Shakespeare's Vast Romance*, p. 87).

28. Schwartz notes Leontes' identification with the orally catastrophic mother and his echo of Lady Macbeth ('Leontes' Jealousy', p. 268; '*The Winter's Tale*', p. 153).

29. This view has been widely accepted since Knight's powerful expression of it (*The Crown of Life*, esp. pp. 88-90). But there have been at least two important recent *caveats* against the sentimentalising of nature's power in the play: Erickson's analysis of the ways in which the associations of women with 'natural' generative and nurturing processes secure patriarchy and limit gender roles (*Patriarchal Structures*, esp. pp. 158-64), and Marilyn L. Williamson's demonstration of the ideological use of the construct 'nature' to mythologise patriarchal power (*The Patriarchy of Shakespeare's Comedies* [Detroit, 1986], esp. pp. 116-21, 129-30, and 161-4).

30. Of the many who recognise that women and the generative forces associated with them are the agents of recovery in this play, see Gourlay ('"O my most sacred lady"', pp. 377-93) and especially Neely, to whose rich account, both in its original form ('Women and Issue', pp. 181-93) and in its revised form (*Broken Nuptials*, pp. 191-209), I am deeply indebted.

31. For the incipient pun on *fault*, see Adelman, *Suffocating Mothers*, ch. 2, note 26. Hermione playfully evokes the same pun in her dangerous conversation with Polixenes ('If you first sinn'd with us, and that with us / You did continue fault', 1.2.84-5).

32. Among the many who see Antigonus as Leontes' scapegoat, see especially Schwartz ('Leontes' Jealousy', p. 260; '*The Winter's Tale*', pp. 156-9), Erickson (*Patriarchal Structures*, pp. 156, 159), and Nevo (*Shakespeare's Other Language*, pp. 116-18); all three see his fate as a complex reworking of Leontes' delusion.

33. The pastoral is generally seen as a corrective to Leontes' court; Lindenbaum sees it specifically as a corrective to Polixenes' pastoral in its embracing of sexuality and change ('Time, Sexual Love', pp. 14-20).

34. Both Lindenbaum ('Time, Sexual Love', p. 18) and Frey (*Shakespeare's Vast Romance*, p. 73) note Florizel's implicit reversal of Lear's position.

35. Perdita is often identified with nature, Venus Genetrix, or Mother Earth (see, e.g., Lindenbaum, 'Time, Sexual Love', p. 18; Gourlay, '"O my most sacred lady"', pp. 387-8; Kahn, *Man's Estate,* p. 219). But Williamson notes wryly that the natural processes embodied in

Perdita are trustworthy because her noble birth proves them 'socially acceptable' (*Patriarchy*, p. 130).

36. Leontes has already prepared for Polixenes' equation by identifying 'gates' with the female genitalia (1.2.197).

37. Leontes' crisis of faith is often noted; see, e.g., Frey, *Shakespeare's Vast Romance*, pp. 78-80. Book I of *The Faerie Queene* suggests how readily the loss and regaining of a beloved woman could serve as an analogy for the loss and regaining of faith. But I am thinking less of the loss of any specific religious faith than of the loss of faith in the world outside the self: what Cavell calls 'scepticism's annihilation of the world' (*Disowning Knowledge*, p. 214). In associating this crisis of faith specifically with the mother's body and with the loss of interior aliveness, and the resolution of this crisis with the return of the capacity to play, I am drawing on the work of D. W. Winnicot (*The Child, the Family, and the Outside World* [Harmondsworth, 1964]). Wheeler's wonderfully rich account of the loss and recovery of trust in a 'hallowed presence' (*Shakespeare's Development*, pp. 82-4) is very suggestive for all the romances and is worked out in detail for *The Winter's Tale* (pp. 214-19).

38. My formulation here follows from Winnicott's sense that the object becomes 'usable' only when it survives destruction and thus is placed outside the sphere of omnipotence; its 'use' comes from the recognition of its otherness, which then enables it to contribute to interior richness ('The Use of an Object and Relating through Identifications', *Playing and Reality* [London, 1971], p. 90). Hermione is obviously the primary object that survives destruction; here I am arguing that her return is mediated for Leontes (who recovers her through Perdita) and for the audience by the position of pastoral as the place that Leontes' destruction of the world did not destroy, the place therefore 'usable' because it is outside the sphere of omnipotent control.

39. The last scene presents something of a challenge to those who would see in the play primarily the recuperation of male bonds (e.g., Kahn, *Man's Estate*, pp. 218-19) or the recovery of control over patriarchal issue (e.g., Williamson, *Patriarchy*, pp. 150-2). Keeping us hungry by refusing to show us the reconcilations with Polixenes and Perdita, Shakespeare creates in us the sense that something is missing, so that we too will be ready to go to Paulina's house with 'all greediness of affection' (5.2.102); and what is missing and longed for is focused in the report of Leontes' cry: 'O, thy mother, thy mother' (5.2.52-3).

40. The (implicitly gendered) contrast between control and emotion is central to Marianne Novy's understanding of Shakespeare (see *Love's Argument* [Chapel Hill, NC, 1984], pp. 9-10, 16-17); she finds the relinquishing of control characteristic of the romance protagonists and essential to the 'transformed images of manhood' in them (pp. 172-4). See especially her moving account of the statue's awakening, where

'imagery of warm flesh and cold stone ... identifies the contrast between emotion and control with that between life and death' (p. 180).

41. The *locus classicus* for this formulation is Sherry Ortner's 'Is Female to
Male as Nature is to Culture?' in *Woman, Culture, and Society*, ed.
Michelle Zimbalist Rosaldo and Louise Lamphere (Stanford,
CA, 1974), pp. 67-87.

42. My formulation here is very close to Novy's (*Love's Argument*, p. 180)
and Neely's ('Women and Issue', p. 191); see also Taylor (*Shakespeare's
Darker Purpose*, p. 45) and MacCary (*Friends and Lovers*, pp. 214-15).

43. See D. W. Winnicot, 'Transitional Objects and Transitional Phenomena', *Through Paediatrics to Psycho-Analysis* (London, 1975), p. 230.

44. I use *we* here to register my sense not only of the degree to which
Shakespeare demands his audience's participation but also of the degree to which the deepest restorations of the end are relatively unin-
flected by gender. The most primitive losses and recoveries are prior
to gender differentiation: though daughters will probably be less
prone than sons to use the language of female contamination to register their sense that the world is alien and potentially overwhelming,
both daughters and sons can find in the recovery of the benign maternal body a figure for the recovery of trust in the world.

45. Among the many who see in Hermione's awakening an allusion to
Shakespeare's specifically theatrical art, see especially Leonard Barkan
('Living Sculptures': Ovid, Michelangelo and *The Winter's Tale*, *English Literary History*, 48 [1981], 661-2) and Cavell (*Disowning, Knowledge*, p. 218). The role of the audience's faith in bringing the statue to
life is commonly acknowledged: see, e.g., Howard Felperin (*Shakespearean Romance* [Princeton, NJ, 1972], p. 242), Frey (*Shakespeare's
Vast Romance*, p. 161), R. S. White (*'Let wonder seem familiar', Endings
in Shakespeare's Romance Vision* [Atlantic Highlands, NJ, 1985], pp. 156-
7), Bruce McIver ('Shakespeare's Miraculous Deception: Transcendence in *The Winter's Tale*', *Moderna Sprak*, 73 [1979], 341-51), William
C. Carroll (*The Metamorphoses of Shakespearean Comedy* [Princeton,
NJ, 1985], pp. 213, 222-3), and especially Nevo (*Shakespeare's Other
Language*, p. 127) and Cavell (*Disowning Knowledge*, pp. 218-21).

46. Many note the healing of play in Act 4, scene 4; see especially Frey's
lovely description of pastoral play and of the ways in which the pastoral restores our faith as audience, reversing the theatre of suspicion
that had preceded it (*Shakespeare's Vast Romance*, pp. 138-44).

From *Suffocating Mothers: Fantasies of Maternal Origin in Shakespeare's Plays*. London:
Routledge, 1992. Used by permission of Taylor & Francis Group.

SHAKESPEARE AND ROHMER:
TWO TALES OF WINTER

Stanley Cavell

Stanley Cavell (1926-) is a contemporary philosopher who writes influentially about Shakespearean tragedy and skepticism, but he also writes about film and about moral perfectionism, especially the kind that he finds in Ralph Waldo Emerson. His detailed reading of the relationship between The Winter's Tale *and Eric Rohmer's* Conte d'hiver *concludes a series of* Pedagogical Letters on a Register of the Moral Life, *which is the subtitle of Cavell's* Cities of Words, *where the following essay appears. That book contains his revised lectures from a course he taught for over a decade at Harvard and the University of Chicago, and he identifies these writings as letters to indicate an intimacy that he wants this work to express and encourage in responding to such texts as we are likely to read in the humanities. That intimacy entails an openness to experience in which we must believe before we can understand. In this final essay Cavell emphasizes Félicie's response to the statue scene in* The Winter's Tale. *He identifies that response as "what Emerson calls thinking," hearkening to an intuition which may otherwise be lost or disowned, like a buried talent. Félicie's interpretation of Hermione's reawakening is immediately contested by her friend Loic, but as the story continues, it turns out to contain existential insight, however debatable it is in theory.*

IKE THE previous chapter, this one concerns both a literary text and a film—in this case, not a film that is a close adaptation of a text, with tantalizing differences, but a film that is something like a commentary on a text. Eric Rohmer's film bears, in French, the title *Conte d'hiver*, which is almost the canonical French title of Shakespeare's *The Winter's Tale*. I shall, to distinguish it from the play, translate it as it is advertised in English, namely as *A Tale of Winter*.

The play and the film are relatives of the genre of narrative I have named the comedy of remarriage. That this narrative ends, not as in classical comedy, with a marriage, but with a remarriage, means, as I have emphasized, that the narrative begins, or climaxes, with a divorce, or some equivalent separation, not at any rate with some simple misunderstanding, or defiance, or confusion (as in *A Midsummer Night's Dream*); so the adventure of getting the pair not simply together (which had already happened), but together again, back together, is not one of overcoming external obstacles to their union, but one of overcoming internal obstacles. What this overcoming requires is not a moral reevaluation of particular actions or decisions that have come between them, but the revision and transfiguration of their way of life. In a phrase, the dimension of morality raised in these narratives is that of Emersonian perfectionism.

Overcoming an inner obstacle is manifested in *A Tale of Winter* as what Rohmer's character Loic calls a resurrection, and characterizes as fantastic. I note his claim in a gesture of gratitude to Northrop Frye, whose *Anatomy of Criticism* made so strong an impression on me when it appeared in the years I was beginning to teach. In Frye's description of Old Comedy the woman of the principal pair undergoes something like death and resurrection. Frye explicitly contrasts this with the example of (unspecified) Hollywood comedy. But some equivalent of resurrection or rebirth is blatant in *The Philadelphia Story* (as Mike carries Tracy like a child in his arms from a body of water and Tracy raises her head to say that she is not wounded but dead), and in *The Awful Truth* (as Lucy, by let's say metempsychosis, becomes Jerry's sister). And since marriage, as I have argued, is an image of the ordinary in human existence (the ordinary as what is under attack in philosophy's tendency to skepticism), the pair's problem, the response to their crisis, is to transfigure, or resurrect, their vision of their everyday lives, something that requires, in words I recall George Eliot gives to Daniel Deronda, "the transmutation of self" which "is happening every day." The form the revision takes I have articulated as recognizing the extraordinary in what we find ordinary, and the ordinary in what we find extraordinary. The particular slant given to this perception in Rohmer's meditation on Shakespeare's *Winter's Tale* can be said to be an interpretation, or transfiguration, of the woman's fatal patience, and impatience, in "The Beast in the Jungle" and in *Letter from an Unknown Woman*.

In Rohmer's film, a pair of young lovers, Félicie and Charles, as they part, having spent an, indefinite portion of the summer together at the seashore (perhaps it is an island), arrange to meet again. Charles is temporarily traveling outside France and can provide no useable address, and the address Félicie gives him proves to be incorrect.

We cut to five years later, some days before Christmas, and find Félicie to be the mother of a daughter, Elise, whose father is the unlocatable man of that summer adventure. With each of the two men now in her life (Loic, a philosopher, and Maxence, the owner of a beauty salon in which she is employed), each of whom wishes to marry her, Félicie discusses her inexplicable dumbness in having given the wrong address to the love of her life. She also discusses with them, and with her splendid mother, with whom she and her daughter live when she is not staying at Loic's house, her ideas about love. She makes clear to each of the men that she does not love him as she loved Charles. She tells Loic that she loves him and is grateful to him for his friendship but is not intensely attracted to him; she is attracted to Maxence physically and, when he tells her he has left the woman he was living with, she decides that she loves him enough to live with him.

She and Elise move to the city of Nevers with Maxence, who has bought a salon there, but the following day she recognizes that, as she tells him, she is not madly in love with him and therefore was mistaken in believing she could live with him. This revelation has something to do with a revelation she had earlier that day while she was visiting a cathedral with Elise, who insisted they go inside (something Félicie herself had no interest in doing) to see the Nativity scene.

Back in Paris, Félicie tells Loic she has not returned to begin again with him. She wants to have his company however, and they go together to a performance of Shakespeare's *The Winter's Tale*, of which Rohmer's film shows most of the final scene of resurrection. The play affects Félicie profoundly. Afterward she and Loic discuss the play and Félicie relates her experience of it to her revelation in the cathedral, where, she announces, she felt alive to her existence in a way she had experienced only once before, five years earlier with Charles. She describes her senses of true and false faith in a way that impresses Loic, not least because he hears in her words an unlettered discovery of insights brought to philosophy by Plato and by Pascal and Descartes, and she concludes that, whether Charles returns or not, she will not live in a way that is incompatible with their finding each other again.

It is by now the day of New Year's Eve. As she and her daughter are returning in a bus—one of the many vehicles, private and public, we have seen them in around Paris—to her mother's house for a family gathering, they encounter Charles. He is with another woman and Félicie, after saying to Charles that she was dumb to make the mistake with the address, grabs Elise's hand and dashes off the bus. The woman Charles is with is a friend who knows about the contretemps with the address and is not surprised when Charles rushes after the pair. What Félicie and Charles find to say to each other in the public street, and how their ecstatic yet ordinary re-encounter is related to the ecstatic and metaphysically extraordinary re-encounter staged at the close of Shakespeare's play, it is a proof of Rohmer's genius to discover.

I have been finding Rohmer's film to contain—more with each viewing—surprising and beautiful confirmations of the sort of claim

I made for *The Winter's Tale* in an essay I published in 1986. At the opening of that essay I note that at the end of Shakespeare's play a dead five- or six-year-old child is left unaccounted for. And I sense that Rohmer's camera's repeated cuts, in *A Tale of Winter*, to five-year-old Elise alone, is as if to assure itself of her existence. Yet confirmation in Rohmer's film of my earlier thoughts on the Shakespeare play was initially hard for me to believe.

Shakespeare's *The Winter's Tale* is split into two parts. The first part comprises Acts 1 through 3, in effect a compressed tragedy revisiting the insane intensities of jealousy interrogated in *Othello* (the madness made starker by the absence of a separate Iago, but lodged in a more emotionally plausible rival). The second part, somewhat longer, comprises Acts 4 and 5, working through its great pastoral celebration of nature in Act 4 to a transcendental, nearly religious, return in Act 5 of reality which tragedy, or something like it, had denied. (How near the religious the return is, and in what sense near, is an explicit question, both of the play and of the film.) The emphasis of my essay on *The Winter's Tale*, extending the preoccupation of my companion essays on Shakespearean tragedy, is on the world-destroying skepticism formed in Leontes' mad state of mind in the first part of the play. Rohmer's film, on the contrary, seems as it were to skip that first half and to begin with an epitomizing of the late-summer festival engaging a country town, which makes up the bulk of the second part of Shakespeare's play. Rohmer transfers the jollity of this pastoral setting to a montage of a pair frolicking on a beach and taking photographs of each other and biking through the woods and fishing and cooking and making love, which seems precisely to avoid the part in which Leontes' madness drives the plot.

So before getting into Rohmer's film's response to, or perhaps its competition with, Shakespeare's play—one may even find in it more generally a declaration of film's competition with theater—let me just indicate what I have argued about Shakespearean tragedy in relation to philosophy's concern, through so much of its modern period, with the crises of knowledge associated with the religious and scientific revolutions of the sixteenth and early seventeenth centuries, linked with the names of Luther and Galileo and Newton. Modern philosophy is familiarly taken to begin with Descartes's subjectifying of existence (as Heidegger envisions the matter), showing the power of doubt to put into radical question the existence of the world and of myself and others in it, retrievable only in my recognition that I cannot doubt that I think, backed by the consequent discovery that my thinking ineluctably recognizes, as it were bears the imprint, of the existence of God. Much of subsequent philosophy—professional, academic philosophy at any rate—has retained the skepticism but lost the route to God, making the existence of the world a persistent, epistemological problem of knowledge perpetually unjustified. My claim for Shakespearean tragedy has been that, in the generation preceding Descartes's beginning of modern philosophy, Shakespeare was already, in the main characters of his tragedies, exploring characters whose destructiveness can be seen to arise out of this epistemological lack of assurance, but in each case directed to a different topic, a different way in which the foundation of a life seems to give way before a moment of doubt, casting the world into a hostile, worthless chaos. In Othello's case it is a doubt, expressed as jealousy, about Desdemona's faithfulness; in the case of King Lear it is about whether he is loved; in Hamlet's case about the worth of human existence, about the curse of being born, of being mortal; in Macbeth's case about the identity or nature of his wife.

In *The Winter's Tale*, Leontes' wish to kill the world, what of it is his, arises from something that, while resembling Othello's consuming jealousy, is more directly related, as I there emphasize, to a response to his wife Hermione's pregnancy, expressed as a doubt that his children are his. My essay on *The Winter's Tale* elaborates an argument for this emphasis; in what follows here I shall simply assume and assert it. Leontes' madness is magnified as it is shown to spread to his doubt that his five- or six-year-old son is his, from its concentration on the unborn child almost come to term in Hermione's body. For this present pregnancy he has at least the grace, or curse, to construct evidence identifying an alternative father, his returned childhood friend Polixenes. That *The Winter's Tale* differs from the plays in which skepticism produces only tragedy—so that it is traditionally classified as one of Shakespeare's late romances (together with *Pericles, Cymbeline,* and *The Tempest*)—I find marked specifically by a peculiarity of Leontes' basis for doubt (whether his children are his), which is (unlike the doubts in the major tragedies, which are about faithfulness more generally, or about the worthiness to be loved, or about the worth of human existence, or about the nature of one's spouse) not a doubt that a woman is apt to be vulnerable to. What would it look like for Hermione to doubt whether her children are hers? I am careful to say that it does not follow that women are in general not vulnerable to what philosophy calls skeptical doubt, only that where they are, their doubt of existence is apt to be expressed otherwise than toward their progeny, and in some emotion other than doubt. (They may have some anxiety about the father of their child.)

I am going to argue that Rohmer does in fact reveal in the figure of Félicie a kind of skepticism (one centered on questions about herself but somehow bound up with her sense or disappointment in others), and that it too is overcome by something that resembles faith but that is also to be distinguished from what we may expect of faith. This suggests that the first, tragic half of Shakespeare's *The Winter's Tale*, as well as its reparative second half, is after all under discussion in Rohmer's *A Tale of Winter*. But if so, then something in Félicie's strangeness to the world, let's call it her stubbornness or perverseness, which everyone around her feels in her—it seems part of her attraction to them as well as of her annoyance or puzzlement to them, say her mystery, her unknownness, something she feels in response to herself—this perverseness must function in her world in something like the way Leontes' extravagant and lethal strangeness functions in his world.

Here, if it can be made out, is a remarkable result, since it means that the consequences of melodramatically tragic action, to which human folly subjects us, is active pervasively, below the level of notice, in the world of everyday existence, the insistent habitat of Félicie. In my various discussions of skepticism, in relation to Descartes, Hume, Kant, Wittgenstein, and so forth, principally worked out in my book *The Claim of Reason*, skepticism *contrasts* with what, in reaction to the skeptical threat, we can see as ordinary or everyday life. Skepticism breaks into that life, with a surmise that I cannot live with, that the world and I and others are radically unknown to me. I *must* find a way to put this doubt aside—perhaps through what Pascal calls the taste for distraction, or what Hume depicts as the desire for sociability, or what Kant calls recognizing the necessary limits of human understanding, or what Wittgenstein calls the limits of my language. But if Rohmer's suggestion is valid, our temptations to skepticism, or say to a knowledge beyond human powers, are unannounced and may be at work anywhere, woven into the restlessness of vacations at the beach as well as into the business of getting along every day with others back in town, walking along the streets with them, and through tunnels and down and up stairs in their company, riding with them in trains, and subways, and buses, and automobiles.

In order to pursue this counter-vision of Rohmer's, I am going to take Rohmer seriously as a thinker, one whose organ of thought is the motion picture camera. "Take him seriously" means grant him the power to be engaging intellectually claims made by writers such as the five he cites specifically. In addition to Shakespeare, there are E. M. Forster, Victor Hugo, Pascal, and Plato. Forster's novel *The Longest Journey* is under discussion early, as Félicie returns to Loic's apartment to tell him she is leaving him for Maxence. The passage in question is one, at the opening of the novel, in which a character imagines a cow standing in a field and—in an epistemological mode made famous by Moore and Russell at Cambridge in the years between the world wars—is moved to speculate (in contrast, as I recall it, with the cow's contentment) on the doubtfulness of our knowledge of the existence of the external world. (There is a comparable cow at the opening of Nietzsche's first Untimely Meditation, on history.) Toward the end of that same evening, Loic recites a poem of Victor Hugo's with immense flair, at the same time both movingly and quizzically, dramatizing an intellectual cast of mind that both attracts Félicie and puts her off. He is identified as a trained philosopher and a believing Catholic, neither of which Félicie trusts. (It may be pertinent that E. M. Forster's *A Passage to India* and Victor Hugo's *Les Misérables* and *The Hunchback of Notre Dame* are significant novels that have also provided the bases of notable films.)

As Loic, later, drives Félicie to his apartment after they have gone together to the performance of *The Winter's Tale* (their going together happens more or less by chance when Félicie visits Loic to tell him that she has suddenly left Maxence, but not in order to return to Loic), their discussion of the play focuses on signature passages in the writing of Pascal and of Plato, neither of whom Félicie has read but whose intuitions—what Loic calls her "instinctive science"—capture something essential in what these monsters of intellect have brought to the cultural table. Loic says, impressed by the accuracy of Félicie's formulations, "You're killing me." It would be a possible measure of Rohmer's seriousness to suppose that he has meant his camera to validate, or discover, the fact that instinctive science, anyway, instinctive philosophy, should be expected to begin in the articulation of an individual's intuition, before or beyond education. (This would form a comment on the debasement philosophy suffers when it arises from articulation without intuition, giving the impression of thoughts as mere, or empty, words. This is a way of putting what distresses both Loic and Félicie, in different, conflicting, ways, in that earlier discussion in his apartment, which touched upon skepticism and metempsychosis, the transmigration of souls, the topics of Pascal and of Plato that come up in the long car ride.)

But what does it mean to say that Rohmer's camera can "validate," or "discover," intellectual origins? What is revealed to it? What attracts its attention? What authorizes its witnessing? A Rohmer film characteristically includes a passage in which a woman is taken out of the ordinary by a transcendental moment, a declaration that the world we are given to see, like the words we are given to mean, is not all the world there is, and not all we mean. A favorite instance of mine is in Rohmer's film *Summer* (also called *The Green Ray*, perhaps to distinguish it from his film *A Tale of Summer*), in which a woman, wandering away from a boring dinner party, becomes lost in an indefinite stretch of trees, and as a wind animates the trees into a state of shivering, the woman begins to sob, one would not say from a fear of being actually lost, and if from a sense of aloneness, then no more from loneliness than from a perspective of a place in nature in which she feels unencumbered, we might say feels no longer out of place, shaken by an ecstatic sense of possibility. (I note that in Rohmer's *A Tale of Winter* there is a shivering tree in the poem of Hugo's that Loic recites.) The ecstatic insight Félicie will attain during the car ride is achieved by evidently opposite conditions. There she and Loic, whose love for her she accepts but cannot return, are not open to stirring wind and sky but enclosed together in a small, cave-like space, cut off from the world, human and natural, wrapped together in the woman's mood.

In that mood, stirred by Shakespeare's play, Loic raises the most obvious question about the play, namely whether the woman at the end is brought magically back to life or whether she is to be understood as not having died. Félicie explains to Loic that, although unlike her he is a believer, he does not recognize faith; as if whether Hermione had died or not died is inessential to the play's issue. Félicie goes on to inform Loic of a fact that he will be surprised by, that on the day she left Maxence in Nevers, she found herself praying, and what is more, praying in a church. So we have accordingly in *A Tale of Winter* to consider two kinds of time—a time of the experience of transcendence (in the church, and at the play) and a time of articulation or understanding of that experience (in the car ride). Freud's name for this temporal relation is *nachträglich* (meaning supplementary or extra), but his use of it (notably in the case of interpreting the primal scene) is not simply that something supplements or augments what has been experienced, but that in returning to what has happened, that is to say, in retrospect, the return reveals it for the first time, as if the first time it happened was in a dream. (I take Emerson's linking of Intuition with Tuition, a link he calls thinking, to be such a relation.) Dreams enter remarkably into Shakespeare's text of *The Winter's Tale*, as when Hermione says to Leontes, "You speak a language that I understand not:/My life stands at the level of your dreams," and Leontes replies, "Your actions are my dreams." These are explicit announcements that what happens requires a time for understanding or recognition. And I note in addition that the idea of what happens leaves its mark on Rohmer's text. Various people say: "It just happened"; "The things that happen"; "It could have happened to anyone." In a Freudian world of human interaction almost nothing *just* happens, so to justify the qualification "just" requires the most careful attention. We shall therefore have to come back to this.

We know as soon as we know that Rohmer is producing a meditation on Shakespeare's play, not merely including comments here and there about certain of its themes, that he cannot avoid the maximum theatrical stake of Shakespeare's structure, namely to consider whether the statue's being replaced by life *holds*, or "works," theatrically, whether the audience is given enough motive to stay with the moment. I know prominent and gifted Shakespeareans who cannot find, or have not found, that that concluding scene does hold them, the scene of awakening or resurrection. This constitutes a drastic criticism of a work that for gifted others achieves the highest level of theater. By "not avoiding the maximum theatrical stake" I mean that Rohmer creates an analogous moment in his film, namely in the return of a long-absent parent.

Whether this moment holds us in Rohmer's film does not so much depend on overcoming scientific incredibility—chance encounters in a bustling city are familiar enough events—as on whether we are held moment to moment, from the recognitions of and by the lover/father Charles to the concluding ecstasy of the line "These are tears of joy" and its repetition by the child, who thereby receives a concept she cannot then and there encompass. Its time of understanding, or revised understanding, if it comes, is years away. The film's attention to the child's absorptions suggests to me that the line joining tears and joy, taken from her mother, begins in her some measure against which to criticize the lesson so much of the world likes to teach, namely that existence is inevitably as melancholy as most grownups assume is natural to the human condition.

But when do we know that Rohmer's film is serious about—is measuring itself against—Shakespeare's play? I suppose an early incontestable moment—a fixed, topological point of identity between these works—is Félicie's self-identification in her conversation with Maxence the weekend she travels to Nevers to visit him in anticipation of joining him permanently with her daughter, Elise. In a long exchange with Maxence, in which his open sympathy evidently confirms her decision to make the move, she gives an explanation of how, at the close of the summer at the beach, she happened to give the man called Charles a false address and of why he had at the time no address to give her, and why she could not be located in a city register because her last name was not that of her mother (who used her maiden name, and with whom she lived when she was not with a man), nor was her name that of her sisters (who had changed their names in marrying). She concludes this exchange by observing, "I'm the girl no one can find." Now this is a fair reference to Shakespeare's Paulina's line that brings Hermione as it were to life: "Turn, good lady,/Our Perdita is found." Since Paulina's line occurs in the final scene of the play, which Rohmer incorporates most of in soon showing Loic and Félicie at the play, Félicie will hear her own line almost repeated back to her as part of her transformative attendance at the play. Do we imagine that Félicie takes Paulina's line to contradict hers, or the other way around? Does she, that is, take herself there as an echo or as a shadow, a negative, of Perdita? Presumably that is under discussion in the conversation in the car ride, which we owe more attention.

Before that, we already have enough undeniable connection between Rohmer's film and Shakespeare's play to be alerted to fainter allusions between them. Take, for example, the pictures that Félicie's daughter Elise draws (five years old, plus, I suppose, a few months; the film, after the opening montage, specifies its setting as across the winter solstice to New Year's Eve) of flowers and a princess and a clown, which can be taken as references to principal motifs of Shakespeare's pastoral Act 4 in Bohemia, where Perdita is queen of the annual sheep-shearing festival. And given the importance in others of Rohmer's films of the perspective in moving from place to place and back again, as if one is at home nowhere, I am prepared to take the pair of visits from Paris to Nevers as some allusion to the move and return from Shakespeare's Sicilia to Bohemia. Indeed I am prepared to consider the connection, perhaps yet fainter, of Félicie with hairdressing as a witty, citified reference to sheep-shearing, since both modes of hair cutting are associated simultaneously with festivals and with money, and represent places where the woman both is and is not in place. (In Shakespeare's festival, Perdita is an unrecognized princess playing the part of its queen.)

A more serious, no doubt, or more explicit connection between the film and the play is Loic's insistence, in the first conversation in his apartment with his intellectual friends, on the difference between religion and magic or superstition, which also recalls lines we hear in the depicted scene from *The Winter's Tale*, as Hermione obeys Paulina's instruction to show life, and Paulina instructs the onlookers, "Start not; her actions shall be as holy as/You hear my spell is lawful"—to which Leontes will respond "If this be magic, let it be an art/Lawful as eating." This oblique association of Loic with Shakespeare's Paulina, marking Loic as the friend and protector of Félicie, thus links Félicie with Hermione as well as with Perdita, a mother as well as a daughter (both of which Félicie is shown to be, unlike any woman in Shakespeare's play).

The play insists on the mother and daughter resembling each other, accented in the briefly shocking moment of incestuous desire when Perdita is presented to Leontes as the betrothed of Florizel (the son of the friend whose death Leontes had sought in his early madness) and Leontes declares that he would ask for her for himself, upon which Paulina instantly intervenes. It is more to Rohmer's point to underscore, rather than incestuousness (suggesting the prerogatives and the unsociability of absolute power), the plain fact that all mothers have begun as daughters, as necessarily as that all who are old were young. That such truths may amount to revelations seems to me re-marked in the way Félicie's wonderful mother accepts the reality of Félicie's erotic life. When to Félicie's saying she prefers Maxence's roughness to Loic's sweetness, her mother replies, "Sweet men are rare," I find myself recalling the opening scenes of Félicie and Charles playing at the beach, as if these are images of her mother remember-ing her own youth. And the mother's acceptance of life, of a future in which she will no longer participate, is expressed in the simplicity with which she remarks, when at the end she sees her granddaughter alone on the living room sofa, having withdrawn from the power of her parents' joyful embraces, "Your mother and papa are together" and asks if she isn't glad.

A comparatively tiny, yet still incontestable, fixed point between the play and the film, and perhaps most puzzling, is the rediscovered father's (Charles's) punctual and happy impulse—having been prompted to ask "Is this my child?" and been answered by Félicie, "Doesn't she look like you?"—to sweep the child up into his arms. When Leontes asked of his five- or six-year-old son, "Art thou my boy?"—having noted, "They say [your nose] is a copy out of mine"—it expressed a sentiment, or presentiment, that sent Leontes (or else was a desperate argument meant to stave off his being sent) into his first open speech of derangement, relating passion to infection and to dreams that ques-tion what is and is not possible. What is the point of this juxtaposition of Charles and Leontes—or is it rather a juxtaposition of Félicie and Leontes, since it is she who asks the question of resemblance between father and child? That she particularly notices noses is shown in her remarking, at Nevers, the nose of a saint's effigy. Earlier we heard her comparing men's looks in conversation with her sister, saying that she agrees her nose is like Loic's and adding that she never liked her nose. (This at once plants the idea of Loic as her brother, which she will later confirm in saying that if they had met in another life they might have been brother and sister, and anticipates the idea that she wants the child to have the father's nose, not hers, hence she as if restates Leontes' question of comparison.)

The point of contrasting Charles with Leontes cannot be to emphasize Leontes' stretch of madness—how can anything empha-size it more than the suddenness and avidity of his own embracing of his madness? And it can hardly be put there to emphasize Charles's normality, since almost anyone is different from Leontes, and cannot be called normal on that account. Perhaps it is to question what would count as normal in an abnormal world, anyway a world in which we have no measure of the normal, we might even say no measure of the natural. The great question of the pastoral sequence, the longest act of the play, may be taken to be whether nature itself, or whether the entire realm of art, can either of them be taken as such measures. It is a world—the human world is one—in which anything can happen; anyone may become lost in it; anyone may be found anywhere. The opening words of Shakespeare's play are: "If you shall chance . . ."

Let us stay with the fact that it is in Félicie's mind that the contrast between Charles and Leontes is made; she would have heard Leontes' questioning of resemblance at the performance of the play we have witnessed her witnessing. So what relation are we to derive between Félicie and Leontes from recognizing that, like Charles, she takes a question bearing on the faces of father and child out of Leontes' mouth, thus momentarily impersonating him? This somewhat deranged displacement may have enough force to push to a crisis what I was calling Rohmer's "seriousness" in invoking his various ingestions, both huge and tiny fragments, of Shakespeare's play, to ask from the beginning what it is in Shakespeare's *The Winter's Tale* that has demanded Rohmer's *A Tale of Winter* as a meditation upon it.

I cited as an opening response to their connection the incontestable allusion of Félicie's "I am the girl no one can find" to Paulina's declaration "Perdita is found"; and now with the further, odder, alignment of a line of Félicie with words of Leontes, I am led to suggest—of course in retrospect, in remembering, in recounting, in reconstituting, in recognizing—that the onset of the meditation is shown in the very fact that the very opening of the film is a montage of summer playfulness on some seacoast a train ride, then a ferry ride, from Paris. (I ask nothing much right off from the knowledge that Shakespeare's tale moving by sea between Sicilia and Bohemia requires imagining that Bohemia has a seacoast, a matter of some unkind merriment or distress to Shakespeare's critics and editors for centuries.) More serious for us is that the opening montage of pleasure ends by recurring to a scene of intercourse whose conclusion motivates the film's first words, as the man says, "You're taking a risk"—making explicit the possibility of pregnancy, something the woman evidently wishes to risk, as her enigmatic, spontaneous laugh in response indicates. I understand this as a sort of materialization of the invisible intercourse that has sacked Leontes' mind ("Go, play, boy, play: thy mother plays, and I/Play too; but so disgrac'd a part, whose issue/Will hiss me to my grave."

In my essay on Shakespeare's play I make a lot of the fact that the body of the play (after the familiar Shakespearean device of a scene of prologue in which an exchange between subordinate characters prepares more of the issues of the world of the play than could be guessed) begins with the words, "Nine changes of the watery star" (that is, the moon), words that mark the fact that Hermione is nine months pregnant (she will deliver a day or two later), and simultaneously mark the time that their speaker, Polixenes, Leontes' brotherly visitor, has been present in Sicilia. It is Leontes' striking together these two facts that ignites his mind. I contend that it is the fact of Hermione's pregnancy that drives Leontes mad, which means that his jealousy of Polixenes is a cover for that madness. (As in my essay on *Othello* I contend that Othello's jealousy of Cassio is a cover for his bewilderment at Desdemona's separate, erotic responsiveness to him, to Othello.) Why it is that the pregnancy threatens Leontes, why he develops a psychic ruse to deny his role in it, I do not suppose we are given to know—perhaps it is because the birth will speak of his mortality, of one who should die after him, perhaps because it signifies his separateness from Hermione, something coming between them. (I am perhaps encouraged in taking Rohmer's preoccupations to heart just here, because of a stunning film he made a few years earlier, *The Marquise of O*, whose subject is a mysterious, as it were fatherless, pregnancy.) Leontes recovers his sanity the instant he learns that both his children are, as he believes, as good as dead.

But how would the conjunction or conjecture of pregnancies affirm a further connection between Félicie and Leontes, rather than simply between Félicie and Hermione? I do not say the conjunction with Leontes is as simple, but I point to a moment in which Félicie's pregnancy is the object of some madness of her own.

Go back to the conversation with Maxence when she visits him in Nevers in anticipation of moving there with him. In trying to explain how she can have given Charles the wrong address—really it was only the wrong town, each town with an unresonant name (like not remembering whether Leontes is the King of Sicilia or the King of Bohemia)—she recalls that she realized her error when she made the same slip "six months later on the birth-certificate forms." So she connects the slip with her pregnancy. Both may be thought to be accidents. She concludes her account to Maxence by declaring—with an explanation that excludes explanation—"I was dumb. Stark, raving dumb." Maxence responds to this in a way that shows what Félicie had described to her mother as Maxence's intelligence, resembling Charles's in being self-won, not self-conscious, but unlike Charles's in lacking refinement. Maxence says: "You can't say 'stark raving dumb.' The expression is 'stark raving mad.'" And when Félicie replies, "You see, I am inarticulate," he returns, "It could happen to anyone."

This exchange is clearly enough a preparation for the re-encounter with Charles on the bus, as Félicie, seeing him only after he has seen

her, and as Elise says "Papa," picks up the thread of the same explanation, in roughly the same tone, averring that she was just dumb, nothing else, whereupon, perhaps noticing that Charles is with the woman
he is seated next to, she takes Elise's hand and dashes with her off the
bus, leaving Charles a confused instant in which to follow, with a parting word to his companion. The difference this time is that Félicie has
given the explanation to the right person. The explanation has never
worked in the past, when she always sounds as if she is saying it to herself and that she doesn't believe it. Charles is the right person because
that there *is* no explanation is precisely what he needs to hear, namely
that there is no impediment between them in the world, that they are
free to pick up the thread where they left it.

A question arises for me here that I may seem to have been
avoiding and which I must not neglect to specify. May Charles be
understood to recover (let us say, by metempsychosis), the figure of
Florizel in Shakespeare's play—the Prince of Bohemia, son of the
man Leontes had imagined in his murderous jealousy to be his wife's
lover? This would seem somehow to follow from my earlier proposal
that Rohmer had transposed Shakespeare's pastoral, from its place as
succeeding the tragedy or (tragedies) of the opening acts of the play, to
the play's opening assertions of nature in the film, preparing the ground
for a miraculous deflection of (if not tragedy, then) misadventure. My
problem with drawing this implication is that the invocation of Florizel
follows, let me say, too mechanically. The other transfigurations (of Loic
out of Paulina, of Félicie out of Hermione and Leontes as well as out of
Perdita, of the girlchild Elise out of the dead boychild Mamillius), each
lend a new cast to Shakespeare's texture. (I might say that I am working
with an idea that Rohmer's film proposes itself as a metempsychosis of
Shakespeare's play.) The idea of Charles as Florizel merely follows from
the empirical fact that he is the only man for Félicie on their summer
island. He has not been shown to perceive, through his love of her, the
royal Félicie in the transitory garb of a festival queen.

It may be of help to ask: Which Shakespearean *pair* does Charles/
Félicie fit? Not exactly Florizel/Perdita, since Florizel does not *return*
to Perdita, nor vice versa. But also not the pair Leontes/Perdita, unless
Rohmer is deliberately stressing the incestuous moment in Shakespeare's narration. And not Leontes/Hermione, if I have perceived
correctly that both of these participate in the figure of Félicie. Just
possibly Rohmer is suggesting that Charles hints of Florizel's fleeing
father Polixenes, as if holding open the question whether there had
been an element of the real in the cause of Leontes' original jealousy.

Perhaps the very instability in identifying Charles's relation to
Félicie's multiple metempsychoses is the cause of my wishing to

describe their reencounter as I did a moment ago, insisting on the rightness of her telling Charles in effect that there is no impediment (on her side) to their, let us say, remarrying. Perhaps we can say: Charles's reference to Shakespeare's play is not to a particular *character*, but rather to a particular *relationship* to Perdita, namely that the man she would give herself to in marriage is felt by her to be, or to have been, under a prohibition from giving himself to her (a prohibition also based on misinformation about, one could say, her proper address). If we say that for her the pregnancy was the impediment, this may be understood, for example, as her fearing that it would cause the man to leave, or cause him to stay for the wrong reason. Here is this film's presentation of a central formulation I have offered of remarriage comedy, that, in contrast to classical comedy, in which a pair who are made for each other face obstacles on the path of finding each other, in remarriage comedy a pair who have found each other face obstacles in maintaining the knowledge that they are made for each other.

Have I said enough, or imagined strongly enough, to satisfy us in shadowing Shakespeare's play with Rohmer's film, where the tale lasts roughly sixteen days, through Christmas to New Year's Eve, rather than roughly sixteen years, as in Shakespeare's telling? I find, for example, that I accept the instruction and the happiness of Rohmer's depiction of a run of dumb luck—can we speak of a dumb miracle? But why isn't it *just* dumb? This option is open to us to take—as it is, more or less, in Shakespeare's conclusion.

Here what I earlier spoke of as Rohmer's raising the issue of the competition of film with theater comes to the surface. Let us ask: What is the difference proposed in Rohmer's film between a photograph's being replaced by life and a statue's coming to life? One might answer that it is the difference between the wondering whether you know that a person exists, is alive, and wondering whether you know the person's identity. The statue is not a reminder, it is not dispensable, in this granting of life, it has a (virtual) life of its own. The dispensability of the photograph is declared when Charles says that he recognized Félicie even though he had no photograph of her. But is the photograph dispensable when, as in the case of the child, it is all she has as proof of her father's identity? His photograph stands for her for his reality the way the crèche stands for her for the reality of the birth of Jesus.

The instantaneousness of still photographs stops time, they are death masks of a time; to add that motion pictures animate these masks might suggest the irreducible (if mostly ignorable) experience of magic in our exposure to photographs, still and in motion. It is a theme of my early book on film, *The World Viewed*, that if we say theater originates in religion and is never fully free of that origin, then we should say that film originates in magic. In both *The Winter's Tale* and *A Tale of Winter*, the relation of art or image to reality is portrayed, or recaptured, as miraculous, specifically as resurrection. But to say so may seem to cheapen or take for granted the value of the work of film, since its version of resurrection is achieved, let's say, automatically. (Film becomes the very picture of a dumb miracle.) But I find that Rohmer's questioning suggests that we as readily cheapen or take for granted the work of theater, the fact that it achieves its version of resurrection (maybe not automatically, but nevertheless) instantaneously, achieves let us say metempsychosis, the replacement in a body of another soul. (If we say both transformations are the province of both film and theater, then we have to specify the difference of proportion in each.) Both transformations are occurrences of our everyday. And Rohmer's great subject is the miraculousness of the everyday, the possibility and necessity of our awakening to it every day, call it the secularization of the transcendental. This makes it seem that the transcendental precedes the secular. Is this wrong? Perhaps our various arts are in disagreement, or competition, over the order of precedence.

There is no denying what Maxence says: What happened to Félicie could happen to anyone. That, however, poses a further question that may take us to a more satisfying place to stop. *What* happened to Félicie?

When Maxence stumbles onto her having as it were failed to say she was stark, raving mad—I do not suppose him to sense that that is perhaps what she *wanted* to say—and having instead said something meaningless, or anyway something that hasn't been given a meaning, namely that she was, or is, stark raving dumb, her interpretation is that she is inarticulate, which we have ample evidence that she is not. The fateful inarticulateness lay in her misspeaking her address to Charles, the thing Maxence will help her remember is called a lapsus, what Freud called a slip, an *acte manqué*—in the Standard (English) Edition of Freud's works, translated as a parapraxis. The issue here is not what motivated the slip but what it signifies as a mental state between being dumb and being mad, what it signifies that it has, with however different effects, the same consequence on her world as Leontes' madness, however motivated, had on his. Namely, it excluded from that world the one each has loved, with whom each has produced a child. (Nothing with so massive a consequence actually counts for Freud as a "slip," any more than it could count as such, I would like to add, in J. L. Austin's work on excuses, which has things as significant, in their way, to say about slips as Freud has.)

The idea of inarticulateness specifically links Félicie's sense of her condition with the inarticulateness of Leontes' derangement, as well as with Othello's decline, as he loses consciousness, into babbling, both cases I have described in terms of world-shattering skepticism, revealing itself as requiring, and desiring, the destruction of language, words having become unbearable. Félicie's sense of inarticulateness, we might say, betokens a milder form of skepticism, an expression of the everyday mistrust of the world, a sort of mistrust of existence and of what there is to say about one's existence. One might think of it as the necessity of exposure to the world as the precondition of knowing it—expressed in those slights, distractions, misgivings, contretemps, defensive silences, withdrawals, reservations, that deal little deaths through your earthly career. It happens to everyone; it is done by everyone. Why Félicie would mistrust the one by whom she becomes pregnant and to whom she was saying goodbye for a while, what madness or rage she may have for a moment felt at his intrusive and absorbing role in what was her transformation into a mother, we shall not know. She is the girl they can never find. Who is not?

But we are shown (or we eventually learn that that is what we are shown) her overcoming of her distance from this man in the presence—no less, no more—of the Nativity scene her daughter is looking at in the otherwise vastly empty church, still in Nevers. In the car ride after the performance of *The Winter's Tale*. Félicie will name to Loic this moment of her presence at the image of divine birth, or more precisely at her daughter's witnessing this image (presented as indistinguishable in itself from human birth) as her having prayed, but not as she was taught to pray as a child. She goes on to describe the experience, with Loic's help, as a meditation, one in which she was not thinking but rather was seeing her thoughts, which came to her as with a total clarity, or with the clarity of totality (she describes herself as feeling full). It is rather a denial or curtailment of Descartes's cogito argument (that I know I exist because I cannot doubt that I think); it is a meditation in which, like Descartes, she overcomes her skepticism, concluding here however by affirming her existence as independent of whether what the world calls the world (or perhaps calls God) is present or absent. She says she felt then that she was herself.

We might say that what Shakespeare's play enabled her to articulate was that she is found, by herself. And since that means, as she says, that she has found Charles within her desire, she can say further (afterward, back in Loic's apartment, as he ratifies their conversation by reading from Plato) that it does not matter whether Charles actually returns. Which is to say, it will not affect how she lives now. Or rather, as she says more precisely; she will live in a way that is not incompatible with their recovering each other.

Loic is moved to say to her in the car—in response to her acceptance of her understanding—that if he were God he would particularly cherish her. She replies: "Then God ought to give me back Charles." And when Loic then indicates that that is too much to ask, Félicie corrects the philosopher: "I am not asking God to give him back." That is to say. He simply *ought* to, it would make the world better. It ought to be better.

Félicie's interpretation of her prayer—intuiting Pascal's Wager on immortal joy and Plato's argument for the preexistence of the soul—is her way of marking the difference of Emersonian perfectionism from utilitarianism, whose calculation of pleasure is anything but Pascalian individual riskiness; and equally from Kantianism, whose universalization by the moral law she denies when, as when Loic once said to her that her words are meaningless to him (it was perhaps when she said she could understand the preexistence of the soul, that she felt that she and Charles had met in an earlier life), she replies, "I saw it; you did not." She acts neither from reason (she once remarks that she doesn't like what is plausible), nor from inclination (she speaks instead of avoiding what is counter to her convictions) nor from hope (startling Loic by saying that not everyone lives with hope, clearly not meaning that she lives with hopelessness). She exists, as her thoughts exist; she loves; she counts herself happy.

Thinking of her happy, I wonder if we have material at hand now with which to give an answer to the question I raised about her enigmatic laugh at Charles's observation, in their prologue, that she is taking a risk. Go back to my observation that Félicie's "slip" concerning her address cannot be understood as a Freudian slip. Since I still imply that her blanking out has significance, what register of significance can or must we attribute to it? At a minimum mustn't there be some sense that she does not want, or is not ready to have, Charles present with the appearance of the child, or, since she is perplexed by herself, does not want to want that?

Her blank, or contretemps, concerning her giving the wrong address, cannot directly be filled in, as if it were replacing a substitute by an original, as a Freudian slip can be, by what Freud calls, in *The Psychopathology of Everyday Life*, "a symbolic representation of a thought." An example reported by Freud is a case of someone's "mistakenly" or "accidentally" using a house key to try to enter his office at night, which becomes interpreted as meaning that the person would rather be entering his house than working at night. What might Félicie's thought have been? To arrive at an articulation of her giving a wrong address we would have to have some reason for her not wanting to be found, specifically not by the man whose child she is bearing. (I assume we have no reason to surmise, as Charles seems to have surmised when they met five years later on the bus, that she had been pregnant with someone else's child.) Don't women want to be with the father of their child, if they love him madly? We know she wants in principle to live with some man, and that she has found neither a sweet nor a bluff man to be possible. If there is meaning in her madness toward Charles it bears on why she is less ready to live with him than with his child. Why would she, in other words, wish to be the girl *he* can never find? Or is it, rather, that it is he to whom she is not prepared to give her address now? As if the woman in Rohmer's film has been confirmed by Shakespeare's play in thinking that men in general, with whom one is in love, are some kind of menace to their child at the time of its birth.

This woman is the antithesis of Lisa in *Letter from an Unknown Woman*. Félicie has no specific reason to believe the man would find the child unwelcome, a threat to his accustomed intimacy and privilege with the new mother, hence a threat to the well-being of the child. Still, Charles did raise the thought of her taking a risk. Did he mean taking a risk not simply of becoming pregnant, but at the same time, for the same reason, a risk in trusting him? Is this enough to cause some skepticism about Charles? She will answer Charles's question, on his return, about whether she has known other men, in a way that indicates that Loic and Maxence have afforded her what experience she has of men. It is not a great deal to go on.

Here is perhaps the simplest hypothesis answering the enigma of her laughter. She laughs at Charles's suggestion of risk (partly no doubt because a risk for mad happiness appeals to her, as in her Pascalian wager; but essentially) because there is no risk, since she knows she is already three months pregnant. This would explain also her detail of filling out a birth certificate six months after she and Charles parted. (There are two scenes of intercourse; my simple hypothesis requires that the earlier, in which the sound track records orgasm, dates her conceiving early in the summer, the later dates the end of summer— the sequence that follows it is of their parting, and her giving her address, after the ferry ride back to shore.)

However ordinary this young woman's tastes and accomplishments are shown to be, we have seen that she is some kind of spiritual genius, in something like Emerson's sense of demanding her uniqueness to be recognized, expressed as her "asking a lot" of men—for example, she wants them to pray for her in church "from the bottom of the heart," meaning to pray as if they *were* her; she wants them to know life from life, not from what others have said about life; she wants them masterful and submissive, intelligent and sweet; sometimes she wants to sleep next to them when she doesn't want to go home, yet does not then want to make love, in this sense wants to be a child taken care of but not even answerable to a wonderful mother (whatever happened to her father, Charles is the only man she takes home to her mother's house); and she wants them to find her without her giving her address, she wants to be *returned* to, freely, to be found as herself, loved madly.

What gives this relatively unlettered, relatively inexperienced young woman so much as the idea that there are such things to want (or to want to want)? Which I imagine comes to the question: Where do the ideas of "instinctive science," or intuitions that become philosophical tuitions, come from? Which philosophers before Wittgenstein and Emerson really care about this sense of the origin of philosophy? I think at once of moments in Descartes (proving the existence of God by means of discovering God's stamp in oneself) and in Nietzsche (understanding the significance of music by understanding the deliverances of the womb). And I think that Rohmer's sense that Plato and Pascal care about such originations is right. But they are perhaps too easy to praise in this regard: I mean too easy to praise without fully knowing whether one believes or understands them.

In a sense there are really three tales in our two texts, but one of the tales is interrupted. The interrupted tale is begun by Mamillius, Leontes' son, the announcement of whose death awakens Leontes to his folly. Near the beginning of Shakespeare's play, Mamillius begins a story that he turns to whisper into his mother's ear. His mother Hermione had asked him for a merry tale but Mamillius, asserting his independent will, replies: "A sad tale's best for winter: I have one/Of sprites and goblins." Then, as Hermione accommodatingly replies "Let's have that, good sir ... and do your best/To fright me with your sprites: you're powerful at it," Mamillius begins: "There was a man .../Dwelt by a churchyard," whereupon Leontes bursts in full madness upon the scene and disarms the intimacy between mother and son. You might say that Shakespeare's tale is about why Mamillius's tale is thus interrupted; or you might say that Shakespeare completes the tale of a man who dwelt by a churchyard, since Leontes has visited Hermione's burial place every day for sixteen years, and at the same time Shakespeare has deferred to Hermione's wish for a merry tale by providing a happy ending at the grave site. You could also say that Rohmer has contested Shakespeare's completion of the tale by declaring that a woman does not know where the man may exist, an ignorance that haunts her own existence as much as any sprite or goblin, and that Rohmer responds to Hermione's readiness to be frightened, say by the almost hopeless odds in the tale, not so much against finding the man as against keeping faith in finding the man.

It is clear enough that Rohmer overcomes our epistemological sophistication with probabilities by giving a child the last words, but more systematically by trusting the infantile economy of the demand for the coincidence of fantasy and reality that film seems born to satisfy—as if our hard-won grown-up work of learning not to wish for the impossible has brought us the danger of forgetting how to believe in the possible. Call it our unnecessary and unwilling suspension of belief.

In *A Tale of Winter*—along with other of Rohmer's sorts of cinematic discovery, such as how to capture the interest in the minimal sense of an event in the world, the fact that in each instant, as Samuel Beckett puts the matter, something is taking its course, or as in Wittgenstein's *Tractatus*: "Not how the world is, but that it is, is the mystical"—Rohmer discovers the vision or interest of film in a world of strangers passing, on their individual mortal paths, and oneself as a passerby among others, each working out a stage of human fate. The vision, as I am calling it, is one in which it comes to us that no one of us need have been in precisely this time and place, coincidentally with the event or advent of precisely each of the others here and now; yet just his scene of concretion is an immortal fact for each of us, each having come from and each going to different concretions, each some part of the event of each that passes.

Emersonian transcendentalism speaks ahead to Rohmer's. From Emerson's "Self-Reliance": "Accept the place the divine Providence has found for you; the society of your contemporaries, the connection of events." Some in my hearing have taken Emerson here to be speaking conservatively, as if not, and urging us not, to disturb events; in short as if his words had been "Accept the place the *society* of your contemporaries has found for you," namely a place of conformity— even though Emerson notes a few lines later that such an acceptance would amount to our becoming "cowards fleeing before a revolution." The place the divine Providence has found for you, on the contrary, among exactly these contemporaries, a place unknown to them, would be that place from which to turn to what it is yours to find.

I add the confession that I associate the little group of three children as the concluding image of Rohmer's film with the opening image of childhood in Wittgenstein's *Philosophical Investigations*—in both of which the child reads to me, among other ways, as the witness of its elders' lives, an image of children as beneficiaries and victims of the unclear world we have to leave to them. The rest of the *Investigations* is then a record of our discovering the capacity to come specifically, concretely, patiently, to their aid in clarifying it, something not perfectly distinguishable from coming to ourselves.

FOR FURTHER READING, VIEWING, AND LISTENING

CRITICAL STUDIES

Alpers, Paul. *What Is Pastoral?* Chicago: U of Chicago P, 1996.

Asp, Carolyn. "Shakespeare's Paulina and the *Consolatio* Tradition." *Shakespeare Studies* 11 (1978): 145-58.

Barber, C. L. "'Thou that beget'st him that did thee beget': Transformations in *Pericles* and *The Winter's Tale*." *Shakespeare Survey* 22 (1969): 59-67.

Barton, Anne. "Leontes and the Spider: Language and Speaker in Shakespeare's Last Plays." In *Shakespeare's Styles*. Ed. Philip Edwards, Inga-Stina Ewbank, and G. K. Hunter. New York: Cambridge UP, 1980. 131-50.

Bate, Jonathan. *Shakespeare and Ovid*. Oxford: Clarendon, 1993.

Battenhouse, Roy. "Theme and Structure in *The Winter's Tale*." *Shakespeare Survey* 33 (1980): 123-38.

Belsey, Catherine. *Shakespeare and the Loss of Eden: The Construction of Family Values in Early Modern Culture*. New Brunswick: Rutgers UP, 1999.

Bennett, Kenneth C. "Reconstructing *The Winter's Tale*." *Shakespeare Survey* 46 (1994): 81-90.

Bergeron, David. *Shakespeare's Romances and the Royal Family*. Lawrence: U of Kansas P, 1985.

Bethell, Samuel L. *The Winter's Tale: A Study*. New York: Staples, 1947.

Bishop, T. G. *Shakespeare and the Theatre of Wonder*. Cambridge: Cambridge UP, 1996.

Bloom, Harold, ed. *The Winter's Tale: Modern Critical Interpretations*. New York: Chelsea House, 1987.

Bristol, Michael D. "In Search of the Bear: Spatiotemporal Form and the Heterogeneity of Economies in *The Winter's Tale*." *Shakespeare Quarterly* 42 (1991): 145-67.

Clubb, Louise. "The Tragicomic Bear." *Comparative Literature Studies* 9 (1972): 17-30.

Colie, Rosalie L. *Shakespeare's Living Art*. Princeton: Princeton UP, 1974.

Egan, Robert. *Drama Within Drama: Shakespeare's Sense of His Art in "King Lear," "The Winter's Tale," and "The Tempest."* New York: Columbia UP, 1975.

Eggert, Katherine. *Showing like a Queen: Female Authority and Literary Experiment in Spenser, Shakespeare, and Milton*. Philadelphia: U of Pennsylvania P, 2000.

Enterline, Lynn. "'You Speak a Language That I Understand Not': The Rhetoric of Animation in *The Winter's Tale*." *Shakespeare Quarterly* 48 (1997): 17-44.

Ewbank, Inga-Stina. "From Narrative to Dramatic Language: *The Winter's Tale* and Its Source." In *Shakespeare and the Sense of Performance: Essays in the Tradition of Performance Criticism in Honor of Bernard Beckerman*. Ed. Marvin Thompson and Ruth Thompson. Newark: U of Delaware P, 1989. 29-47.

Felperin, Howard. *Shakespearean Romance*. Princeton: Princeton UP, 1972.

Forker, Charles. *Fancy's Images: Contexts, Settings, and Perspectives in Shakespeare and His Contemporaries*. Carbondale: Southern Illinois UP, 1990.

Frey, Charles H. *Shakespeare's Vast Romance: A Study of "The Winter's Tale."* Columbia: U of Missouri P, 1980.

Hartwig, Joan. *Shakespeare's Tragicomic Vision*. Baton Rouge: Louisiana State UP, 1972.

Henke, Robert. "*The Winter's Tale* and Guarinian Dramaturgy." *Comparative Drama* 27 (1993): 197-217.

Hunt, Maurice. *"The Winter's Tale": Critical Essays*. New York: Garland, 1995.

Hunter, R. G. *Shakespeare and the Comedy of Forgiveness*. New York: Columbia UP, 1965.

Kaplan, M. Lindsay and Katherine Eggert. "'Good queen, my lord, good queen': Sexual Slander and the Trials of Female Authority in *The Winter's Tale*." *Renaissance Drama* ns 25 (1994): 89-118.

King, Ros. *The Winter's Tale* (The Shakespeare Handbooks). Basingstoke: Palgrave Macmillan, 2008.

Knapp, James. "Visual and Ethical Truth in *The Winter's Tale*." *Shakespeare Quarterly* 55 (2004): 253-78.

Kurland, Stewart. "'We Need No More of Your Advice': Political Realism in *The Winter's Tale*." *Studies in English Literature* 31 (1991): 365-79.

Lamb, Mary Ellen. "Engendering the Narrative Act: Old Wives' Tales in *The Winter's Tale*, *Macbeth*, and *The Tempest*." *Criticism* 40 (1998): 529-53.

Lewin, Jennifer. "'Your Actions Are My Dreams': Sleepy Minds in Shakespeare's Last Plays." *Shakespeare Studies* 31 (2003): 184-204.

Lyne, Raphael. *Shakespeare's Late Work*. New York: Oxford UP, 2007.

Martindale, Charles, ed. *Ovid Renewed: Ovidian influences on literature and art from the Middle Ages to the twentieth century*. Cambridge: Cambridge UP, 1988.

Martz, Louis L. "Shakespeare's Humanist Enterprise: *The Winter's Tale*." *English Renaissance Studies: Presented to Dame Helen Gardner in Honour of Her Seventieth Birthday*. Ed. John Carey. Oxford: Clarendon, 1980. 114-31.

Matchett, William. "Some Dramatic Techniques in *The Winter's Tale*." *Shakespeare Survey* 22 (1969): 93-108.

Mebane, John, ed. *Cymbeline, The Winter's Tale, and The Tempest: An Annotated Bibliography of Shakespeare Studies, 1864-2000*. Fairview: Pegasus, 2002.

Morse, William R. "Metacriticism and Materiality: The Case of Shakespeare's *The Winter's Tale*." *English Literary History* 58 (1991): 283-304.

Mowat, Barbara A. *The Dramaturgy of Shakespeare's Romances*. Athens: U of Georgia P, 1976.

_____. "Rogues, Shepherds, and the Counterfeit Distressed: Texts and Infracontexts in *The Winter's Tale*." *Shakespeare Studies* 22 (1994): 58-76.

Neely, Carol Thomas. *Broken Nuptials in Shakespeare's Plays*. New Haven: Yale UP, 1985.

Nuttall, A. D. *William Shakespeare: "The Winter's Tale."* London: Edward Arnold, 1966.

Orgel, Stephen. "The Poetics of Incomprehensibility." *Shakespeare Quarterly* 42 (1991): 431-7.

Overton, Bill. *The Winter's Tale* (The Critics Debate). Atlantic Highlands: Humanities Press International, 1989.

Palmer, Daryl W. "Jacobean Muscovites: Winter, Tyranny, and Knowledge in *The Winter's Tale*." *Shakespeare Quarterly* 46 (1995): 323-39.

Parker, Patricia. "Sound Government, Polymorphic Bears: *The Winter's Tale* and Other Metamorphoses of Eye and Ear." In *The Wordsworthian Enlightenment: Romantic Poetry and the Ecology of Reading*. Baltimore: Johns Hopkins UP, 2005. 172-90.

_____. "Temporal Gestation, Legal Contracts, and the Promissory Economies of *The Winter's Tale*." In *Women, Property, and the Letters of the Law in Early Modern England*. Eds. Nancy E. Wright, Margaret W. Ferguson, and A. R. Buck. Toronto: U of Toronto P, 2004. 26-49.

Paster, Gail Kern. *The Body Embarrassed: Drama and the Disciplines of Shame in Early Modern England*. Ithaca: Cornell UP, 1993.

Platt, Peter G. *Reason Diminished: Shakespeare and the Marvelous*. Lincoln: U of Nebraska P, 1997.

Potter, Nicholas. *Shakespeare's Late Plays: A reader's guide to essential criticism*. Basingstoke: Palgrave Macmillan, 2009.

Pyle, Fitzroy. *"The Winter's Tale": A Commentary on the Structure*. New York: Barnes and Noble, 1969.

Raman, Shankar. "Death by Numbers: Counting and Accounting in *The Winter's Tale*." In *Alternative Shakespeares 3*. Ed. Diana Henderson. New York: Routledge, 2007. 158-80.

Rhu, Lawrence F. "Competing for the Soul: On Cavell's Shakespeare." In *Stanley Cavell and Literary Studies: Consequences of*

Skepticism. Eds. Richard Eldridge and Bernard Rhie. New York: Continuum, 2011.

———. *Stanley Cavell's American Dream: Shakespeare, Philosophy, and Hollywood Movies.* New York: Fordham UP, 2006.

Sanders, Wilbur. *The Winter's Tale.* Twayne's New Critical Introductions to Shakespeare. Boston: Twayne, 1987.

Schalkwyk, David. "'A Lady's 'Verily' Is as Potent as a Lord's': Women, Word, and Witchcraft in *The Winter's Tale.*" *English Literary Renaissance* 22 (1992): 242-72.

Snyder, Susan. *Shakespeare: A Wayward Journey.* Newark: U of Delaware P, 2002.

Sokol, B. J. *Art and Illusion in "The Winter's Tale."* Manchester: Manchester UP, 1994.

Taylor, A. B. *Shakespeare's Ovid: The "Metamorphoses" in the Plays and Poems.* Cambridge: Cambridge UP, 2000.

Traub, Valerie. *Desire and Anxiety: Circulations of Sexuality in Shakespearean Drama.* New York: Routledge, 1992.

Watson, Robert N. *Back to Nature: The Green and the Real in the Late Renaissance.* Philadelphia: U of Pennsylvania P, 2006.

———. *Shakespeare and the Hazards of Ambition:* Cambridge: Harvard UP, 1984.

PERFORMANCE CRITICISM: STAGE AND FILM

Draper, R. P. *The Winter's Tale, Text and Performance.* Basingstroke: Macmillan, 1985.

Gilbreath, Alexandra. "Hermione in *The Winter's Tale.*" *Players of Shakespeare 5.* Ed. Robert Smallwood. New York: Cambridge UP, 2003. 74-90.

Jones, Gemma. "Hermione in *The Winter's Tale.*" *Players of Shakespeare 4.* Ed. Robert Smallwood. New York: Cambridge UP, 1998. 153-66.

McCabe, Richard. "Autolycus in *The Winter's Tale.*" *Players of Shakespeare 4.* Ed. Robert Smallwood. New York: Cambridge UP, 1998. 60-70.

Rothman, William. "Tale of Winter." *The "I" of the Camera: Essays in Film Criticism, History, and Aesthetics.* New York: Cambridge UP, 2004. 325-29.

Sher, Antony. "Leontes in *The Winter's Tale.*" *Players of Shakespeare 5.* Ed. Robert Smallwood. New York: Cambridge UP, 2003. 91-112.

Tatspaugh, Patricia. *The Winter's Tale* (Shakespeare at Stratford). London: Arden Shakespeare, 2002.

Williams, George Walton. "Exit Pursued by a Quaint Device: The Bear in *The Winter's Tale.*" *The Upstart Crow* 14 (1994): 105-9.

FILM AND SOUND RECORDINGS

Butley. Dir. Harold Pinter. Perf. Alan Bates, 1974. Kino Video, 2003. DVD.

A Tale of Winter. Dir. Eric Rohmer. Perf. Charlotte Véry and Frédéric van den Driessche, 1992. Artificial Eye, 2004. DVD.

The Winter's Tale. Dir. Jane Howell. Perf. Jeremy Kemp and Anna Calder-Marshall, 1981. Ambrose Video, 2000. DVD.

The Winter's Tale. Dir. Robin Lough. Perf. Antony Sher and Alexandra Gilbreath, 1999. Kultur Video, 2005. DVD.

The Winter's Tale. Dir. Stanislav Sokolov. Home Box Office, 1994. Videocassette.

The Winter's Tale. Perf. Sir John Gielgud and Dame Peggy Ashcroft, 1961. Caedmon Audio, 1999. Audiobook.